Practical Data Quality

Learn practical, real-world strategies to transform the quality of data in your organization

Robert Hawker

BIRMINGHAM—MUMBAI

Practical Data Quality

Publishing Product Manager: Kaustubh Manglurkar

Associate Publishing Product Manager: Heramb Bhavsar

Senior Editor: Tiksha Abhimanyu Lad

Technical Editor: Sweety Pagaria

Copy Editor: Safis Editing

Project Coordinator: Farheen Fathima

Proofreader: Safis Editing

Indexer: Rekha Nair

Production Designer: Alishon Mendonca

Marketing Coordinator: Vinishka Kalra

First published: September 2023

Production reference: 1180923

Published by Packt Publishing Ltd.
Grosvenor House
11 St Paul's Square
Birmingham
B3 1RB, UK.

ISBN 978-1-80461-078-7

www.packtpub.com

To Ollie and Evie, who are my inspiration and motivation. To Emma, for supporting me through all the late-night writing and editing sessions. To Mum, Dad, and Andrew, for lifelong encouragement and incredible support.

– Robert Hawker

Foreword

Data practitioners have, for many, years been aware of the importance of having good quality data, but it seems that it is only in recent years that many business users are understanding the need for good quality data. Poor data quality has always caused a myriad of problems for organizations, but far too often is just considered something that you must live with or work around. This has never been true, but it has been challenging to convince business users of this! In recent years there has been a growing demand for better quality data and with the rapidly growing momentum of Generative Artificial Intelligence (AI) there is more need than ever to have well understood, good quality data. Afterall, AI can only ever be as good as the data it learns from, so it is absolutely vital that good quality data is used to train Large Language Models.

I've been helping corporates and large public sector organizations understand and manage their data better for more than 20 years. Typically, people turn to me because their data is a mess, and they need help unraveling it, or because they realize that they are pouring cash into new initiatives that are failing because of poor quality data.

I was honored when Robert asked me to write this foreword. I am primarily known for my expertise in data governance, but the two data management disciplines of data governance and data quality are so interrelated, that it is often difficult to know when one stops and the other starts. Most organizations embark on their data governance journey with the primary purpose of improving the quality of their data. However, data quality initiatives that are not supported by a data governance Framework tend to be tactical and short lived at best. I like to describe their relationship as symbiotic. To be successful, all data governance practitioners need to be well versed in data quality and all data quality practitioners need to be knowledgeable about data governance.

As a former long standing board member of DAMA UK (the UK Chapter of the Data Management Association), I chaired a working group that published a white paper in 2017, outlining six key dimensions to use when measuring data quality. It took a huge amount of effort on the part of the working group to firstly agree on a set of "standard" dimensions and then to provide advice on how they can be used. The white paper was extremely well received and is often quoted and referred to (indeed it is mentioned in Chapter 2 of this book) but it is only a short publication focusing on one small facet of data quality. If you are just starting out in data quality, it does not give you the complete picture or provide practical steps that you can take to improve the quality of the data in your organization. That is where this book comes in.

This book doesn't just focus on what you need to do, but gives you an understanding of what bad data is and the impact of poor data quality on your organization. After all, you will need to convince numerous stakeholders to let you embark on data quality activities in the first place.

Rob takes you through the basic principles, key concepts and terminology, including an explanation of the relationship between data governance and data quality and why you need to embrace both.

He tackles the challenge of estimating the benefits likely to be delivered (I discovered early in my career that "I will find and solve some data quality issues, which will probably save you money" just doesn't cut it as a successful business case) but most importantly this book gives you a detailed plan, along with a clear understanding of the activities you need to tackle, in which order, as well as practical advice on how to undertake them successfully. It includes everything you need to know from how to select the right data quality tool to the people you will need to support you, through data discovery and profiling, measuring and monitoring data quality, through to the all-important remediation activities.

There are a number of complex concepts that you need to get your head around when working on a data quality initiative and I admire the way that Rob uses his extensive experience in the field to explain these in a simple, accessible way, providing excellent examples and use cases, along with examples of frequently-made mistakes to bring it all to life.

Solving data quality issues may seem like a simple easy thing to do, but delivering successful sustainable results involves more than you might initially think. This book gives you a complete plan to deliver sustainable data quality improvements which will significantly contribute to the success of your organization.

I encourage you to delve into this excellent book, apply its principles, and start improving the quality of the data at your organization!

Nicola Askham

The Data Governance Coach

www.nicolaaskham.com

Contributors

About the author

Robert Hawker started his career as a chartered accountant before making the leap into data in 2007. He led data teams within two global implementations of SAP, looking after master data management, data ownership and stewardship, metadata management, and, of course, data quality over a 14-year period. He moved into analytics in 2017 and now specializes in Microsoft Power BI training, implementation, administration, and governance work. He lives in the UK and shares his experiences through conference and blogs.

I would like to acknowledge the support of the following people:

Nicole Hartley for her support as a technical reviewer and for being a great colleague and friend for more than 15 years.

Nicola Askham for her fantastic foreword, general encouragement and support in approaching DAMA.

Nigel Turner who was asked to review a chapter to ensure I had correctly referenced DAMA content, but provided a really valuable technical review as well.

Miles Reah for all the work in planning the structure of the book and great feedback on the first 5 chapters I wrote.

Tiksha Abhimanyu Lad for being a true partner through the writing and editing process. The book is much better with her contributions and she kept my morale high throughout with her encouraging messages.

About the reviewers

Nicole Hartley has an extensive IT background and over 10 years of hands-on experience in data governance working for a multinational telecommunications organization – most prominently, on a large-scale digital transformation program, requiring a strong focus on data quality.

In her personal life, Nicole devotes her time to her family.

Miles Reah has over 8 years' experience of working as a data governance consultant with a wide range of clients across multiple major industries. Miles is **Data Management Capability Assessment Model** (DCAM) certified by the **Enterprise Data Management Council** (EDMC) and has built up extensive knowledge of data governance, data quality, and data lineage during his career. Miles has been part of large and small-scale data governance teams and has seen the power of good data quality. He has experience in implementing data quality frameworks, policies, and controls in a variety of situations. Miles often speaks at universities, sits on speaker panels, and writes thought pieces about data governance/data management.

Table of Contents

3

The Business Case for Data Quality   61

4

Getting Started with a Data Quality Initiative   93

Part 2 – Understanding and Monitoring the Data That Matters

5

6

7

Part 3 – Improving Data Quality for the Long Term

8

Data Quality Remediation 203

9

Embedding Data Quality in Organizations 231

Preface

Practical Data Quality is about how to take your organization from a basic awareness of a data quality problem to a position of having data good enough to truly underpin success.

The book begins by explaining how bad data can affect an organization's process efficiency, decision-making, and ability to remain compliant. It then establishes the key concepts you need to understand to be successful with data quality and the end-to-end process I have used to transform data throughout my career.

The book goes on to explain each step of the data quality journey, starting with creating a business case and managing the hectic period at the start of an initiative. Then the book establishes the typical stakeholders you will need to engage with through the process, how to work with them to identify which data to focus on, and the specific rules that the data should comply with.

Next, it shows how to monitor data against the rules that have been established and how to actually start correcting the data.

To close, the book explains how to embed good data quality practices into the day-to-day activities of your organization and outlines best practices and challenges to be avoided in your work.

By the end of the book, you will have a complete outline of how you can transform data quality in your organization, armed with examples to catch the interest of your stakeholders, and templates to accelerate your work.

Who this book is for

The book is aimed at anyone intending to improve data quality in their organization. The book outlines the basics of data quality for people new to the topic, but provides insights into every step of the data quality life cycle, using real-world examples and templates to accelerate progress. Typical readers are business leaders, such as chief operating officers or chief executive officers, who see data adversely affecting their success and data teams, such as analytics or governance teams who want to optimize their data quality approach.

What this book covers

Chapter 1, The Impact of Data Quality on Organizations, explains the importance of data quality and defines what is meant by bad data.

Chapter 2, The Basics of Data Quality, explains key data quality concepts, including the typical roles involved, the data quality improvement cycle, and the overall fit of a data quality initiative into a wider data management program and organization.

Chapter 3, The Business Case for Data Quality, explains how to calculate the costs and benefits of a data quality initiative, combining these with qualitative matters into a compelling business case for funding.

Chapter 4, Getting Started With a Data Quality Initiative, identifies the activities which are required immediately after a business case approval, such as supplier and tool selection, hiring, early remediation activities and planning. It provides a framework to ensure that all these activities make progress at the required rate early on.

Chapter 5, Data Discovery, explains how to understand business strategy and how it links to data, processes, and analytics. Once this is understood, the chapter explains how to perform a data profile and interpret the results to derive the first data quality rules.

Chapter 6, Data Quality Rules, explains how to derive a full set of business data quality rules, covering all the key elements including defining rule scope, thresholds, dimensions, and weightings. Well developed rules identify the data which does not meet the required standard efficiently and in a repeatable fashion.

Chapter 7, Monitoring Data Against Rules, outlines the various dashboards and reports required to efficiently and effectively monitor data quality against business rules.

Chapter 8, Data Quality Remediation, explains how to use the data quality dashboards and reports to prioritize and then deliver data quality improvement activities.

Chapter 9, Embedding Data Quality into Organizations, describes how to ensure that data quality improvement does not finish when the active initiative ends, , by ensuring it becomes part of day-to-day business practices.

Chapter 10, Best Practices and Common Mistakes, outlines the key best practices for a successful data quality initiative and the common mistakes that reduce the effectiveness of the work. The book ends with an analysis of how new technology such as generative AI will impact work in this field.

To get the most out of this book

You should have a basic understanding of how businesses operate, including the following:

- Awareness of how organizations are structured, including different departments and organizational practices
- Awareness of key processes in organizations such as procure to pay or order to cash
- Awareness of key systems in organizations such as ERP systems and CRM systems
- Awareness of data management concepts such as master data management, data ownership, and stewardship

Templates and diagrams

We have made some templates and diagrams available in the book's GitHub repository here: `https://github.com/PacktPublishing/Data-Quality-in-Practice`.

The content included is as follows:

File name	Description
Chapter 1 – Data Governance versus Process Speed Diagram (Figure 1.3	A diagram used in the book that people may wish to tailor to their own presentations.
Chapter 2 – Business Case Template (*Figure 2.3*)	A template created for the book to show how you can provide quantitative calculations for your data quality initiative.
Chapter 2 – Typical One-Page Plan (*Figure 2.1*)	A one-page plan template that could be used as a starting point.
Chapter 6 – Report Hierarchy Diagram (*Figure 6.2*)	A diagram used to show how the various data quality dashboards relate to one another. This could be used in a presentation to generate ideas and feedback.
Data Quality Dashboards v2	Power BI reports developed to support the book in the monitoring chapter. To open this file, you will need to download Power BI Desktop from Microsoft (for free). Please note, in Power Query, the path to the source data file was removed for security reasons. Please do not apply changes (that is, use **Apply Later** when you open the report). If you use **Apply Now**, the data will disappear from the report and it will no longer be possible to explore it.
Data Quality Remediation Prioritization v	Another Power BI report – this time showing the prioritization work for the remediation chapter. The same notes apply as for Data Quality Dashboards v2 – the source file link was removed, so changes should not be applied.

> **Tips or important notes**
> Appear like this.

Get in touch

Feedback from our readers is always welcome.

General feedback: If you have questions about any aspect of this book, email us at customercare@ packtpub.com and mention the book title in the subject of your message.

Errata: Although we have taken every care to ensure the accuracy of our content, mistakes do happen. If you have found a mistake in this book, we would be grateful if you would report this to us. Please visit www.packtpub.com/support/errata and fill in the form.

Piracy: If you come across any illegal copies of our works in any form on the internet, we would be grateful if you would provide us with the location address or website name. Please contact us at copyright@packt.com with a link to the material.

If you are interested in becoming an author: If there is a topic that you have expertise in and you are interested in either writing or contributing to a book, please visit authors.packtpub.com.

Share Your Thoughts

Once you've read *Data Quality in Practice*, we'd love to hear your thoughts! Scan the QR code below to go straight to the Amazon review page for this book and share your feedback.

https://packt.link/r/180461078X

Your review is important to us and the tech community and will help us make sure we're delivering excellent quality content.

Download a free PDF copy of this book

Thanks for purchasing this book!

Do you like to read on the go but are unable to carry your print books everywhere?

Is your eBook purchase not compatible with the device of your choice?

Don't worry, now with every Packt book you get a DRM-free PDF version of that book at no cost.

Read anywhere, any place, on any device. Search, copy, and paste code from your favorite technical books directly into your application.

The perks don't stop there, you can get exclusive access to discounts, newsletters, and great free content in your inbox daily

Follow these simple steps to get the benefits:

1. Scan the QR code or visit the link below

https://packt.link/free-ebook/9781804610787

2. Submit your proof of purchase

3. That's it! We'll send your free PDF and other benefits to your email directly

Part 1 –
Getting Started

Data quality initiatives can be difficult to get off the ground. It is not easy to identify clear quantitative benefits up front, and not all stakeholders inherently have an understanding of how damaging poor data quality can be.

In the first four chapters of this book, you will gain an insight into the key concepts that are fundamental to a data quality initiative, such as the roles involved, how the activities fit into a broader data management program, and the end-to-end data quality improvement cycle. You will learn how to create a compelling business case for a data quality initiative, which should lead to the required funding to make meaningful progress. The book will guide you on how to make an impactful start immediately after the business case is approved.

By the end of this part, you will be able to fully articulate what a data quality initiative will comprise, from start to finish, and explain the benefits and costs involved in depth.

This part comprises the following chapters:

- *Chapter 1, The Impact of Data Quality on Organizations*
- *Chapter 2, The Principles of Data Quality*
- *Chapter 3, The Business Case for Data Quality*
- *Chapter 4, Getting Started With a Data Quality Initiative*

The Impact of Data Quality on Organizations

Data quality is often one of the most neglected topics in organizations. It becomes part of the culture of the organization to make statements such as *The data for that report comes from our CRM system – but be warned: the data quality isn't great* or *Sorry, I can't answer that question because our data just isn't good enough to support it.* How often do you hear these statements repeated month after month – and even year after year?

When data quality is neglected in this way, it impacts the following:

- The effectiveness of business and compliance processes
- The ability to make high-quality decisions from reporting
- The ability to differentiate your organization from the competition
- The reputation of the organization with customers, suppliers, and employees

Organizations cannot leverage new technologies, such as AI and ML, to get the most out of their data. Those lofty ambitions to monetize data as a product all too often must be shelved.

Poor data quality is also an invisible drain on productivity. Every employee in an organization is impacted by poor data quality in some way – whether it is a report that doesn't include all the information they need or a business process that they can't complete because key data is missing. Eventually, people stop reporting the issues and create new (often highly complex) processes to deliver the required outcome despite the data quality problems. The problem of data quality is often considered to be too complex and too costly to resolve – leading to people searching for ways around the problems.

Take the example of a manufacturing organization with a highly automated product master data creation process. The products needed to be extended to the various manufacturing plants and sales organizations. This was done using tables containing rules (for example, field X should contain value Y for Italy and value Z for Germany). The process of creating products took just seconds but the underlying tables of rules had not been kept up to date, so this systematically created incorrect data for three products in one country. The incorrect data was carried over into sales invoices that reached customers. The product master data had a flag that, if ticked, meant an additional charge needed to be made for packaging. This flag was incorrectly left blank for the three products. A total of more than ten thousand invoices were distributed in six weeks without the additional packaging fee. A small issue had a substantial impact!

After reporting the product data issue consistently for many weeks – with no action taken to resolve the issue – the sales team established a process to manually correct each invoice before it reached the customer. This work was so repetitive that employee attrition became an issue. This was one of a raft of similar issues within this organization that was invisibly draining away its potential.

Does this sound like a familiar story in your organization? If so, I hope that this book helps you find a path forward.

The value of this book

I realize it is never easy to find the time to read a book like this one. There are so many business books you could read to improve your performance and that of your organization. Most people have started to read a number of similar business books and never made it all the way through.

So, why invest your valuable time in this one? I hope that I will help you understand which of your data is bad, which of that data matters, how to get that data quickly from bad to *good enough* – and to keep it there. This is the meaning of **Practical Data Quality**.

The approach outlined in this book helped take an organization that had such poor data that it was literally struggling to keep the lights on in its premises, to a point where data quality was considered a strength. (This organization had such poor data that it could not get payments to its utility providers and very nearly had a power supply suspension.)

The rate of progression was high. In just weeks, data quality improvements were made for the highest priority issues. Within 6 months, an automated data quality tool was in place to identify data that did not meet business needs, and processes were in place to correct the data. After two years, data quality was fully embedded in organizational processes, with new employees given training on the topic and data quality scores close to 100% of the targets. If you follow the approach in this book and you have the right support from your organization, you should be able to achieve similar results.

Importance of executive support

I firmly believe that the approach in this book is the right one. However, even the right approach can fail without the right support from executives.

In the example organization, the support that was required was relatively easy to obtain. The situation had been so bad that the leadership team could see that data quality was a major issue that was affecting revenue, costs, and compliance matters – the three topic areas that typically capture the interest of executive boards.

The data quality team was asked to report on data quality monthly to the board and every time a concern or blocker was raised, actions were immediately defined to move them out of the way.

In most organizations, data quality issues are not so severe that their impact is plain to see right up to the executive level. The issues are well known to those on the front line of the business, but people work hard to smooth the rough edges of the data before it reaches the executives. Processes and compliance activities are impacted, but not severely enough to cause a complete breakdown that executives will become aware of. Business and IT executives often have different priorities and different languages when talking about data and data teams must often bridge these divides.

The following chapters will outline an approach that will help you surface these issues in a way that will influence executives to support data quality initiatives.

The remainder of this chapter will cover the following main topics:

- What is bad data?
- The impacts of bad data quality
- The typical causes of bad data quality

What is bad data?

The first topic is about defining what is meant by bad data. It rarely makes sense to aim for what people might consider perfect data (every record is complete, accurate, and up to date). The investment required is usually prohibitive, and the gains made for the last 1% of data quality improvement effort become far too marginal.

Detailed definition of bad data

What do I mean by bad data?

In summary, this is the point where the data no longer supports the objectives of the business. To drill into this in more detail, it is where the following occurs:

- Data issues prevent **business processes** from being completed in the following ways:
  - On-time (for example, within **service-level agreements (SLAs)**)
  - Within budget (for example, the headcount budget has to be exceeded to keep up with agreed time constraints)
  - With appropriate outcomes (for example, products delivered on time)

- Data issues mean key information is not available to support **business decisions** at the time it is required. This can be because of the following challenges:

  - Missing or delayed information (for example, selecting products to discontinue based on profit margins, but no margins are available for key products in reporting)

  - Incorrect information (for example, competitor margin is presumed to be X% but is 5% lower than this presumption in reality, due to an error in data aggregation)

- Data issues cause a **compliance risk** – this can be where the following occurs:

  - Data that must be provided to a regulator is not available, is incomplete, incorrect, or is delayed beyond a regulatory deadline

  - Data is not retained as per privacy laws – such as the **General Data Protection Regulation (GDPR)** in the EU

- Data does not allow the business to **differentiate** itself from its competitors where data is sold as a product (for example, a database of customer data) or as part of a differentiated customer experience.

Data that contributes to any of these types of issues to the point that business objectives cannot be met would be considered bad by this definition.

The level of data quality is rarely consistent across business units and locations within a company. There are usually pockets of excellence and areas where data has become a major problem. Often, the overall progress of a business toward its objectives can be seriously impacted by significant failures within just one business unit or location.

One organization I worked with had a strongly differentiated product that was achieved through great R&D and thoughtful acquisition activity. The R&D team carefully managed their data and kept the quality high enough to achieve their business objectives. The Operations team was less mature in their management of data, but their data quality issues were not severe enough to prevent them from meeting their main objectives. They still managed to produce enough of their differentiated product for the organization to predict extremely high sales growth. However, the Commercial team had inherited low-quality customer master data (heavily duplicated, incorrect, or missing shipping details primarily) from an acquisition, and some of the possible sales growth was not achieved. As part of a customer experience review, a major customer commented, "you can have the best products in the marketplace, but if it becomes hard to do business with you, it doesn't matter."

Bad data versus perfect data

We already mentioned that the investment to get to *perfect data* rarely makes economic sense. Having bad data does not make economic sense either. So, how should organizations decide on what standard of data is *fit for purpose*?

The answer is complex and will be covered in more depth in *Chapter 6*, in the *Key features of data quality rules* section, but in summary, you must define a threshold at which you deem the data to be fit for purpose. This is the point where the data allows you to achieve your business objectives.

The trick is to make sure that the thresholds you define are highly specific. For example, most people would consider a tax ID for a supplier to be a mandatory element of data. It is tempting to target a data quality score of 100% (in other words, every row of data is perfect) for data like this, but in reality, thinking must be much more nuanced.

In many countries, small organizations will not have a tax ID. In the UK, for example, it is optional to register for VAT until company revenue reaches £85,000 (as of 2022). This means that the field in a system that contains this data cannot be made mandatory when collecting the data. A data quality threshold has to be set at which data will be considered fit for purpose.

> **Note**
> To manage this truly effectively, you would segregate the vendors into large enterprises and smaller organizations. You would set a high threshold (for example, 95%) for large enterprises, and a much lower threshold (for example, 60%) for smaller organizations.

To get this rule perfect, you might even try to capture (or import from a source such as the Dun and Bradstreet database) the average annual revenue for the past 3 years for a supplier when adding them to your system. You would then specify a high threshold for those who had revenue over the tax registration level. This would be a time-consuming rule to create and manage because you would need to capture a lot of additional data and the thresholds would change over time. This is where judgment comes in when defining data quality rules – is the benefit you will gain on making the rule specific worth the effort to obtain/maintain the information you need?

If you are not specific enough with your targets, data may be flagged as bad inappropriately. When tasked with correcting it, your colleagues will notice *false negatives* and lose faith in the data quality reporting you are providing them with. In this example, a supplier is being chased for a tax ID, only to find they do not have one. These false negatives are damaging because the people involved in your data quality initiative start to feel they can ignore the data failures – it is the classic "boy who cried wolf" tale in a data quality context.

Now that we have introduced the basics of bad data, let's understand how this bad data can impact an organization.

Impact of bad data quality

In November 2018, a Gartner survey found that "Poor data quality costs organizations an average of $11.8M per year." The same survey also found that "57% of organizations don't know what bad data quality is costing them."

Quantification of the impact of bad data

It is usually incredibly difficult to be this precise when thinking about the monetary impact of data quality issues. When looking at these two quotes together, there is a further curiosity. Presumably, the number of $11.8m per year comes from the 43% of organizations that **did** calculate what bad data quality was costing them. By implication, then, we do not get from this survey what the organizations who are **not** measuring this suffer in terms of losses from poor data quality. To quote Donald Rumsfeld from 2002, these organizations are operating with "unknown unknowns."

Those that do not even measure the impact of poor data quality ironically are likely to have the worst data quality issues – they are completely ignoring the topic. It is like in education – the student who constantly worries about their test results and fears failure is usually more successful in the end than their more relaxed counterparts who rarely (if ever) bother the teacher.

The measurement also lacks sophistication. It would be helpful, for example, to understand how this number changes for large organizations and in different geographies. $11.8m is almost irrelevant for a company with tens of billions of dollars in revenue but is a make-or-break figure for more modestly sized organizations.

The other challenge with this number (which will also be discussed in *Chapter 2*) is that the dollar cost of data quality issues is inherently difficult to accurately and completely measure. For example, it might be possible to identify the personnel cost of the effort expended while contacting suppliers to collect missing email addresses. However, this is just one data quality issue of an unknown number. Do you really have time to identify the effort being expended on all these manual data correction activities in your company today and quantify them? What about the missed revenue from situations where a customer is impacted by poor data quality and decides not to trade with you again? Do you even know that is why they chose to stop trading with you? The reality is that there is rarely time to get holistic answers to these kinds of questions when working to get a data quality initiative off the ground. At best, illustrative examples are provided to show the known impacts of data quality. This is typically not what senior executives expect and this often means data quality initiatives fail before they can even begin.

In truth, no one knows how much bad data quality costs a company – even companies with mature data quality initiatives in place, who are measuring hundreds of data points for their quality struggle to accurately measure quantitative impact. This is often a deal-breaker for senior leaders when trying to get approval for a budget for data quality work. Data quality initiatives often seek substantial budgets and are up against projects with more tangible benefits.

At an investment board meeting in a previous organization, a project in which I was involved was seeking approval for a data quality initiative. In the same meeting, there was a project seeking approval to implement an e-invoicing solution. This was an online portal for suppliers to log onto and submit invoices electronically against purchase orders and track their payments from the company. This project had a clear business case – it was expected to reduce supplier queries about payments by 50% and allow a reduction in the number of full-time employees in that area. The board was challenging and, in the end, approved the e-invoicing project and rejected our initiative.

Six months later (and with irony that was not lost on the team), the e-invoicing project was not able to go live on time because it was identified that the supplier master data quality was too low. The go-live would have caused chaos because basic system functionality required the email and VAT fields for suppliers to be populated with a much higher level of completeness and accuracy than was available.

Both fields were in the scope of the data quality initiative, and our team had raised these concerns previously with the e-invoicing project team. The outcome was that the project had to be delayed by three months and the resources (costly consultants) had to be paid to complete the testing activities again.

What were the learnings from this experience?

Firstly, it is critical to start small. Pick one type of data (for example, customer or product data) where you know there are issues. The type of data you choose should be one where you can give tangible examples of the issues and what they mean to the company – in terms of revenue, costs, or compliance risks. Request a modest budget and show the value of what you have delivered through the issues that you have detected and resolved.

Secondly, make it part of your strategy when trying to obtain approvals to explain to key stakeholders (for example, business sponsors) *why* it is hard to quantify the benefits of data quality. Remember that they are used to seeing projects with quantitative business cases and they need a mindset shift before considering your data quality initiative. Meet with decision-makers individually before an approval board and make sure they understand this. Not everyone will be supportive, but in taking this approach, hopefully, enough debate is sparked to give you a better chance of approval.

Impacts of bad data in depth

We will now explore each element of our bad data definition in more depth. This section aims to outline in depth how poor data quality can affect organizations to help you look for these impacts in your own organization.

Process and efficiency impacts

Many organizations introduce SLAs for key processes – for example, 24 hours to create a new account for a new employee. These SLAs are critical because other processes are designed with an expectation that the SLA is met. For example, a hiring manager might be told that an employee can be onboarded within two weeks from the initial request. If one of the sub-processes (for example, new account creation) is delayed, this can lead to an employee arriving on site and being unable to be effective. Poor data quality can often cause SLAs to be missed. For example, if a new employee record is incorrectly assigned to an old organizational unit, the relevant approvals may not be triggered by the hiring manager and other leaders. This is surprisingly common – when re-organizations take place, legacy organizational units are often left in place.

> **Note**
>
> Every organization I have worked with asks for a response to a similar statement in their employee survey: "Processes at the organization allow me to be effective at work." This statement always received the most negative response in the survey. When studying the text comments in response to this statement, I found that a significant percentage (around 30%) related to issues with data quality.

Here are further typical impacts on the organization when bad data causes SLAs to be missed:

Typical Impacts	Example(s)
The impacts are diverse. They can include the following: • Employee dissatisfaction. It is frustrating when processes you rely on at work take longer than they should. • Inability to start a business relationship (for example, supplier, customer, or employee) on time. • Inability to meet a contractual deadline with an existing business partner. • Missed opportunities – customer buys a product from a competitor.	A contract is signed with a supplier to start providing a service. The supplier has been used for many contracts in the past and there are multiple versions of this supplier in the system already. Procurement has to work out which version of the supplier record to associate the contract to, and this takes 2 weeks, against an SLA of 48 hours. The supplier is not able to provide resources on time as there is no purchase order, and resources are assigned to another project. It takes a further 4 weeks for appropriately skilled staff from the supplier to become available, leading to a 6 week delay in a critical project.

Table 1.1 - Impacts and examples of missing SLAs

When bad data quality causes issues with processes, another impact can be on the budget for running that process. The organization of teams running processes is based on a certain level of expectation for process efficiency. Often, leaders and Human Resources professionals do not check the level of data quality before establishing teams. There is an assumption that data is of high enough quality to be used in the process and there is no resourcing allowance for remedial work. When data quality is not fit for purpose, then the team may not be correctly sized, resulting in the following impacts:

Typical Impacts	Example(s)
• The team must be augmented above the existing headcount to cope with additional effort caused by bad data quality. Often, augmentation is via contractors or consultants and the cost in these cases is usually 30-50% higher. • If the team cannot be augmented, the existing team is asked to cope with higher demands. This can lead to stress-related absence and higher employee attrition. Hiring replacement employees is costly (hiring costs, training costs, lost knowledge, and so on).	The accounts payable team for one business unit discover that invoices are routinely coded to another business unit by mistake. Invoices must be manually re-coded to the correct business unit before month-end processes can start. The month-end deadline is not adjusted; therefore, the team effort level is higher.

Table 1.2 – Impacts and examples of incorrectly sized teas

When processes are unexpectedly impacted by data quality issues, it may not be possible to rapidly augment the team. In these situations, the focus of the team running the process is split. They must manage data quality issues on top of their usual tasks:

Typical Impacts	Example(s)
If a team cannot be augmented, the following can occur: • The quality of outputs may fall to an unacceptable level – leading to complaints from business partners or mistakes that take additional effort to resolve. • Particular elements of the process may be prioritized – such as large customers ahead of smaller customers. Eventually, this leads to reputational damage through customers publicizing poor experiences.	The accounts payable team can process payments for key suppliers. Key suppliers include those who provide raw materials for manufacturing. However, utility suppliers are not included in the priority list and are not paid on time, leading to facility utility outages. Manufacturing is halted while the issue is resolved.

Table 1.3 – Impacts and examples of poor data quality on teams that cannot be augmented

Tables 1.1, 1.2, and *1.3* provide many of the typical impacts of data quality in the area of processes and efficiency. Many of those who are impacted by these will also be impacted again when they start to use reporting and analytics.

Reporting and analytics impacts

The main purpose of reports is to provide summarized data in a way that quickly conveys relevant information to a user and allows them to make a decision or help them with their day-to-day activities. Summarizing data can often mean that end users of reports are not best placed to detect data quality issues. The more senior the stakeholder, the more difficult it is for them to detect gaps in the data because they are looking at the highest level of summarized data.

For example, the following simple column chart shows the count of road traffic collisions in the UK in 2010 (source: https://www.kaggle.com/datasets/salmankhaliq22/road-traffic-collision-dataset).

Accidents by Date and Weekday vs Weekend

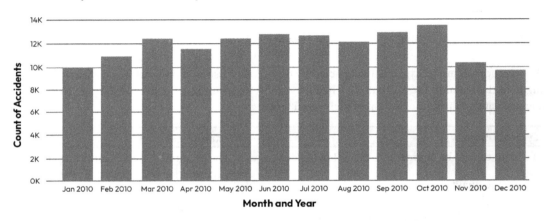

Figure 1.1 – Road traffic collision chart with missing data in November 2010

November 2010 looks like one of the best months in terms of collisions. Only December is better. However, a full week of data has been removed from November 2010 – but there is no way that the end user of this report could know that. Here is the correct chart:

Accidents by Date and Weekday vs Weekend

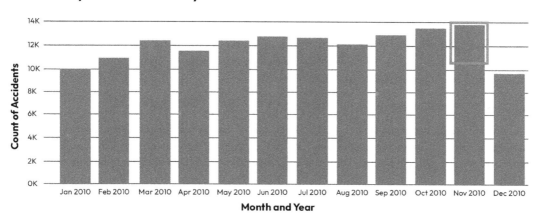

Figure 1.2 – Corrected road traffic collision chart

Here, we can see that November is actually the worst month of the year. There could be other major data quality issues in this dataset that an end user would find hard to detect – a whole region of the United Kingdom could be missing, for example. Some collisions could be misclassified into the wrong region.

All of these issues could drive incorrect decision-making. For example, the Department of Transport in the UK could decide to ban certain types of roadworks on major roads in October every year with a catch-up activity in November. In reality, this could drive a major increase in collisions in a month that is already the worst in the year.

In addition to the process and reporting impacts I've described so far, bad data can mean that an organization struggles to remain compliant with local laws and regulations. Let's explore the impacts and risks that can arise from issues with compliance.

Compliance impacts

Data quality issues can impact compliance for any organization – even those outside of regulated industries. Most companies have a financial audit every year and those with data quality issues will find that process challenging. The modern approach of external auditors is to assess internal systems, processes, and controls and, wherever possible, rely on those controls. The auditor tests that controls were in operation instead of checking the underlying records.

Historically, auditors would perform what they called a substantive audit where they would try to observe documents to support a high enough percentage of a particular number in the accounts. For example, if accounts receivable (amounts owed to the company by other companies) was £1m, the auditor would look for invoices to the total of around £600k and check that they had been properly accounted for (that is, they were unpaid at the period end). This would give them confidence about the whole balance of £1m.

In modern auditing, where controls are found to not be operating effectively, the auditor will exit from the controls-based approach and return to the substantive audit. This increases the audit fee substantially because of the time involved; it also consumes time from your internal resources. In the worst cases, auditors may actually qualify their audit opinion where there is an inability to obtain sufficient appropriate audit evidence. This qualified opinion appears in the company's financial statements and is a huge red flag to investors.

However, companies in regulated industries have another set of challenges to face.

In Financial Services, the regulators request submissions of data in a particular taxonomy so that they can compare different financial institutions. The goal (particularly following the Lehmann Brothers collapse and resulting global financial crisis) is to ensure that institutions are being prudent enough in their lending to avoid future financial disruption. When the data is received by the regulator, it must meet stringent quality checks and submissions are frequently returned with required changes. Regulators will strengthen their oversight of an organization if they see poor practices in place. Strengthened oversight can even lead to institutions being required to retain more capital on their balance sheets (that is, reduce the amount they are lending and making a profit with!) if they lack confidence in management. Banking regulators have even introduced specific regulations for their industry about data governance. In Europe, the Basel Committee for Banking Supervision wrote a standard (BCBS 239) with the subject "Principles for effective risk data aggregation and risk reporting." It includes principles such as "Governance, accuracy and integrity, completeness, timeliness," and many more. See https://en.wikipedia.org/wiki/BCBS_239.

In pharmaceutical companies, medicinal products and devices are highly regulated by bodies such as the FDA in the United States and the MHRA in the United Kingdom. These regulators examine many aspects of a pharmaceutical company business – manufacturing, commercial, R&D, quality assurance, and quality control to name a few. Regulators expect to be able to inspect a site of the company with little to no warning and a data review would be a key part of this.

For example, deviations are a critical part of the pharmaceutical company data model. These are issues that are raised with any part of the company's operations that can contribute to patient outcomes. They can be raised when something goes wrong in manufacturing, in a clinical trial, or even when an IT project does not go to plan. Regulators will inspect deviations, and if data quality is poor, the regulator may choose to apply their statutory powers to remedy the situation. The most serious issues can result in sites being shut down until improvements can be made. This has financial and reputational consequences for organizations, but the ultimate goal of regulation is to keep human beings safe. Data quality in pharmaceutical companies can be a matter of life and death!

The level of scrutiny and the risk of managing data poorly is so high for companies in these industries that investment in data governance in general tends to be higher. However, it should be noted that data initiatives in these organizations tend to move slowly because of the level of documentation and compliance required for implementation work.

More and more organizations are going beyond using data just for processes, reporting, and compliance in modern economies. We've already covered how these areas are impacted by bad data. If an organization is aiming to create or enhance streams of revenue by including data in their products or by making data itself the product, bad data can be disastrous.

Data differentiation impacts

There has been a major growth in businesses that use data to drive a revenue stream. An example of this is where data is a product in its own right (or part of a product), such as a database of doctor's offices (GP practices) in the UK, that is kept up to date by the owning company and sold to pharmaceutical companies to help with their sales pipelines and contact details.

Data is also often used by organizations as part of a differentiated customer experience. For example, online retailers use algorithms based partly on purchase history to present relevant recommendations to customers. If this purchase history were incomplete, the recommendations would lose relevance and fewer people would be enticed into their next purchase.

In these cases where the data itself is the product or part of the product, data quality is under the greatest scrutiny. It is no longer just your organization that is impacted by the quality issues – your customer is directly impacted now as well, leading to complaints, loss of revenue, and reputational damage. If you sell a range of data products, the low quality of one product might affect the sales of all data products!

Finally, and probably most seriously, there is the risk that where business partners (customers, suppliers, or employees) are exposed to poor data from your organization, the issue enters the public domain. With the prevalence of social media, a relatively isolated data quality issue posted by an influential person can harm the reputation of your company and give the impression that you are hard to do business with. At one organization the commercial team was talking to multiple customers about pricing for the year – which varied across different customers. The data quality of the source system was poor and was exported and combined with spreadsheet data to make it complete. This export was broken down into different spreadsheets to be shared with each customer. Unfortunately, one of the master data analysts made a mistake and sent the whole export to one of the customers – revealing other customers' prices to that customer. This was a significant data breach and led to the employee being dismissed and the customer relationship breaking down as they saw that other customers were paying less for the same products, and they lost confidence in the organization's ability to manage their data. This did not reach social media channels but became widely known in the industry and I saw it quoted as an example of poor practice in another company's data training. It would just take a similar mistake to occur on data about individuals and there could be a GDPR breach with accompanying financial penalties and unwanted press attention. Data quality issues lead to workarounds with data, and workarounds lead to mistakes. Mistakes like these can destroy a business.

With all the negative impacts we have described, it can sometimes be hard to understand how organizations reach a point of having bad data in the first place. It is important to understand how this has occurred in your organization so that meaningful change can be made to avoid future re-occurrences.

Causes of bad data

Any of these impacts can cause critical damage to an organization. No organization deliberately plans for data quality to be poor enough to be impacted in these ways. So, how do organizations end up impacted in this way? How does an organization neglect data sufficiently so that it can no longer achieve its objectives?

Lack of a data culture

Successful organizations try to put a holistic data culture in place. Everyone is educated on the basics of looking after data and the importance of having good data. They consider what they have learned when performing their day-to-day tasks. This is often referred to as the promotion of good data literacy.

Putting a strong data culture in place is a key building block when trying to ensure data remains at an acceptable level of quality for the business to succeed in its objectives. The data culture includes how everyone thinks about data. Many leaders will say that they treat data like an asset, but this can be quite superficial. Doug Laney's book, *Infonomics*, explains this best:

"Consider your company's well-honed supply chain and asset management practices for physical assets, or your financial management and reporting discipline. Do you have similar accounting and asset management practices in place for your "information assets?" Most organizations do not." (Laney, 2017)

Laney makes an interesting point. Accounting standards allow organizations to value intangible assets – for example, patents, copywrites, and goodwill. These are logged on an asset register and are depreciated over time as their value diminishes. Why do we not do this with data as well? If data had a value attributed to it, then initiatives to eliminate practices that eroded that value would be better received.

We will return to this in later chapters, but for now, suffice it to say that having a data culture is a key building block when striving for good data quality. Many organizations make statements about treating data as an asset and having a data culture, without really taking practical steps to make this so.

Prioritizing process speed over data governance

There is always a contention between the speed of a business process and the level of data governance involved in the steps of that process. Efforts to govern and manage data can often be seen as red tape.

Sometimes, a desire for a high process speed comes into conflict with the enforcement of these rules. There may even be financial incentives for process owners to keep processes shorter than a certain number of days/hours. In these cases, process owners may ask for the data entry process to be simplified and the rules removed.

In the short term, this may result in an improved end-to-end process speed – for example, in procurement, initial requests may be turned into purchase orders more quickly than before. However, as shown in *Figure 1.3*, a fast process with few data entry rules will result in poor data quality (box 1) and this is unsustainable.

In all these cases, the organization experiences what we call data and process breakdown – the dreaded box 2 in *Figure 1.3*. The initial data entry process is now rapid, but the follow-on processes are seriously and negatively impacted. For example, if supplier bank details are not collected accurately in the initial process, then the payment process will not be completed successfully. The accounts payable team will have to contact the supplier to request the correct details. If the contact details have also not been collected properly, then the team will have a mystery to solve before they can do their job! For one supplier, this can be frustrating, but for large organizations with thousands of suppliers and potentially millions of payments, processes are usually highly automated, and gaps like these become showstopping issues:

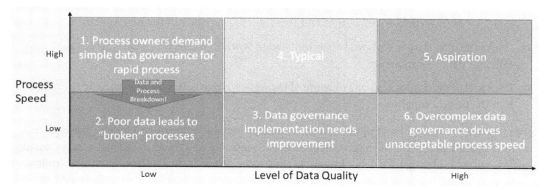

Figure 1.3 – Balance of process speed and data quality – avoiding data and process breakdown

When establishing new processes, most organizations start in box 3, where the rules have been established but they are inefficient. For example, rules are applied in spreadsheet-based forms, but the form must be approved by three different people before data can be entered into a system. Some organizations (typically those in regulated industries) move further to the right into box 6 – where the data governance is so complex that process owners feel compelled to act. This often leads to a move back to box 1 – where the process owner instructs their team to depart from the data governance rules, sacrificing data quality for process speed. Again, this brings the data and process breakdown scenario into sharp focus.

Through technology, organizations tend to move to box 4 – for example, a web-based form is added for data input that validates data, connects to the underlying system to save the valid data, and automatically orchestrates approvals as appropriate. As these processes are improved over time, there is the opportunity to move to box 5 – for example, by adding lookups to databases of companies (for example, Dun and Bradstreet) to collect externally validated supplier data, including additional attributes such as details of the supplier risk and company ownership details. In the best cases, good master data management can contribute to a higher process speed than would otherwise have been possible.

There can be significant shifts in an organization's position within this model when there is great organizational change. This might include a re-organization which might remove roles relating to data management, or a merger with another organization.

Mergers and acquisitions

Often, in merger and acquisition scenarios, two different datasets need to be brought together from different systems – for example, datasets from two different ERP systems are migrated to a single ERP. Often, these projects have extremely aggressive timelines because of the difficulties of running a newly combined business across multiple systems of record and the cost of maintaining the legacy systems.

When data is migrated in an aggressive timeline, the typical problems are as follows:

- Data is not de-duplicated across the two different source systems (for example, the same supplier exists for both former organizations and two copies get created in the new system)

- Data is migrated as-is without being adjusted to work in the new system – which may have different data requirements

- Data was of poor quality in one or more of the legacy systems, but there is no time to enhance it in the project timeline

After a merger, there is usually a significant investment in the harmonization of systems and processes that cover the migration process. If the migration process encounters these problems and bad data is created in the new systems, a budget is rarely set aside to resolve the problems in a business-as-usual context.

Summary

In this chapter, I began to explore how bad data can impact an organization and the people who work within it. I started to explain how organizations unintentionally reach an unfavorable position in terms of data quality. I hope that these topics resonate with you and help you understand how your organization got to this point and what barriers it might be experiencing to its current and future success.

Chapter 2 will outline the key concepts which need to be understood about data quality prior to embarking on improving it. It will also outline the book's approach to managing data quality. This is used to structure much of the rest of the book - with each chapter representing a part of the approach.

References

The following reference was provided in this chapter:

- https://www.gartner.com/smarterwithgartner/how-to-improve-your-data-quality: Gartner predicts that by 2022, 70% of organizations will rigorously track data quality levels via metrics. This sounds positive, but it means that 30% of companies are not even tracking problems. It is also likely that many of the 70% only do this tracking in certain business units or geographies or are at an early stage.

The Principles of Data Quality

2

In *Chapter 1*, I described the problems that organizations experience as a result of poor data quality. From this point on, the book will focus on facing those problems and resolving them in a sustainable manner.

This chapter will outline an end-to-end approach that I recommend, and each subsequent chapter will explore all the important aspects of each stage of the approach.

First, the chapter will provide an appropriate background and context. This context will include an explanation of data governance and the role of data quality within it, an outline of the generally accepted principles and terminology associated with data quality work, and finally, details of the main stakeholders that you will need support from and how they can help.

Therefore, in this chapter, we will cover the following topics:

- Data quality in the wider context of data governance
- The generally accepted principles and terminology of data quality
- Stakeholders in data quality initiatives
- The data quality improvement cycle

By the end of the chapter, I hope that you will have a good overview of how a data quality initiative might run from start to finish and be interested in learning more about each stage in detail.

Data quality in the wider context of data governance

Before explaining all the elements of a data quality initiative in detail, it is important to recognize that data quality is ideally implemented alongside a data governance initiative.

It is possible for data quality to be implemented as a standalone activity, but there are benefits from complementary activities related to data governance. The following sections outline the various aspects of data governance.

Data governance as a discipline

The focus of this section is mainly on data governance, but it is important to explain that data governance is actually part of a wider concept called "data management." Data management covers all aspects of how data is treated in an organization. For example, data management includes the following:

- Data quality
- Data privacy
- Master data management
- Data warehousing and business intelligence

DAMA UK offers a complete explanation of data management in their **Data Management Body of Knowledge (DMBoK)**, which is available from their website: `https://www.dama-uk.org/`.

Data governance is part of data management and is foundational to each of its aspects. However, in this section, I will make reference to both data privacy and **Master Data Management (MDM)**, which are related to but not part of data governance.

The purpose of this section is not to offer an exhaustive guide to data governance and its related concepts. My goal in this chapter is to provide sufficient insight into the discipline such that you can understand the place of data quality within it and how the main elements of data governance can help in a data quality initiative.

> **Note**
> Data governance refers to the collection of people, policies, processes, and tools that an organization uses to ensure that data is fit for the purpose it is created and stored for.

There are many definitions available through a simple internet search – they are all very similar to this one. Data governance has been established as a discipline for a long time now, and the passage of time has led to a level of similarity across the various definitions.

Data governance can seem like quite a theoretical discipline sometimes. In some organizations, the data governance approach can be utopian – with the reality on the ground bearing little or no resemblance to the policies and processes that have been produced. For those of you who think of data governance in this way, this chapter includes a scenario that will be referred to as each aspect of data governance is explained. The scenario should help to ground the concepts in the real world.

Scenario for data governance examples

In this section, I will outline an example organization that I will refer to when explaining each element of data governance.

The company for this scenario manufactures engines for a variety of motor vehicles. The engines vary from small 100cc-capacity go-kart racing engines to much larger motorcycle engines. The customer base includes the following:

- Direct sales to individual private go-kart racing teams
- Direct sales to motorcycle owners
- Go-kart racing shops
- Motorcycle dealers

Customer details are captured during online sales processes and through salespeople who conduct field sales work. These are entered into a **Customer Relationship Management** (**CRM**) system and are copied automatically into an **Enterprise Resource Planning** (**ERP**) system.

Scenario requirements, the proposed solution, and the challenge

Senior marketing leaders in the example organization are looking to increase sales through an increase in direct marketing, ideally through electronic channels (email or social media) to minimize print media costs. They will use email to encourage people and organizations to post about the company on social media, and in return, the best posts will receive company merchandise (stickers, posters, and clothing, with some signed by a well-known racing driver).

The organization has created a data platform that is intended to be a single source of truth for data requirements. This platform includes a data lake and warehouse and is connected to data visualization tools.

The marketing team is encouraged to take data from this platform for two reasons:

- They need to analyze the data to decide which customers should be included in the marketing activity and to what extent. The tools associated with the data platform are better able to handle this data analysis than the systems of record (ERP and CRM).
- They are dealing with large data volumes, and there are concerns that the performance of the systems of record (ERP and CRM) will degrade due to the processing power required for the data analysis. Managing this through the data platform (which is updated daily from the source systems) will mitigate this risk.

When the marketing team follows this advice, they immediately run into issues. The issue is that only around 4% of the records they analyze contain valid contact details that would work for the electronic marketing channels. They are missing valid email addresses. Customers have been able to input deliberately incorrect emails on certain records.

How data governance can help in our scenario

There are many aspects of data governance that can be applied in this scenario to assist with the challenge. The first of these is ownership of the data.

Data ownership

Data ownership involves identifying an individual in an organization to take accountability for an entity of data, such as a customer. The data owner is given a list of roles and responsibilities, and they are the "driving force" behind improving the area they own.

In our engine manufacturer example, the customer email address might be owned by the sales department. The head of sales is the data owner who takes overall accountability.

After a significant period of uncertainty, because ownership of data in the organization is not well documented, the marketing team contacts the head of sales. The head of sales (as the data owner) is surprised that the percentage of valid email addresses is so low and starts an investigation.

The investigation uncovers that the marketing team have not chosen the correct field to use from the data platform. In this case, the use of the wrong field would be completely avoidable with appropriate definitions of data, available to all.

Data definitions

Once of the key responsibilities of a data owner is to ensure that good quality data definitions exist in a data catalog for their area of accountability.

These definitions should be detailed and specific, and any terms that are used across multiple definitions should be used consistently – for example, always using *revenue* or *sales* but not both.

In our engine manufacturer example, we find that there are actually five different email address definitions for customers, applying differently to different types of customers:

- For the direct sales customers, there is one email address field. This usually applies to individuals or small organizations where only one email address is required.

For the more complex corporate channel customers, four different email addresses are captured:

- An email for accounts receivable.
- An email for sales and marketing.
- An email for customer care – for example, for the customer service department to use to communicate with the customer when they have an issue with an engine.
- An email for deliveries – for example, arranging a delivery to a location at a time when it can be safely received. The cost of the engines manufactured by our example company is significant, so large batches of sales are delivered by appointment.

The CRM system contains fields labeled as `Email address 1`, `Email address 2`, `Email address 3`, and `Email address 4`. The data definitions provide sufficient guidance to understand the difference. The following table is an example of how these definitions might look:

CRM field	Scope	Business name	Data definition
Email address 1	Direct sales customers	Email address	A field used to capture an email address used for all communication with the customer. For online customers (usually the small go-kart teams and motorcycle owners ordering fewer than five units), this is the only email address captured. It is used for multiple purposes. The purposes are as follows: • Contact regarding sales invoices and their payment. • Promotion of products and offers, and order-related contact (delivery notifications and returns information).
Email address 1	Corporate channel customers (shops and dealers)	Accounts receivable email address	A field used to capture an email address that can be used to follow up with a customer regarding payment. It is entered manually by sales people in CRM for larger customers who order through the corporate channel. The data is used only for the purpose of contacting a customer regarding sales invoices and their payment.
Email address 2	Corporate channel customers (shops and dealers)	Sales and marketing email address	A field used to capture an email address that can be used to promote products, make offers, or discuss potential deals with a customer.
Email address 3	Corporate channel customers (shops and dealers)	Customer care email address	A field used to capture an email address that can be used to contact the customer in the event of recalls, or service requests that the customer raises. This is entered manually by sales people in CRM. It can also entered by customers when creating a service request ticket after a sale has occurred.

Email address 4	Corporate channel customers (shops and dealers)	Delivery email address	A field used to capture an email address that can be used to contact the customer about a delivery (or collection in the event of a return). This is entered manually by sales people in CRM. This email address is at the customer location level. This means that each customer can have many delivery email addresses maintained – one per delivery location.

Table 2.1 – An example of data definitions for data governance

In *Table 2.1*, there are technically only four fields where email addresses are captured in the CRM system, but there are five data definitions. This is because the business usage of the Email address 1 field is so different for the direct sales customers that this must be captured as a separate definition. The scope of the data definition is critical to the understanding of the user of the definitions in this case.

In our example, the investigation requested by the data owner identified that the data platform contains all four of these email address fields, but the marketing team had identified only the Email address 2 field in the data platform.

To help make this example more understandable, the following table outlines the state of the data in each of the email address fields:

Customer type	Field	Completeness	Comment
Direct sales (10,500 customers)	Email address 1	100%	Required for order, invoice, and delivery emails
Corporate channel (1,500 customers)	Email address 1	72%	Relatively well completed
Corporate channel (1,500 customers)	Email address 2	30%	The sales team did not routinely collect this information
Corporate channel (1,500 customers)	Email address 3	35%	The sales team did not routinely collect this information
Corporate channel (1,500 customers)	Email address 4	80%	Out of the full set of customers, 80% had at least one location with a valid email address

Table 2.2 – An example of data completeness for email addresses at an engine manufacturer

Using only the Email address 2 field meant that the marketing team was only seeing a completion rate of 3.8%. This is calculated by looking at the total number of customers (10,500 direct plus 1,500 corporate customers) and understanding that only 30% of the 1,500 corporate customers had a value in this field (the calculation of overall completeness then is 450 divided by 12,000).

The data owner's team was able to inform the marketing team to also look at `Email address 1`, and then the calculation of completeness changed to 91%. The marketing team would be much happier with this outcome.

However, the data owner then raises a new issue. Although data privacy is not considered part of data governance (it is part of the wider concept of data management), data owners often have a keen interest in this work as well. As the owner of the customer master, the data owner is aware of data privacy requirements, and they ask for further investigation into the proportion of direct sales customers who have given permission to receive sales and marketing content.

Knowledge of how data is used

Data owners have a responsibility to talk to consumers of data and understand how the data is used. They may need to provide guidance if the usage of data is not appropriate. There are two implications of this:

- Processes must be in place to notify key stakeholders of important activities that involve the data they have an interest in

- Policies must be in place around how data can or cannot be used, and these policies must be in line with local laws and regulations

The policies should be reflected in the data catalog. There will be further details on this in the data catalog section that follows.

For our engine manufacturer example, the data owner becomes aware of the intent to email a large number of customers and provides further input related to their data privacy responsibilities. The owner requests that two further checks be introduced into the data analysis:

- Check whether the marketing consent flag (another field in CRM) has been marked as `Yes` for each direct customer record

- Check whether the country of the customer is one where promotional emails are acceptable under local laws and regulations

Once these checks have been completed, the percentage of customers who can be contacted drops to 58% because only 6,510 of the direct customers consented to marketing. The marketing team will need to rework their assumptions to assess whether the campaign will be successful or not, but they will at least avoid being in breach of local laws and regulations (risking fines) related to privacy.

Components of the data catalog

The previous two sections on data definitions and data usage respectively are part of a wider data governance concept called the *data catalog*. The catalog will also include other key elements such as the following:

Element	Explanation	Importance
Field status	Outlines which fields are mandatory, business-mandatory, or optional. Business-mandatory means that the data should be provided if it is available, but there is recognition that it might not be available. For example, a VAT number is mandatory if a business is registered for VAT, but if they are not registered, there is nothing that you can do to collect this data.	Defining which fields are mandatory provides the basis for validations, training, and data quality rules about the completeness of data.
Data domain	The area of the organization that owns this data type. For example, customer data would be owned by the sales team.	This is important in defining which data owner takes accountability for this item.
Data standard	A data standard at a field level would detail how the data in a field should be captured. For example, a field such as `Customer name` might have a standard such as *Full name of the company, matching the legal name on the register of companies in the relevant country.*	Data standards can form the basis of data quality rules and process documentation used to train those who enter data into systems.
Field length and data type	Some data catalogs will include the expected length of a field and the type of data within it. For example, the name of the customer must be less than or equal to 35 characters and should be formatted as text.	This also can be valuable from a rules and training perspective. However, this is often not included in data catalogs because they are often intended to be system-agnostic. In other words, the business can define how the data should be without the constraints of a particular technology. When the data is then created in a system, it is scanned by specialist tools called Metadata Management tools. These tools connect to data sources such as CRM or ERP systems and catalog all the fields, their lengths, data types, and so on.

Table 2.3 – The key elements of a data catalog

A data catalog should be part of the DNA of an organization. There should be a high level of awareness of the existence of the catalog (driven by mandatory training on a regular cadence and for new joiners).

In my view, the catalog should be run a little like Wikipedia. By this, I mean that *anyone* should be able to submit a change to an element, such as a definition. The change should then be governed by appropriately authorized people, such as data stewards (a role that is explained later in the chapter). It can be rejected if it is incorrect, or approved and incorporated if it is correct. In my experience, when there is a heavy reliance on a small number of people to actually write content for the catalog, it does not flourish.

In the *Data governance tools and MDM* section, I will outline how metadata management tools bring the data catalog concept to life.

Bringing this back to our engine manufacturer example, if a data catalog existed in the organization, then the marketing team would have been able to do the following:

- Understand early on who to speak to about the data because the catalog would contain the data owner and data steward names
- Understand that there were multiple email address fields with different purposes and scopes

A data model

Most data governance initiatives include an effort to create a conceptual data model. This is system-agnostic and is a diagrammatic business representation of how different types of data are associated with one another in the organization.

The model will include the following:

- Key business "entities" of data, such as customers, addresses, orders, products, product types, suppliers, employees, and deliveries.
- The relationships between these different entities, such as the following:
  - One customer may have the following:
    - Many delivery addresses
    - Many orders
    - Many deliveries
  - One product may have the following:
    - Many orders
    - One product type
    - One supplier (assuming it is not a generic product that can be bought from multiple suppliers)

- The model is used to ensure that there is a good understanding of how data is structured within an organization. This can help with data engineering and visualization, as well as system design. Critically, it also helps to ensure data design decisions are made with a full understanding.

Returning to our engine manufacturer, the data model would make it clear that each customer would have multiple delivery addresses. The `Email address 4` field would be on the delivery address entity rather than the customer entity, and it would be clear to the users of that field that each customer should have at least one email address for each delivery address, and it would not be sufficient for the customer to have just one email address overall in this field.

An efficient, well-governed data management processes

A key part of data governance is to manage how data is created and updated. Commonly, these processes are referred to as **CRUD** processes (meaning create, read, update, and delete). The following table explains the meaning of each of these with an example:

CRUD component	Explanation and example
Create	A business process is completed and new data needs to be created to support it. For example, a contract is signed and a new customer record is then created in the CRM and ERP systems.
Read	Data in the system is consumed without being changed in analytics processes or downstream business processes (for example, in a sales order).
Update	Over time, records become outdated, or new fields may be added, requiring an update to the customer. The update of a record encompasses many different aspects. It can be a simple change to a record, or it can involve blocking or unblocking a record for transactions in a system. For example, blocking a customer for future sales where there is a payment issue, or unblocking a customer who has now settled a balance.
Delete	Deletion of data involves closing down active transactions, retaining the data for a period of time for tax reasons or for business analysis (for example, trending of sales over time), and then physically deleting it from a system.
	In reality, deletion is not very common. Organizations often mark records for future deletion but never actually remove the data from a system. This is sometimes because the retention period means that there is a long gap between marking for deletion and when the record can actually be deleted, and the action to actually delete is forgotten.
	For example, when a customer is no longer transacted with (perhaps they have gone out of business), the data might be deleted after a retention period.

Table 2.4 – An explanation of CRUD in MDM

Organizations that invest in data governance will work hard to ensure that these processes are properly reviewed and designed effectively for their specific needs. The process review would need to consider the following:

- **The different roles that need to interact in the process**: For example, customer data typically needs input from a customer, a sales team (details of the contract terms agreed with the customer), and a finance team (creditworthiness) before it can be fully activated.

- **Training of these individuals**: People inside and outside an organization need to have sufficient guidance to be able to input useful data on the first attempt. Internal users need to understand the importance of this for the success of the organization.

- **Validations of the data at the point of entry**: For example, checks to ensure mandatory information is provided and is valid.

- **Approvals of the data through the process**: For example, sales may propose a credit limit for a customer, but finance would need to approve it. A data governance team may also approve every record to ensure it is compliant with policies and standards.

- **Different systems of record that need to receive the data**: In all organizations, data will need to be propagated to different systems before transactions will fully function. For example, a customer may be entered into a CRM system, but it would also need to be in an ERP system so that the customer's payment can be processed, and stock can be appropriately allocated.

- **Duplication checks**: When new data is created in a system, it is critical to try to avoid duplication. The customer experience, for example, is negatively impacted where duplicate records exist. The customer may find that each statement from the organization shows only a subset of their transactions, and they have to piece together the information.

Going back to *Figure 1.3* in *Chapter 1*, it is very important to balance validation, governance checks, and the speed of the data process. If speed is prioritized over governance, then data will deteriorate, but if governance is prioritized over speed, eventually the participants and owners of the process will look to avoid governance. Either situation leads eventually to a poor outcome.

In our engine manufacturer example, investment in the data process could have made the marketing team's request easier:

- In the example, the completeness of the sales and marketing email address field for corporate customers is very low (30%). The sales team has not been routinely collecting this data.

- The organization now has a clear and strong purpose for this information.

- The data creation process could be strengthened by training the sales team on the importance of the information and also by introducing reminder messages when a record is saved without this data being completed. However, it would not be possible to add an error message to prevent saving the data because it is acceptable for the corporate customer to decline to provide an email address for this purpose.

A further consideration for the CRUD processes in the organization would be the potential use of MDM tools, ensuring that there is a single source of truth for customer data that covers the fields in both the CRM and ERP systems. At present, it appears that the customer exists in both locations, with CRM focusing on contact details and sales and ERP focusing on the allocation of stock, delivery, and customer payments. This can lead to complications such as the following:

- Different system IDs for the same customer
- Fields that exist in both systems are updated in one system and not the other, causing synchronization issues

Later in this section, the various tools that can support a data governance initiative will be outlined. The discipline of MDM will also be covered in greater detail. As stated previously, this is not part of data governance. Data governance defines the desired processes, and then the MDM activity automates them. This is a good example of where data governance creates the foundations for other related disciplines. MDM is included in this section because there are close ties between data quality and MDM.

Data policies

Linked closely to data processes, *data policies* are a foundational element of data governance. The policies are used by data owners to communicate their intentions and expectations in relation to the data they are accountable for.

The policies required will differ across different organizations. The following table provides a list of the policies that I have seen successfully implemented at a number of organizations:

Policy	Details
Duplication	Provides a clear definition of what is considered to be a duplicate record.
	Many people expect that it should be sufficient to simply state that duplication is not allowed.
	Unfortunately, organizations are usually more nuanced than that.
	At one organization I worked with, there were some suppliers who supplied physical products but also owned land that the organization needed to pay rent for. When a contract ended for the physical product supply, the supplier was disabled in the system, and rent payments also stopped. This led to the utility supply for the equipment on the land being cut off, which impacted the customers of the organization.
	Following this, the duplication policy made it acceptable to have two instances of the same supplier for two entirely different business models.

Active/inactive data	This policy defines when a particular type of data should be considered inactive. For example, if the organization has not ordered from a supplier for 18 months, has not paid that supplier for 6 months, and has no remaining open items with the supplier, then this policy might define that the supplier is inactive.
	The policy also defines what action should be taken when a record is deemed to be inactive. For example, the record should be blocked or marked ready for deletion.
Retention	Linked to the preceding policy, this policy defines how long data should be retained in an organization for different types of data.
	Inactive records should be deleted completely after a specified period, which may be defined by taxation law or other regulations.
Data quality	The data quality policy should define the following: • Broad expectations of an organization in regard to data quality – for example, every individual takes accountability for the data that they can impact • How data quality issues are to be managed – for example, when they should be escalated • Roles and responsibilities for data quality issue management

Table 2.5 – Important data governance policies for organizations

The policies outlined in *Table 2.5* can form the basis for data quality requirements. For example, the active/inactive data policy will be used to identify data that should be considered inactive and ignored from a data quality remediation perspective.

The duplication policy will help to define a set of data quality rules that can be used to identify potential duplicate records.

Returning again to our engine manufacturer example – the active/inactive data policy would be helpful to identify customers who are no longer active. A decision could then be made on whether to send them marketing content to try to restart the relationship. The alternative would be to accept that the relationship has ended (perhaps because it appears that they are no longer in business).

Known quality of data

Of course, a key part of data governance is to ensure that the quality of data is at least known and ideally improved over time to avoid negative business impacts.

Linking this back to our engine manufacturer example - because the organization did not have a data quality measurement capability, the marketing team had to find out independently that only 58% of records could be contacted for marketing purposes. This was because the customer data had missing email address data and a lack of consent. Had a proper data quality measurement process been in place, the data would have been of known quality to enable proper forward planning. The marketing project should have been able to anticipate this and put a data cleansing exercise in their plan.

As the rest of the book focuses on data quality, this will be sufficient for now on this subject.

This concludes the exploration of the various people, process, and policy elements of data governance and leaves us with only one remaining aspect to consider – technology.

Data governance tools and MDM

The preceding sections provided an insight into the people, process, and policy elements of data governance. The only remaining element is the use of tools. Although I consider tools to be an essential element of a successful data governance strategy, it is important to emphasize that they can only truly add value when delivered alongside other elements.

We will now explore the main categories of tools widely used in the marketplace for data governance and MDM.

Data quality tools

In this section, we will not explicitly talk about how data quality tools fit into a data governance initiative. Much of the book is about this (particularly *Chapters 5* and *7*), so more content here would be superfluous. However, it is important to explain that a data quality tool cannot deliver a positive outcome without appropriate actions on the people, process, and policy side.

For example, working to implement a data quality tool without having clearly defined data ownership could lead to the following situations:

- You can identify data quality rules, but there is no one to make decisions on which to prioritize
- You can identify areas of data that require improvement, but no one feels empowered to take resources from other activities and move them to work on data quality remediation
- You lack the support at a senior level to get budget approval for your data quality initiative

A further illustration of this relates to the presence of data definitions. I would not say that good data definitions are a prerequisite for a successful data quality tool implementation, but they most definitely help. In fact, you will find that you will do most of the work to produce a good data definition when defining the rules. Here is a detailed example of this:

- An organization identifies that employees who have left are not automatically deactivated in all IT systems. The retained access is a security risk.

- A rule is created that states that "employees with a status of L or P in the HR system `employee type` field must have a status of `0009` in the employee account directory `status` field."

- Clearly, without further background information, this technical explanation of the rule is only meaningful to HR and IT system subject matter experts.

- To provide that background, a design document is written to explain the business purpose of the rule and what it means in business language. This might look something like this:

  - **Employee type**: A field used by the HR area of the business to understand the status of an employee in their relationship with the organization. `Employee type` indicates whether an employee record is an active employee (`A`), a pensioner (retired employee) (`P`), a leaver (`L`), on extended leave (`EL`), or a resigned employee (with a leave date in the past) (`R`).

  - **Status**: The `status` field in the employee account directory is used by the IT team to indicate whether an account is still able to log on to the organization's systems and whether single sign-on to underlying applications will work. The status options are `0001` (active), `0009` (disabled), and `0002` (email only).

  - The data quality rule identifies all employees who are of status `L` (leaver) or `P` (pensioner) and identifies their status in the employee account directory.

  - If the status is `0009`, then the row of data is considered "passed."

  - If the status is `0001` or `0002`, then the rule is considered "failed." Note that a second rule might check the inverse – in other words, that no employees who are active from an HR perspective have a disabled IT account. (I am sure I am not alone in having had my IT account deactivated when still employed and trying to work hard!)

It is clear that a good data definition can easily be produced from this, and therefore, data quality rules and data definitions complement one another.

The examples given focused on data quality tools and how they are supported by business concepts. However, the same principle applies to master data and metadata management tools. The following sections explain these tools and their role in data governance in greater depth.

MDM tools

MDM tools are often deployed based on the foundations provided by data process work within data governance. An MDM tool is a specialist tool that is intended to improve the process of creating and changing master data, through automation, validation of data, and the ability to integrate with other systems effectively. MDM tools are often used as a single source of the truth for master data.

MDM tools can operate in different scenarios depending on the needs of a business. The different options to implement MDM tools are described in the following sections.

Central MDM

This is where the entire process of creating and updating master data is managed by an MDM tool in a semi-automated fashion. A process I implemented in an MDM tool at a previous organization supported supplier MDM and had the following steps:

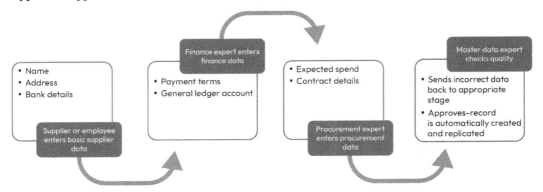

Figure 2.1 – An MDM process example

This implementation began with an existing process that was well defined but lacked automation. The data was entered into Microsoft Excel spreadsheets and emailed between each party contributing data. The final step was a data entry process from a master data clerk who needed to cut and paste data from Excel into a system of record. There were very few validations in place, and often, the data provided could not be entered into the system without being corrected. This led to interpretation from master data clerks who did not want to return to the start of the process.

The MDM tool automatically posted approved data into the system of record and applied all the system validations at the point of entry, without committing data into the system in case it had to be rejected. This significantly improved the speed of the process and led to valuable personnel cost savings.

The MDM tool was also used to replicate data to multiple receiving systems. For example, two ERP systems needed the same copy of the supplier data, as well as contract management and supplier relationship management systems.

For data types where a third party actually provides the majority of the data (for example, suppliers or customers), it has become much less common for the MDM tool to be the first point of entry in central MDM scenarios. Cloud-based procurement tools such as SAP Ariba and e-commerce platforms such as Shopify have become stronger at collecting master data. They not only make the data collection process easy for the supplier or customer but also validate data using external data sources. For example, email addresses, bank details, and postal addresses are all validated when entered, and errors or warnings are provided to the person inputting the data. Where an MDM tool might previously have been the master system, collecting data from the supplier or customer and writing it into procurement or e-commerce platforms, the process is more commonly reversed now. These platforms collect the data and pass it to an MDM system, which then collects internal information (for example, the procurement and finance information in *Figure 2.1*) in a semi-automated fashion and then distributes it to the internal systems that need it.

From a data quality perspective, this means that when correcting issues with data, it is not sufficient to target only the MDM system for improvement – the cloud procurement and e-commerce platforms (or indeed any platform that is part of the data creation process) must also be considered.

Consolidation scenarios

A consolidation scenario recognizes that data may need to be created and changed in several different systems of record, and it looks to bring the data together into a single "golden record."

For example, if an organization has different ERP systems in three different regions, managed by different master data teams, it may be necessary for all of them to be able to create data independently, at least for a period of time. This will ensure they can be reactive to the needs of their region.

However, the organization still needs to have a single view of the data. For example, much better conversations can be completed with a global customer where there is a full view of the business relationship with them in all three regions. Perhaps the customer buys much less in the Asia-Pacific region as a percentage of their revenue than in the North American region. To be able to analyze this in the analytics teams in the organization, there must be a way to link the three customer records in the various regional ERP systems together. The MDM tool can perform a matching activity and automatically assign a common identifier to all the common customer records.

Further information can be captured about the customer in the "golden record," which is not necessary for ERP transactions but helps the overall business relationship with the customer.

In our engine manufacturer example, the data was entered into a CRM system and copied into an ERP system. It is likely that there would be additional data required in the ERP system that would not be needed in the CRM system – for example, the bank details of the customer if the organization needed to provide a refund, or the general ledger account to reconcile the customer to.

An MDM tool could be put into place to manage the whole process of creating a customer. The customer could be given access to a web page that was linked to the MDM tool and asked to enter data. There would be validations in place to make it easier for customers to get their data correct on the first attempt. For example, the email address could be checked by sending an email in which there is a link that the user must click before they can complete their registration. Once the CRM element of the data is complete, the MDM tool will send the data to the CRM system and then prompt ERP users to add any ERP-specific data. The MDM tool would then validate this data before sending it to the ERP system.

Sometimes, investment in MDM-driven processes does not return the required value. In my experience, the data volumes have to be relatively high, and the process must have significant complexities that the MDM tool can partially automate.

Metadata management tools

Metadata management tools are generally better known as **data catalog tools**. They provide a single location to store everything we know about our data – but not the data itself. Metadata is the "data about the data" and includes the following content I referred to in the earlier *Components of the data catalog* section:

- Ownership of data
- Definitions of data
- Data quality rules
- Other information relating to specific systems:
  - Technical details of fields in systems – technical names, field lengths, and field types
  - The lineage of data – how it moves from sources through to target systems and reports

Examples of these tools include Microsoft Purview, Informatica Cloud Data Governance & Data Catalog, Collibra Data Intelligence Cloud, and Alation Data Catalog.

These tools usually have two distinct capabilities:

- A business glossary, which is the business-driven content from the data catalog, curated by people with deep subject matter expertise in the business meaning of the data
- A technical data catalog, which is populated by scanning the systems of record and then describing the data that is found

The challenge with these two distinct components is linking the two together. For example, a field on product data called `Material Group` in an SAP ERP system would have a technical table/field name of `MARA/MATKL`. There might be a business glossary term called *product type* and then a detailed definition of this. The `Material Group` field could be the physical system instantiation of the product type business concept, and the two should be tied together – but it is not easy to see this unless you are both a business process and SAP ERP expert.

Linking the two together is critical when organizations want to bring data quality into the mix. When you start to measure data quality systematically, this provides the opportunity to embed the current level of data quality into the data catalog.

For example, when an end user sees a column of data in a report, they can press a defined hotkey on their keyboard (this is part of the functionality of many of the metadata tools) and trigger the data catalog to appear. The catalog will offer the business glossary term that matches the report column, and it can show information such as the following:

- The definition
- The owner

- The lineage (in other words, which system did the data originate from, and what has happened between the source and the report?)

It is this last point on the lineage where data quality information becomes important. If the data quality of the field is known, then it can be displayed as part of the metadata. The report user can see that the completeness of the data is only 60% for the column that they try to use. They might even be able to see that if the report sourced its data from the same field in a different system, the completeness level is higher.

To complete our engine manufacturer example, the metadata tool would have offered the ultimate guide to the marketing team for their requirements. They would have been able to see all of the email address fields, fully defined, with a single view of the completeness of the data available. They would have been able to see the field that would show whether customers had consented to have marketing content sent to them, and they would have had access to privacy policies. The metadata tool would bring everything they needed all together in one place.

Metadata management tools can offer a single view of everything that an organization knows about its data, including, critically, the current level of data quality.

This concludes the explanation of the data governance and MDM tools that your organization might use in its pursuit of data improvement.

How data quality fits into data governance and MDM

Up to this point, this chapter has focused on helping you understand the important concepts of data governance. This section will now explain the interactions between the data quality initiative and the overall data governance and data management effort.

In my view, the intended end result of investment in data management is to ensure that data becomes – and remains – fit for purpose. Of all the areas of data management, I have always been most interested in data quality initiatives because they are the "results business" of data management. By this, I mean that the success of the whole data effort is reflected in the numbers that data quality tools show. Has the average data quality score improved this month? Can we see that this improvement has made our organization a little more effective?

It is clear that success in a data quality initiative is dependent on the efforts put into other data building blocks, but the results from a data quality initiative often also indicate improvements that can be made to the way that data governance and other aspects of data management work. It is, therefore, a very symbiotic relationship between data quality and the rest of the data management disciplines.

For example, data ownership is a key part of the success of data quality work, but data quality work becomes a key part of measuring the success of data ownership. Data quality rules will expose areas with inadequate data ownership by highlighting worsening scores.

To complete the topic of data quality within data governance, the following section will outline the key interactions between the two.

Data governance, MDM, and data quality touchpoints

This section outlines each aspect of data governance described earlier in this chapter and explains how each can help or be helped by data quality work.

The following table can be used as a reference guide in a data quality initiative to ensure that there is sufficient interaction between teams in the data governance area:

Area	Benefits of data governance for a data quality initiative	Benefits to data governance from a data quality initiative
Data ownership	Help in prioritizing which areas of data need the most attention. Accountability for the data quality rules. Ability to assign resources to data quality initiatives – both people and financial.	A quantitative view of where data is improving or worsening.
Data definitions	Data definitions can significantly accelerate the creation of data quality rules. If data definitions exist, the person who created them can be contacted again to support the development of data quality rules.	Data definitions are often refined and improved by the work done in a data quality initiative.
Knowledge of how data is used	Knowledge of how fields are used helps determine how important they are and, therefore, their priority for data quality work.	When combining knowledge of how data is used with clarity on the level of data quality, the result is valuable. For example, if you know that a field is used for a critical compliance purpose, and you also can check the data quality before the data is sent to the regulator, then you can proactively prevent issues.

Data model	Where a stakeholder asks for a focus on a particular set of data, a data model can show the dependencies with other related data. For example, to improve customer data for analytics purposes, the data model will show that not only does the customer data need to be improved but also all the dimensions. A dimension might be the list of sales managers who sell to customers. For example, if the sales manager's line manager field is not available in that dimension, it would negatively impact an analysis of which parts of the sales team are performing best.	Defining data quality rules can provide great information to help improve a data model. For example, a data quality rule might show a distinction between different types of customers that is significant enough to be reflected in the data model. This could be a realization that some customers are dealers, who sell on to end user customers, while other customers are direct end users. The data model might be updated to show these two different types of business models separately because they would sell through different channels.
Efficient, well-governed data management processes	Well-documented data processes can help a data quality initiative establish which data is most important from a quality perspective.	Data quality rules can be reused in data management processes. Previously unknown rules can be added as validations when creating or changing data.
Data policies	Data quality initiatives will use data policies as an input. For example, data quality reports will generally filter out inactive data (to avoid expending effort on correcting data that is no longer useful), and data policies will define the circumstances where data can be considered inactive.	Data quality initiatives will give rise to new policies (for example, a policy on how to handle data quality issues through forums) but generally do not directly impact existing data quality policies.
MDM tools	MDM tools can be a great source of data for a data quality tool. If the MDM tool provides a single golden record that combines data from multiple underlying sources, the data quality tool can access that instead of all the sources. This can reduce cost, but it is important that no data transformation happens between the true source and the MDM tool for this to be useful.	Some MDM tools are able to connect to a data quality tool and reuse the rules at the time of data entry. The data quality tool becomes a repository of validations that the MDM tool can apply. This saves costs because validations do not have to be developed by the MDM tool implementation.

Data catalog	The data catalog can provide significant time savings when implementing a data quality tool because the definitions, owners, lineage, and other important and useful information are readily available.	The information from a data quality initiative can enrich a data catalog. If users can see the lineage of their report (where the data comes from and how it is transformed) along with the quality of the data at each stage, it gives the best opportunity for business issues caused by bad data to be understood and resolved.

Table 2.6 – A summary of the interactions between data quality initiatives and key aspects of data governance

The preceding reference guide can be used as a starting point to work with the data governance team in your organization (if one exists). It can be made specific to your organization and serve as a promise between the sub-teams of how they will work with one another.

So far, the chapter has explained every main aspect of data governance initiatives and outlined the relevance of each of these to data quality.

The remainder of the chapter will explain the basics of the data quality discipline to prepare you for the concepts referred to in the rest of the book.

Generally accepted principles and terminology of data quality

Data quality as a recognized discipline has been around for a long time. Many organizations and individuals have developed methodologies that have developed our collective thinking and improved outcomes. This section aims to lay out the recognized principles and explain the terminology that every seasoned data quality professional should understand.

Naturally, this section builds on the work of many data governance experts, and there are many references to other existing content, particularly DAMA International (https://www.dama.org/cpages/home). Having said this, the section also includes my own interpretation and views on these accepted concepts as well as practical examples to bring them to life. The first part of this section outlines the basic concepts of data quality.

The basic terms of data quality defined

In *Chapter 1*, I outlined in detail what is meant by "bad data" and the impacts of bad data on organizations. Outlining this in such detail makes it much easier to define the overall concept of data quality simply.

Definition

The level of data quality in an organization is the extent to which data can be used for its intended purposes.

The intended purposes mentioned in the definition refer to the areas outlined in *Chapter 1* in the definition of bad data, namely issues with business processes, decision-making, compliance, and differentiation of an organization from its competitors.

In the following table, we will define the key data quality terms that we will refer to throughout the book. Many of you will already understand these terms but may know them by different names. It is, therefore, important to define them so that they are contextualized for the remainder of the book:

Term	Definition	References
Data quality rules	A data quality rule is logic that is applied to each row of a dataset, which can determine whether a row of data is correct or incorrect.	*Chapter 6* outlines every aspect of data quality rules in detail.
Data quality dimensions	Data quality dimensions are a way of organizing the various data quality rules into themes. For example, data quality rules that assess whether data is missing or not would be mapped to the "Completeness" data quality dimension.	DAMA UK published a white paper in October 2013 on data quality dimensions called *The six primary dimensions for data quality assessment.* This paper provides the data quality dimensions used in the majority of organizations, and this chapter builds on that white paper.
Failed records	Failed records are rows of data that have been run through a data quality rule and deemed incorrect – for example, a record that is supposed to contain a value but is actually found to be empty. The inverse, of course, would be known as a passed record.	*Chapters 6 and 7* both discuss failed records extensively.
Data quality issues	Data quality issues are where failed records are analyzed to ascertain their impact on an organization, with the aim of agreeing on a resolution action.	These are mentioned throughout the book.
Data profiling	Data profiling assesses a set of data and provides information on the values, the length of strings, the level of completeness, and the distribution patterns of each column.	*Chapter 5* outlines the whole process of identifying data quality issues and how profiling can translate these into rules.

Data quality monitoring	The process of reviewing the current status of data quality in an organization, using reports that aggregate the results of rule checks.	*Chapter 7* outlines the reporting required as part of data quality monitoring.
Data quality remediation	The activity to correct data quality once issues have been identified and prioritized.	*Chapter 8* covers this in depth.
Data domains	A data domain is a logical grouping of data. It can be by data object (for example, customer or employee) or by process area (for example, commercial data or HR data).	These are mentioned throughout the book.

Table 2.7 – The key definitions of data quality-related terms

Most of the preceding topics are covered in greater depth in other chapters. Data dimensions, however, are referenced throughout the book and require some further explanation in the following section.

Data quality dimensions

In the early days of my career, I worked as an auditor with a Big Four accounting firm. My job was to check that the financial statements of my clients were a fair reflection of their real financial performance and position.

In order to check this, we were encouraged to check their books and records for *completeness* and *accuracy*. These two terms are transferrable to a certain extent, from the financial audit world to the world of data quality. One of the factors that drew me to data quality was the fact that I inherently and immediately understood what people were talking about when they referred to these dimensions in our initiatives.

In this section, I will reference the recognized data quality dimensions as outlined by DAMA UK in the white paper *The six primary dimensions for data quality assessment* (henceforth referred to as the "DAMA white paper") and provide examples from my own experience of applying these.

Completeness

The first and simplest of the dimensions is completeness. Completeness is defined by the DAMA white paper as "*the proportion of stored data against the potential of '100% complete'.*"

Data quality rules are put in place that define when a value *should* be present in a field, and then each row is checked. The sum of the rows that contain values is then compared to the total number of rows in the scope of the rules.

We will return to the engine manufacturer example:

- The organization has 50,000 products set up in its ERP system

- There are a number of data quality rules set up for completeness for this dataset

- For now, we will assume that all the rules apply to all 50,000 products:

Rule	Rule result
Each product should have a batch number	62%
Each product should have a location	90%
Each product should have a date of manufacture	40%
Each product should have a product type	98%
Overall completeness score	**74%**

Table 2.8 – A simple illustration of completeness across multiple rules

This is a very simple example. In reality, there will be different types of products in this dataset, and some of the rules may only apply to a subset of them. In the following example, we will assume that engine parts make up 32,000 out of the 50,000 products, and only engine parts need a batch number and date of manufacture:

Rule	Number of records assessed	Rule result
Each product should have a batch number	32,000	97%
Each product should have a location	50,000	90%
Each product should have a date of manufacture	32,000	63%
Each product should have a product type	50,000	98%
Overall completeness score	**Not applicable**	**87%**

Table 2.9 – An illustration of completeness where rules apply to only a subset of records

Completeness is a useful data dimension because it is so easily understood by stakeholders. Data quality professionals usually get a lot of recognition for a statement along the lines of "*the completeness of our product data has improved from 59% to 80% in the last six months*." This is not necessarily true for other data quality dimensions. For example, if you substitute "*completeness*" for "*timeliness*" in that statement, there will likely be many more questions asked.

It is very important not to focus too hard on completeness. In one organization I worked at, the focus was so strong on completeness that end users started to prioritize putting *any* data into a field rather than putting the *right* data into it. This is why it is critical to consider the dimensions together.

Uniqueness

The next dimension that is outlined by the DAMA white paper is uniqueness. It is defined by DAMA as *"no thing will be recorded more than once based upon how that thing is identified."*

The end of this definition takes us back immediately to the *Data policies* section in this chapter. The data policy is where an organization should define what identifies a unique row of data. This is not as straightforward as it sounds, as the following example will show.

We will consider supplier data duplication. You might decide to base uniqueness on the address of a supplier. If you have two suppliers with exactly the same address, then there is an assumption of duplication.

We all know, however, that large office premises are often shared – for example, one floor per company. Unless we have the floor numbers for the different entities, this is not a reliable indicator of duplication on its own.

We might consider using the company name to help us match records with potential duplicates. The following screenshot of company names from the UK Companies House website illustrates how this can be problematic. This is a publicly available register of companies, and I searched `apple service` as an example:

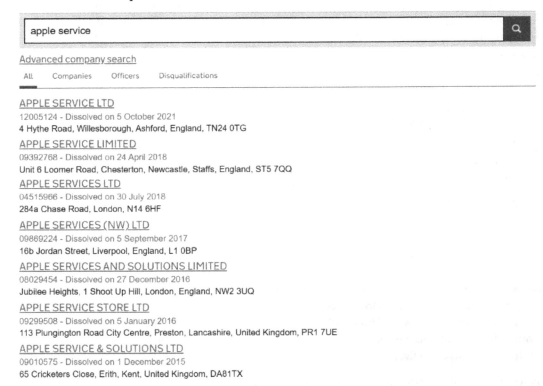

Figure 2.2 – An example of the similarities in company names

> **Note**
>
> *Figure 2.2* is used under the Open Government License (`https://www.nationalarchives.gov.uk/doc/open-government-licence/version/3/`). It contains public sector information licensed under the Open Government License v3.0.

It is very hard to identify the specific company of interest based on the company name alone.

Another option might be to use identification numbers such as a **Dun & Bradstreet** (**D&B**) identification number (called a DUNS number), tax number, or company registration number. These are unique identifiers and can often uniquely identify an organization. The challenge with these tends to be a lack of completeness. Suppliers may not provide this data immediately – it may only come with the first invoice, and an organization may not remember to go back to the supplier record and update it with this information.

> **Note**
>
> A DUNS number is an identifier for a unique legal entity provided by Dun & Bradstreet – a global provider of business decisioning (for example, decisions about providing credit and supplier selection) and data and analytics.
>
> You can read more about the DUNS number on the company's website here: `https://www.dnb.com/`.

In reality, the way to check for uniqueness is to create a check that incorporates all of these together. This is covered in greater depth in *Chapter 7* in the *Managing duplicates* section.

Finally, some organizations may choose to allow duplication in certain situations. I gave one example of this when talking about data policies earlier in the chapter. There is another good example in the HR and IT area. Generally, organizations will have rules that employees should be unique but with some exceptions in certain circumstances. Employees often require elevated IT access (in order to log on and maintain remote servers, for example), and in some organizations, this can require a second employee record. One record is used for the day-to-day HR responsibilities, and the other is simply to allow a second IT account to be created for elevated privileges to be in place. It might be possible to eliminate this practice over time (for example, by allowing two IT records to be associated with a single HR record), but it might take six months to make this change. For the six-month period, this would be an allowed exception – where data quality rules and reports do not flag the admin account as a duplicate. This is important to ensure that the HR team does not see "false positive" results in their failed data reporting and lose faith in the data quality reports.

In my experience, there are not usually many data quality rules associated with uniqueness. Duplication tends to be managed by creating a report, as outlined in *Chapter 7*.

Timeliness

The DAMA white paper moves on next to timeliness. DAMA defines this as *"the degree to which data represent reality from the required point in time."*

I often find that organizations use accuracy instead of timeliness for data quality rules which could fall into this category. DAMA recognizes this and states that accuracy is a dimension related to timeliness. I believe timeliness is "under-utilized" because the action that must be taken for failures on a timeliness rule will be different from the action taken for one related to accuracy.

For example, a rule that checks whether any cost centers in an organization are owned by employees who are marked as leavers might often be classified as an accuracy rule. I think this is better classified as a timeliness rule because what it tells us is that when an employee leaves, cost centers must be updated on a timely basis. There should be a routine check to see whether they own cost centers, and if they do, then a re-assignment to an employee who is remaining with the organization should be made on the same day. In most ERP systems (where cost centers usually exist), it is possible to apply a change on a future date, so this is perfectly feasible.

Other real examples of rules for timeliness from my experience include the following:

- A check to ensure that a customer credit check is not more than three months old at the time of a sales order being raised. Credit worthiness can rapidly change for a company, and therefore, the recency of credit checking is critical.

- A check in a data warehouse to ensure that the data has been refreshed in accordance with an agreed schedule. For example, if the data is meant to be updated daily, then all new records and changes to existing records up to the current date minus one day should be in the data warehouse.

- A check to ensure that customer address data has been checked or updated in the last six months before dispatching stock with a value of more than $1,000.

- A check to ensure that no medicinal products are sent to a location where the license ID of the medical practitioner (for example, a doctor, registered nurse, or pharmacist) has not been checked in the last 12 months.

Validity

The next dimension is defined by DAMA UK as *"data are valid if it conforms to the syntax (format, type, range) of its definition."*

Along with completeness, this is the most commonly used dimension and will probably have a large number of data quality rules associated with it. This dimension is best explained with examples, as follows:

- Employee data is checked for a valid social security number. This varies by the country that the employee is based in:

  - In the UK, the format checked for is *XX 11 11 11 X* (where *X* is an alpha character and *1* is a numerical character)

  - In the US, the format checked for is *111-11-1111* (where *1* is a numerical character)

- Customer email addresses contain the appropriate components:

  - An @ sign is included

  - A domain appears after the @ sign (not necessarily a real or valid domain – there'll be more on this later)

  - The suffix is correct – for example, `.com`, `org`, or `.co`

- Zip or postal codes are in the appropriate format for the country the address is based in:

  - In the UK, the format checked for is *XX1(1) 1XX* (with the same notation as before; the second *1* is in parentheses to indicate it is optional as it applies only to London)

The key takeaway from the DAMA definition and my examples is that data is only checked against an expected format, type, or range. It is not checked to confirm that it is real. For example, `rob@ hawker.com` is a valid email address, but it is not accurate. It is not my email address, and the `hawker.com` domain is not a valid domain at the time of writing (perhaps I should reserve this and build an online empire!?).

This comparison to reality is where the accuracy data dimension comes in.

Accuracy

The accuracy dimension is defined by DAMA UK as "*the degree to which data correctly describes the "real-world" object or event being described.*"

The key part of this definition is the fact that rules associated with this dimension must compare data to an authoritative source of some kind. For example, an email address validity rule can check that the domain provided is a real domain. If we can connect to a database of all existing domains and compare email addresses to it, then we can check whether that part of the email address is valid. Note that we still cannot easily check the part before the @ sign.

In reality, rules that truly address accuracy are usually more difficult and expensive to implement because they involve access to a third-party resource. A good example of this is supplier data, and my experience of working with an organization called D&B. There are many references in this book to using the services of **D&B** because they have a large and accurate database of organization data that can be used to check the accuracy of internally held data. The success of their business is based on the accuracy of the company data in their database. At previous organizations I worked with, we would compare our data to D&B's database and create rules to assess where our data differed from theirs. These rules were good examples of the appropriate use of the accuracy dimension.

Another good example comes from Nigel Turner from Global Data Strategy (`https://www. linkedin.com/in/nigelturnerdataman/`). At one of Nigel's former organizations, physical validation of electronic equipment was required to ensure the accuracy of data. It was critical to that organization to ensure that equipment was correctly identified and assigned to the right customer.

In the early days of my career when I was a financial auditor, I encountered another example of this. A client that sold rice had large silos containing the product at their premises. Cameras were positioned at observation windows at various points of the silo to enable the quantity (and value) of rice to be remotely ascertained. During a difficult period, the company wanted to increase the value of the rice on its balance sheet because of financial problems, and so they used glue to affix rice to the inside of the observation windows! The silo was made to look fuller than it really was. This is an example of an issue with data quality related to the accuracy dimension. Following this, the data quality was routinely checked by an auditor climbing the ladder to inspect the rice from the top of the silo – not a simple task for those of us who do not enjoy heights!

In organizations like this where physical assets define success or failure, this kind of approach may be required.

Consistency

The final dimension that DAMA UK outlines is consistency. DAMA UK defines this as *"the absence of difference, when comparing two or more representations of a thing against a definition."*

This dimension becomes relevant when comparing data that should be the same across different data sources in your organization. A very typical example of this is employee data. Employee data is pervasive in organizations. It usually begins its life in HR systems, before being propagated to identity management systems (such as Microsoft's Azure Active Directory) and then applications that the employees use (such as Microsoft Office 365 applications, SAP ERP, and CRM systems).

In each of these places, there will be a simple record of the employee, including their name, email address, and expiry date (if they are a contractor). It is a very common problem for employee data to be out of sync across these systems. This lack of synchronization causes some very common problems in organizations. I suspect many of you reading this will have suffered from one or more of these at some time:

- Contractors have their employment extended in the HR system, but this does not propagate to the IT systems, and they are locked out of their machines or their applications

- Employees need to perform a new function – such as claiming for out-of-pocket expenses – but they have to set up a new profile in the expenses system (in other words, they incorrectly do not exist in the expenses system)

- Employees change their name (for example, through marriage), and this name change is reflected only in a subset of the applications where they have a profile

- Employees change their bank account details in the HR system, but the expenses system still holds the old account details

- Employees move departments, but their information and access are still commensurate to their previous roles

These are all examples of inconsistencies between different systems, and the rules that are created for this dimension can be some of the most valuable. Imagine if we introduce data quality rules that help an organization find resolutions to all these common problems. The employee experience would be so much more positive, and a lot of time would be saved.

General advice on data quality dimensions

Data quality dimensions are a fundamental part of data quality work. They offer a great way of aggregating the results of individual rules, but more importantly, they act as a prompt to ensure that a wide range of data quality rules have been considered.

For example, I typically see a split of data quality rules across the dimensions as follows:

Figure 2.3 – An approximate split of data quality rules across dimensions at most organizations

This bias toward completeness and validity is because these are usually the most obvious and most easily delivered rules. They focus on data in just one system within an organization and rely on basic knowledge of the data, which is important, and the expected formats and types.

It is important to look at which data quality dimensions you address with the population of rules that you identify and, more importantly, the dimensions that you neglect.

When looking at the examples of the rules I've provided against each dimension, it is clear that leaving out any one dimension will mean that some important rules are missed.

In my experience of working with data owners, with the appropriate research to identify the right set of rules, the split of rules against dimensions might look more like the following:

Figure 2.4 – A more balanced distribution of rules across dimensions

This obviously varies from dataset to dataset, and more effort is required to identify the rules. It is harder to achieve, but ultimately, a balance of rules against all the dimensions should add more value.

In this section, we explained the various terms that we will use in the rest of the book and focused on the key concept of data quality dimensions. This will be useful in later chapters (*Chapters 5, 6, and 7* in particular).

The next section moves on to the various stakeholders who are typically involved in data quality initiatives.

Stakeholders in data quality initiatives

Data quality initiatives require wide-ranging discussions and support from an organization. This section aims to outline each of the stakeholder types and explain the following:

- Their role
- The typical profile of people in these roles
- What help they will need to provide in a data quality initiative

Different stakeholder types and their roles

Clearly, every organization has its own way of organizing itself. There are no two organizations with an identical internal structure. However, over the last 15 years, a number of data governance role names (for example, data steward) have become standard across different geographies and industries. The content of these roles has become more and more consistent over this period. This section will outline these roles.

The roles that are outlined are not necessarily allocated as full-time positions. Often, people are given these roles on top of their "day job." Sometimes this is advantageous because the person cannot fulfill the data element of their role without being in the position that they are in. However, sometimes, it is detrimental to the person and the organization because the data element of the role is beyond the individual's capacity and, therefore, is neglected.

The various roles will be explored, along with a recommendation as to whether the role would be an additional responsibility on top of an existing role, or whether the role would be full-time. Prior to exploring the roles, we must understand an organization concept called the "hub-and-spoke" model.

The hub-and-spoke model

Most organizations now operate what is called a "hub-and-spoke model" for data and analytics work. In this model, there will be a "central hub" of roles, often led by a chief data officer (a role that is outlined in the following table). This team sets the vision and strategy for data and analytics and ensures organization-wide consistency in how data and analytics work is carried out. The hub will work to identify people within each business unit of the organization who they can partner with. These roles (led by data owners) are typically called "spoke" roles. There are alternative models, but the hub-and-spoke model is now so common that the remainder of the chapter assumes that this is how your organization is working.

A useful analogy for the hub is to think of it like a government of a country. The government will write a set of laws, and the police and legal system will ensure those laws are enforced. The hub is similar in this regard. The hub creates a framework (a set of laws if you will) for data governance that every spoke can then interpret and implement (and enforce!). Having introduced this concept, I will now explore each set of roles in turn.

Hub roles

The following table explains the hub roles that are relevant to data quality:

Stakeholder type	Role outline	Nature of role
Chief Data Officer (CDO)	The CDO is accountable for both data governance and analytics for an organization. This will include all aspects of data governance, data engineering, data science, and reporting. They may have their own budget but will typically partner with other parts of the organization, ensuring that activities that are data-related are coordinated and working toward an agreed vision and strategy. More mature organizations (from a data perspective) may have a CDO, but it is still very common for this role to not exist in organizations. In organizations without a CDO, the support required may come from another member of the executive team, such as a **Chief Technology Officer (CTO)** or a **Chief Financial Officer (CFO)**. In some organizations, there may be a head of data and analytics at a more junior level who effectively acts as a CDO.	Full-time.
Data governance lead	This role would be part of the CDO's leadership team and responsible for the overall data governance effort, including data quality. Their role is to help set the overall data governance strategy and ensure that data owners are in place and engaged across a business.	Full-time.
Data quality lead	The data quality lead is responsible for driving the data quality aspect of data management forward. They will be the person leading all the activities outlined in *Chapters 5, 6, 7, 8, and 9*.	Full-time.

Table 2.10 – An explanation of the hub roles relevant to data quality

There are other important roles in the central hub, but these are of less relevance to the data quality aspects of data governance. For example, there could be a data catalog lead, who would be very valuable to consult with during a data quality initiative, but their support would be organized by the data governance lead, who is included in *Table 2.10*.

Spoke roles

The following table provides an explanation of the various spoke roles. These roles are duplicated for every business function. For example, there will be one (or more) of these for finance, commercial, HR, production, supply chain, and so on:

Stakeholder type	Role outline	Nature of role
Data owner	The data ownership role was outlined already in the *How data governance can help in our scenario* section, but they are mentioned again in this table for completeness. The data owner role is fully accountable for the data governance and quality of a particular domain of data – for example, commercial data.	Part-time – the data owner must be a senior stakeholder in the business area where their data is used.
Data steward	The data steward role is usually appointed by the data owner to play an active and day-to-day role in all data governance activities for their domain. They will implement the work that the owner prioritizes. The data steward will perform all the detailed activities, such as collecting data definitions and reviewing them, defining and approving data quality rules, and documenting and improving data creation and change processes. They report issues to the data owner and ask them for support and to make key decisions.	Full-time, but sometimes several stewards are appointed part-time. This can be valuable because the stewards continue with the day-to-day management of data in their other roles.
Data champion	Data owners and stewards are extremely common roles. The data champion is less common, but where I have seen it used, it has been very valuable. The champion usually works across a number of different data domains and helps to ensure that they work consistently. For example, if there is a VP of operations at the board level in an organization, they might appoint a separate data owner for every area they own, which might include supply chain, manufacturing, and engineering. However, they might also appoint a data champion to drive consistency. The champion role can be very useful because it can identify where synergies can be applied. For example, if all three sub-functions mentioned in the preceding paragraph write a policy on the identification of duplicate data, the champion can help them work together to do this consistently.	Part-time. This role is commonly filled by a team member from a process excellence team.

| Data producer | Data producer is the term for people in an organization who actually create data in systems. For certain data, such as cost centers, this will be a small group of people who receive and action requests to create or change data in the relevant system. For some data, such as employee data, there will be a "self-service" process to update data that every employee will take part in. In this case, everyone becomes a data producer.

People are not generally appointed to this role. This role is part of their day-to-day activities, and a data quality initiative may look to identify them so that they can be supported to create and maintain data in line with newly created or agreed rules. | Part-time. The creation or change of data is part of their day-to-day role. |
|---|---|---|
| Data consumer | Data consumers are those in an organization who use data. This is usually everyone in the organization to a greater or lesser extent. This role becomes more meaningful when we narrow it down to a specific circumstance.

For example, if we find an issue with duplicate supplier data, we know there are two key consumers of this data:

- The payments team, which needs to pay the suppliers

- The spend analytics team, which needs to understand how much is spent holistically with each organization

In this case, it helps to be able to identify these data consumers because they can be notified of the duplication issue and given guidance on how to work around it. | Part-time. The consumption of data is part of their day-to-day role. |
| Process lead | Many organizations have global process leads or owners in place. This can quite commonly be the same person who takes on the data owner role. If there are two different roles in your organization, it can be very valuable to work with the process owner. They can provide great insight into how the processes are impacted by data quality issues and, therefore, can be ideal to suggest which data to focus on. | Part-time. |

Table 2.11 – The spoke roles relevant to data quality initiatives

So far, I have simply listed the roles and described what they do. In order to make this section more practical and valuable, I will now describe what each role might be required to do to support a data quality initiative.

How data governance roles help a data quality initiative

The following table outlines what each role might practically contribute during a data quality initiative:

Role	Example contributions to DQ initiatives
CDO	<ul><li>Overall sponsorship of the initiative – providing some budget and helping to coordinate with data owners to obtain a further budget</li><li>Design and implementation of a suitable organization structure in data and analytics – for example, establishing the role of data quality lead</li><li>Ensuring data quality is on the agenda at the board level</li><li>Signing off key decisions such as tool selection, or which functions (for example, finance or commercial) are included in the scope</li></ul>
Data governance lead	<ul><li>Sets the overall direction for data governance and how data quality fits in. Ensures that other parts of the data governance agenda support data quality, as described in the *Data governance, MDM, and data quality touchpoints* section in this chapter.</li><li>Coaches and supports the data quality lead. The data governance lead will usually have had their own direct experience in data quality initiative work.</li><li>Ensures that data quality findings influence the work of other areas of data governance. For example, if a data quality finding means that an MDM process must change, the data governance lead will set this as an objective for their data process lead.</li></ul>
Data owner	<ul><li>Provision of a portion of their budget</li><li>Support and time from people in their teams (for example, in testing data quality rules; see the *The implementation of data quality rules* section in *Chapter 6* for more details)</li><li>Signing off the scope for their function (for example, which data quality rules will be delivered and which will be excluded)</li><li>Influencing other senior leaders in their function and beyond</li></ul>

Data stewards	• Provision of data definitions as input to data quality rules
	• Suggesting data quality rules
	• Identification of the right people in their function to identify further data quality rules
	• Explanation of existing data processes and structures
	• Involvement in testing – either personally, or by coordinating testers in their function
	• Reviewing testing completed by others
	• Support with communication to their function upon going live
	• Support through the remediation phase, ensuring that identified data quality issues are properly prioritized
Data champion	• Provides an unbiased cross-functional view of priorities. For example, if both finance and commercial data owners want their scope to be included in the initiative, the data champion can find the best solution for an organization as a whole
	• Provides an end-to-end view of the impacts of a data quality issue. For example, if the finance team maintains data but the commercial team members are the ones who use that data, the champion can represent the interests of both.
Data producer	• Provides subject matter expertise on how data is collected and input into systems
	• Provides subject matter expertise on how underlying systems use particular fields – for example, selecting the "hold" status for a supplier means that no purchase orders can be issued, but they can still be paid
	• Implements agreed changes to data creation and change processes when it is identified that current processes cause data quality issues
Data consumer	• Explains clearly what they need from the data and where data is not fit for purpose as it stands
	• Contributes to data quality rules

Table 2.12 – The contributions of various roles to data quality initiatives

You may note that one role is missing from *Table 2.12* – the data quality lead. This was excluded simply because it is the role that provides all of its time to a data quality initiative. As outlined in *Table 2.11*, the data quality lead will organize and lead every step of the data quality initiative from start to finish.

In this section, we have explained a number of roles that are commonly in place in organizations that have started on their data governance journey. If none of these roles are formally in place in your organization, please do not worry. They may not be officially appointed, but there will be people who are in positions to perform these roles. It might be the VP of IT instead of a CDO (not something I recommend, but a common practice!), and your data owners may not know that they are data owners, but they can be treated as such and provided with the relevant support if they are guided correctly.

The final part of this chapter is an outline of the end-to-end data quality cycle that I have developed through my experience with various organizations.

The data quality improvement cycle

Different organizations clearly have very different challenges. They are in different locations around the world, with different local laws and regulations. They are in different industries – some closely regulated and some with minimal regulation. However, in my experience, the process that needs to be followed to improve data quality is consistent across all organizations. I have seen success with this process in multiple industries and various parts of the world.

The process I will outline is not "rocket science" – it is a logical and simple approach that I believe most organizations will benefit from. It is the basis of the rest of the book's structure. Each chapter from now on (with the exception of *Chapters 4* and *10*) will focus on a particular part of the data quality improvement cycle.

The following diagram provides an overview of the cycle:

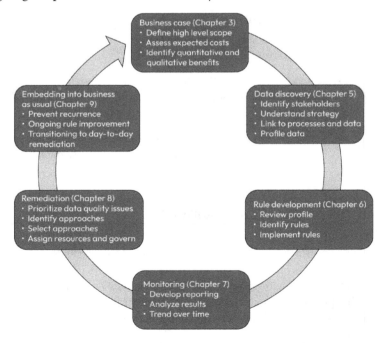

Figure 2.5 – The data quality improvement cycle

The first point to note is that this is a cycle. Organizations starting with data quality have to select a subset of their data to focus on (for example, supplier data, cost center data, or employee data) as part of a high-level scoping activity before the business case is prepared. They need to complete all phases of this cycle for that set of data. It is possible to start on another set of data when still working on the first, but usually, some of the benefits need to come to fruition before an organization will sanction that. Usually, these benefits start to be visible in the remediation phase, and it may be possible to get approval for a second data quality initiative while in the remediation and embedding into **business as usual** (**BAU**) phases for the first subset of data.

Sometimes, you will focus more than once on a single set of data. Perhaps the scope of rules was too large to deliver in a single initiative with a tight timeline. Supplier data may have been the focus the first time, and a second iteration of rules for supplier data might be the focus for the second cycle.

For some instances of the cycle, it may be possible to miss out steps. For example, the business case step might not be required if the success of the first cycle was so significant that a new cycle was already budgeted for. The data discovery from the first cycle might have identified a sufficient workload so that you can simply prioritize the next tranche of rules without going through the full discovery again. The parts that are required for all cycles are rule development, monitoring, remediation, and embedding into BAU.

The following subsection will briefly explain the different phases of the cycle, so this section can be used as a guide for which chapters of the book to refer to for more details.

Business case

The business case element of the cycle is about getting support for your data quality initiative. This will typically need to be financial support so that appropriate resources and tools can be made available.

In order to do this, the high-level scope of the initiative needs to be agreed upon first. This does not need to be a final agreed scope but just enough detail to be able to estimate the costs and benefits.

The costs and benefits then need to be estimated. *Chapter 3* provides models and strategies to identify the costs and benefits, which can be very challenging with data quality work.

Data discovery

The outcome of this phase is to get a detailed scope agreed upon in which you will deliver data quality improvement. This starts with understanding the business strategy of an organization and understanding what impedes progress in delivering this. Once this has been understood, the focus shifts to linking the strategy issues to processes and the underlying data.

Once these links have been made, the data quality initiative can show that it plans to work on improving data that directly affects the ability of the organization to execute its strategy.

To start the process of improving data, the initiative needs to find out more about it, and a technique called **data profiling** is used to do this. Data profiling provides statistics about the data, highlighting information such as the minimum, maximum, median, and mode values.

Rule development

Data profiling results will generate some of the first data quality rules that will be considered for delivery. The rest of these rules come from workshops within the business, with the profile results to support the conversations in these workshops. Once the rules have been identified and each aspect of the rule has been documented (for example, rule thresholds and rule weightings; all the concepts will be defined in *Chapter 6*), then implementation work can begin.

This part of the initiative is effectively a form of IT implementation work. A data quality tool will be connected to the sources of data that need to be evaluated, and rules will be developed in the tool. There will be a phase of testing, which has many nuances that are specific to data quality work (again, outlined in *Chapter 6*).

Monitoring

Once data quality rules have been delivered, an organization needs to identify the best way to communicate the results to leaders and those who need to take action.

Typically, a suite of reports is developed that allows a range of stakeholders to get what they need. Senior stakeholders (such as the CDO or data owners) will be able to see the overall status of their areas of interest and the trends. Stakeholders such as data quality leads and data stewards will be able to see this high-level view but also a more detailed rule-by-rule view, showing the number of records checked and how many passed and failed.

Operatives such as the data producers who typically correct data in a remediation phase will need reports that allow them to see the failed records one by one, in a context where they can easily make corrections.

The results can be trended over time to see which areas of the organization make positive progress with data quality and which need some support.

Remediation

Once the data quality issues are known after the monitoring phase, it is time to correct the data. This is usually managed like a project within a data quality initiative. Eventually, the desire is for teams who create and change data to routinely do this correctly and improve the data where they see issues. However, most organizations start from a low base and need a dedicated phase and resources in place to make progress.

The remediation phase requires a prioritization effort now that the largest gaps in the data are known, and then an appropriate approach to remediation has to be defined.

Once the approach is agreed upon, the remediation activity begins and must be governed through forums that regularly review the status and risks or issues.

Embedding into BAU

BAU means the activities that are performed day to day in an organization as part of the standard roles fulfilled by employees. In other words, no additional project funding is needed to deliver these activities.

The end goal of any data quality initiative is to have remediation continue beyond the project phase described previously into BAU. This means that business teams continually use the monitoring tool to identify the latest status and proactively continue to raise data quality scores beyond what was achieved in the remediation phase.

Another key part of this work is to look at the causes of the known data quality issues and find ways to prevent them from re-occurring. This might involve providing training to data producers so that they know that a field has to contain values in a certain format henceforth.

Finally, it is also important to keep rules up to date as systems of record change and processes change. There has to be a BAU route to identify the required changes and deliver them without a live initiative in place.

The data quality improvement cycle has now been outlined "in a nutshell" in this section. The chapters referred to in the diagram in *Figure 2.5* provide a great deal of detail on all these concepts and offer real-life examples that should help you get stakeholder support.

Summary

This chapter has been about ensuring that all readers have a common understanding of the key underlying concepts in the book. Data quality initiatives are normally a subset of the work that happens in a data management team, and therefore, a thorough understanding of data management, and particularly data governance, is important.

The success of any data quality initiative relies on the interest and support of stakeholders at all levels. The chapter has outlined all these roles and how they can help the initiative.

Finally, the chapter outlined the end-to-end process that has helped me be successful with data quality work in my career to date.

The next chapter will describe arguably the most difficult phase of the end-to-end process – the business case for data quality. Most initiatives fail at this point. Indeed, some of my initiatives failed at this point, and the lessons I learned (the hard way) inform what will be discussed.

References

The following reference was used in this chapter:

- DAMA UK's white paper – *The six primary dimensions for data quality assessment*

The following authors contributed to this white paper:

- Nicola Askham – The Data Governance Coach and DAMA UK committee member
- Denise Cook – Senior Manager, Data Governance, Security & Quality, Lloyds Banking Group, Fellow of the BCS
- Martin Doyle – CEO, DQ Global
- Helen Fereday – Data Management Consultant, Aviva UK Health
- Mike Gibson – Data Management Specialist, Aston Martin
- Ulrich Landbeck – Data Management Architect, Microsoft Corporation
- Rob Lee – Group Head of Information Architecture, Lloyds Banking Group
- Chris Maynard – Director, Transforming Information Ltd
- Gary Palmer – Chief Alchemist, Information Alchemy, and Charter Member of IAIDQ
- Julian Schwarzenbach – Director, Data and Process Advantage, and Chair, BCS Data Management Specialist

3

The Business Case for Data Quality

In this chapter, I will focus on a key step of any data quality initiative – how to explain the need for it internally in the organization and get the support required to get started. *Chapter 1* established that data quality initiatives do not always get assigned as much value as other initiatives. In this chapter, I will explore the reasons behind this in greater depth and what can be done to maximize the chances of a successful outcome.

I will consider what motivates decision-makers, how their decisions are typically made, and how to position data quality in this context. Then, I will explore the elements of a successful data quality initiative (people, processes, and technology) and how to estimate the costs. The chapter will also discuss how to create a picture of the likely benefits of your initiative in a way that convinces decision-makers to support you. It will give practical examples of successes and what contributed to these outcomes.

In this chapter, we're going to cover the following main topics:

- Activities, components, and costs
- Developing quantitative benefit estimates
- Outlining qualitative benefits
- Anticipating leadership challenges

Activities, components, and costs

Quantitative business cases are essentially made up of two components – expected benefits and expected costs. We must now start to look at the components that will make up the costs of our data quality initiative. We are going to determine how to analyze those costs and decide what should be included or excluded.

Activities in a data quality initiative

Before it is possible to understand the components of cost for a data quality initiative, you need to understand the activities that are usually required from start to finish. This section lists the typical activities in phases.

Chapter 2 outlined the data quality improvement cycle.

In my experience, the organization iterates through this cycle continuously and each iteration requires funding. This chapter will examine a single journey through the phases and identify the expected costs and benefits associated with it.

The first iteration usually requires more significant funding because key elements of the data quality strategy have to be established for the first time (for example, a data quality tool). Therefore, in this chapter, I will focus on that first iteration.

The activities that are part of the phases of the improvement cycle will be used to identify the costs for the business case later in this chapter. The following table outlines the main activities from each phase:

Project Phase	Typical Key Activities	Covered In
Business case	• High level scoping activity (for example, processes such as procure to pay or data objects such as suppliers) • Create a high-level plan, including milestones and resources • Create a detailed plan for the discovery phase • Identify and document benefits • Identify and document costs • Obtain business approval • Assess data privacy requirements • Start initiative governance (that is, team meetings or steering committees)	This chapter.
Data discovery	• Identify key stakeholders • Understand business strategy and link to data quality issues • Identify key data quality issues to be resolved • Log and prioritize high-level requirements • Link to processes and data • Profile data	*Chapter 5*

| Rule development and monitoring | Design phase:

 • Log detailed requirements
 • Agree on detailed initiative scope
 • Design data quality rules
 • Design a security model (if necessary)
 • Write design documents showing how these rules will be implemented
 • Create a detailed project plan for the remaining phases
 • Perform first setup activities for data quality tool(s)

 Build phase:

 • Connect to data to be quality-checked
 • **Extract, transform, and load** (**ETL**) data if necessary
 • Create data quality rules
 • Create data quality reports
 • Design the test approach and scripts
 • Unit test individual rules and reports

 Testing phase:

 • Create test scripts
 • Execute end-to-end testing (project team)
 • Train test users
 • Execute user acceptance testing (end users)
 • Resolve defects
 • Review test results
 • Conduct a go/no-go meeting

 Go-live:

 • Move all work into the production system (cutover)
 • Train end users
 • Provide access to end users
 • Run the initial pilot
 • Support pilot users one-on-one
 • Roll out to a broader user community | *Chapter 6* and *Chapter 7* |

Remediation	• Prioritize data quality issues and identify the appropriate approach for remediation • Create a remediation plan and regularly review its progress • Run the reports and propose a remediation plan • Govern remediation activities	*Chapter 8*
Embedding into BAU	• Identify root causes to prevent re-occurrence • Establish a business-as-usual change process to add/change rules outside of the project • Transition to day-to-day remediation and track the benefits • Present data quality rule results to stakeholders on an ongoing basis • Kick off data quality governance bodies – data quality issue review meetings, steering committees, and so on	*Chapter 9*

Table 3.1 – Typical activities in each phase of a data quality initiative

In *Table 3.1*, the rule development and monitoring phases from the data quality improvement cycle have been combined into a single row. These phases combined are effectively the implementation of a data quality tool. The activities in these phases are similar to those of any other IT implementation activity and are broken down into design, build, test, and go-live activities. These will be referenced later in this chapter.

You may be thinking about different project methodologies because the sequence of activities can vary based on the selected methodology.

Waterfall versus agile

As for any project or program, two different delivery methodologies can be followed. Many organizations use a "waterfall" approach – meaning that there are clear and distinct phases to the initiative and usually a single go-live toward the end of the initiative. Other organizations choose to use an Agile (Atlassian provides a good definition of Agile and various tutorials on their website: `https://www.atlassian.com/agile`) approach, where there are typically many go-lives with small incremental scopes included. The activities that are required are broadly the same across both approaches. Irrespective of the delivery methodology, the initiative must do the following:

- Develop a plan
- Select a tool and set it up
- Connect to data
- Design, build, and test data quality rules and data quality reports

Table 3.1 assumes that a "waterfall" methodology is being used.

Delivery frameworks

Organizations usually have a framework for initiative delivery that includes various documents or "work products" that need to be completed. There will be different documentation requirements at each organization. Industries with higher external regulatory requirements will typically impose greater documentation requirements. For example, pharmaceutical companies will usually expect an assessment of whether the project could impact patient safety – often called a GxP assessment. GxP is defined at `https://en.wikipedia.org/wiki/GxP`. Essentially, GxP is shorthand for the good practices that must be applied to ensure the safety of any product that's consumed or used to treat a human being for any medical condition. The GxP assessment will be accompanied by a risk assessment to inform the scope of the test phase. Understanding the delivery methodology of the organization is key to understanding how to get started with a data quality initiative. Once the methodology has been understood holistically, it is time to focus on what is required for the early phases.

Early phases

As mentioned in *Table 3.1*, the subsequent phases of the typical initiative will be covered in *Chapters 7, 8,* and *9*. In this chapter, we will deep dive into the activities in the planning and business case phase.

This phase is all about getting the approval that you need from senior leaders (usually via some kind of investment board) to deliver your initiative in end-to-end. Usually, this phase will be led by a data quality manager at an organization. This person would usually be part of a data management group, with a role dedicated to measuring and managing data quality. This person should have familiarity with the broader concepts of data governance and an understanding of data quality tools. It is very helpful if this individual has experience with your business and understands the key factors for its success.

In organizations with a lower level of data maturity, a role like this won't exist yet. In these cases, where the data management journey has probably not even started yet, it may be too soon to start a data quality initiative with a specific scope. Sometimes, a senior leader in IT will be asked to start looking at data quality. In these cases, our recommendation would be to start looking for examples of data quality that are causing problems in the organization and use these to create a simpler business case. This simple business case would be a calculation of the cost of bringing on one additional person dedicated to data quality. The only benefits necessary for the business case would be enough to cover that person's expenses.

That person would then be tasked with starting a discovery phase in an initiative like the one outlined earlier. The *Developing quantitative benefit estimates* and *Developing qualitative benefits* sections ahead should help you identify the areas you should explore to make the case for this foundational data quality role.

Assuming that this role does exist, there are typical activities they will complete up to and including the receipt of the coveted approval.

High level scoping

The scoping activity is all about determining the initial scope. Usually, *any* part of an organization will have data quality issues when you put them under a microscope. You could find yourself trying to focus on all functions and all locations at the same time. This is usually a recipe for failure unless the organization is particularly small.

So, how do you ascertain which areas of the business to focus on? The theoretical answer to this is that you should perform a detailed review of every part of the business, covering the following:

- Business objectives
- Current impediments to achieving these objectives
- **Root cause analysis** (**RCA**) into these impediments, dividing them into process issues, technology issues, and data issues
- Compare the results across all functions/locations and identify the most impactful data issues – in other words, those that are causing the most significant impediments to those all-important business objectives

However, this book is about practical data quality, and in reality, this theoretical approach is unlikely to succeed for the following reasons:

- It will take too long – by the time you finish, the review of the first conversations you had will be out of date.
- Many business areas will have other priorities occupying their teams and will not see data quality as important. This means they will not make time to support your RCA.
- Some stakeholders are nervous about their data quality issues having greater visibility. They know there are issues and a data quality initiative will expose these to their peers.
- Comparing how impactful data quality issues are is rarely objective – every stakeholder believes their issue should be the top priority.

The practical approach is to push on the open doors – in other words, try to identify the stakeholders who already have concerns about data quality and are actively looking for help. Those stakeholders usually have some prior experience with data quality and already understand that some of their impediments are caused by underlying data quality issues. Sometimes, you will identify stakeholders who intuitively understand data quality and become ardent supporters. These stakeholders may not have prior data quality experience but after just a few interactions with an expert, they realize that the issues they've been managing are caused by data quality problems.

For example, at one organization I worked with, the most severe data quality issues were in the supply chain area. The senior leader in that area was very aware of the data quality concerns and the impact they were having on their area. They were, however, unwilling to work with our team:

- They did not want to expose the supply chain data quality issues to their peers on the board
- They had their own approach to managing data quality and wanted to pursue that

The approach was to ask a third-party organization to cleanse the data as a "one-off" exercise. This investment was not positive for the organization because the third party applied generic data quality rules that didn't specifically apply to the data of this organization. Some improvement was made, but the worst issues remained untouched. The data which was improved quickly returned to a poor quality level again, as there was no handover into a business-as-usual state.

Another senior leader in the organization (the CFO) was experienced with data quality issues and knew that a lot of the problems affected their team. They supported and championed the data quality initiative. Their element of the initiative became a showcase that we put in front of other leaders. This showcase led to the supply chain leader asking to run a second data quality initiative with the team and actually, the benefits obtained were much more significant than those for finance. The finance project unlocked these benefits by demonstrating a strong track record of delivery and success.

The high level scoping phase should produce sufficient clarity on the focus areas for the initiative to produce the business case. For example, details of the process areas or data objects which will be included, and the broad timeline (for example, 9 months). The Discovery phase covered in *Chapter 5* will produce the full detailed scope which the initiative will deliver.

Planning and business case phase

Once the high level scope and timeline is established, the full planning and business case activity can begin. I will explore all the key activities listed in *Table 3.1* in depth and identify the key challenges.

Data quality tool selection process

This may seem out of place – very early on in our initiative, I focus on a technical matter at a stage where there aren't any detailed requirements yet. The reason for this is that the costs of a project will vary depending on the decision around a tool. Some initiatives will start without any tool – in other words, using existing capabilities, such as data warehouses, visualization tools, and spreadsheets to manage data quality monitoring.

Other teams will choose highly regarded tools from suppliers such as Informatica or SAP, which come with a certain amount of cost, and some may use open source tools.

It isn't necessary to completely finalize this decision at this stage, but it is important to have an approximation of a data quality tool cost in mind so that you can put a sensible figure into your business case.

High-level plan

In the high level scoping activity, just the broad time scales are established – in other words, is the work expected to run over 6 months, 1 year, or some other time scale? The high-level plan in this section provides a moderate level of detail – enough to estimate resource requirements so that costing can be established. Quite often, the time and resources spent on the initiative will be the most expensive part of the initiative.

For example, if a testing phase is going to be 6 weeks long and requires one full-time data quality rule builder to support any defects raised, then a cost can be estimated. The rate of the rule developer can be estimated (for example, US $400 per day) and a total cost ($12,000) can be put into the cost section of the business case.

The high-level plan outlines the high-level activities required for the initiative in rows and the time that each is expected to take in columns. The plan is usually simple enough to fit on a single page, as shown in the following diagram:

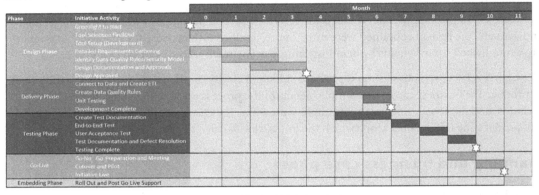

Figure 3.1 – Typical high-level plan

Note that *Figure 3.1* does not include the high-level scoping activity. The assumption is that there are sufficient internal resources to complete this without dedicated funding. This early phase establishes the basic scope of the work and allows an accurate timeline to be determined. This is a prerequisite for developing a high-quality business case. Similarly, this chapter does not include the main detailed discovery phase covered in Chapter 5. Some organizations may choose to include this in the business case - particularly where there is a lack of internal data quality resources to conduct this phase without the support of a third party consulting organization.

It is typical for activities to overlap across phases. For example, the test approach documentation and test scripts are dependent mainly on the design documentation. It is prudent to allow development work to progress to a certain extent before writing test documentation. Developers often notice issues in the design early on and have to revise it in the first few weeks of their work.

A detailed plan for the design phase

At this stage, it is common to create the next level of detail for the design phase. This phase will kick off immediately when the project is (hopefully!) successfully approved. This plan will often be created in a work management tool (such as Microsoft Project, Monday.com, or Atlassian Jira) because they allow you to manage the following:

- A hierarchy of tasks

- Dependencies between tasks and automatically updating dates when tasks fall behind

- Assigning resources to tasks

Here is a typical example of a detailed plan from Jira. In this plan, the main tasks that appeared as lines in the high-level plan in *Figure 2.1* are now shown as "Epics" with a set of detailed tasks nested underneath. An Epic is a summary-level activity that's used to group detailed tasks. Its purpose is to allow users of the plan to operate at a summary level and only explore the detailed tasks where they need to. The Epics in *Figure 2.2* correspond to the phases shown in *Figure 2.1*. This detailed plan shows the next level of detail for the Tool Selection Finalized and Tool Setup (Development) lines from the high-level plan:

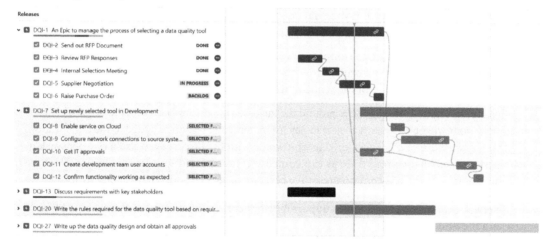

Figure 3.2 – Typical detailed plan for the detailed design phase

You can observe the status of each task, the start/due dates, the resource assignment (against the first five rows), and the dependencies between tasks (the faint gray lines connecting tasks). The different colored bars indicate the tasks themselves and the sequence in which they should be completed. The length of the bar indicates the length of the phase and the sub-task.

Once the plan has been completed to a reasonable level of detail, it is possible to start thinking about how much each activity might cost the organization. Both the costs and benefits need to be identified before a meaningful business case can be created.

Identify and document benefits

This part is the most challenging of the planning and business case phase – and will be covered in much more depth in the *Developing quantitative benefit estimates* and *Developing qualitative benefits* sections of this chapter.

In a nutshell, this is the process of identifying the key benefits that will get the initiative the support that it needs from those who can grant a budget. It will rarely be possible (for reasons explained later in this chapter) to give a total benefits figure – but usually, sufficient benefits can be identified to justify the initiative's cost.

Identify and document costs – scope of costs

This element of the planning and business case phase usually requires a model to be developed that can be used to identify the costs involved in delivering a data quality initiative.

The starting point for a cost model is to identify the scope of costs to be included. Key considerations for this include the following:

- What is the scope of the initiative and how does it impact the resource requirements at each stage?

- What key roles do you need in your data quality initiative and what does each role typically cost? For example, the typical annual salary of a data quality developer might be US $60,000.

- What percentage of a **full-time employee's** (**FTE's**) time will be required to fulfill each role? For example, do you need a project manager for 3 days per week or 5 days per week? This determination is a function of the scope of the initiative.

- What are the organizational policies around the inclusion of personnel costs in project work? Some organizations will only expect a project to pay for incremental resources added to the organization. Other organizations will expect anyone who works with the project even half a day per week to be part-funded by the project. Costs can come from unexpected sources sometimes. Here are some examples of the less common resource costs we have seen added to data quality initiatives:

  - Network engineers (required to support network connections between the data quality tool and the underlying data sources)

  - Database administrators (required to explain the data model in the source and provide access)

  - Application security teams (required to set up roles used by the data quality tool to access the data and also to set up a security model for the data quality reporting itself)

  - Information privacy experts (required to assess whether any data had a data privacy implication under legislation, such as the **General Data Protection Regulation** (**GDPR**) in the EU, and if so, what needed to be done to manage privacy risks)

  - Procurement and legal specialists (required to help select a data quality tool and implement a contract with a supplier)

- Does the initiative require any new software licenses or hardware? Some organizations expect the first year of these kinds of costs to be project-funded and then embedded into a business-as-usual budget.

Identify and document costs – people cost modeling

Once the scope of the costs is known, a more detailed model has to be produced based on the initiative's scope and the effort required to deliver it. The various project roles play a greater or lesser role in the initiative in different phases and this has to be taken into account.

To illustrate this, I have created a set of business case templates and completed them for a typical data quality implementation initiative (I have used Microsoft Excel for these templates because they are easy to share, but they would be more visually impressive in other tools). The final output, which would form the people costs estimate, is shown here:

Resource	Phase	FTE Effort Requirement	FTE Cost
Project Manager	Discovery Phase	0.2	1,333
	Planning and Business Case Phase	1.0	13,333
	Design Phase	1.0	26,667
	Delivery Phase	0.6	12,000
	Testing Phase	0.6	20,000
	Go Live	0.4	5,333
	Embedding and Remediation Phase	0.2	1,333
Data Quality Architect	Discovery Phase	0.2	1,333
	Planning and Business Case Phase	0.2	2,667
	Design Phase	1.0	26,667
	Delivery Phase	1.0	20,000
	Testing Phase	1.0	33,333
	Go Live	0.6	8,000
	Embedding and Remediation Phase	0.2	1,333
Data Quality Developer(s)	Discovery Phase	0.0	0
	Planning and Business Case Phase	0.0	0
	Design Phase	0.4	10,667
	Delivery Phase	2.0	40,000
	Testing Phase	2.0	66,667
	Go Live	1.0	13,333
	Embedding and Remediation Phase	1.0	6,667
Data Quality Tester(s)	Discovery Phase	0.0	0
	Planning and Business Case Phase	0.0	0
	Design Phase	0.0	0
	Delivery Phase	0.5	10,000
	Testing Phase	1.5	50,000
	Go Live	0.0	0
	Embedding and Remediation Phase	0.0	0
Business Users	Discovery Phase	1.5	10,000
	Planning and Business Case Phase	1.0	13,333
	Design Phase	0.5	13,333
	Delivery Phase	0.0	0
	Testing Phase	1.5	50,000
	Go Live	1.5	20,000
	Embedding and Remediation Phase	1.5	10,000
Total Resource Costs			487,333

Figure 3.3 – Typical people cost outline for a business case

This outline provides a list of each of the roles needed to deliver the initiative and how much time is required from them during each initiative phase. The time estimate is provided in a **full-time equivalent** unit of measure in the **FTE Effort Requirement** column. This is a common unit of measure in business cases that compares the number of days of effort to the time a full-time worker would spend working for the business in 1 year. The FTE Effort Requirement numbers are example figures based on a recent project conducted but would vary depending on the scope of the initiative.

Alongside this template are several sub-templates:

- A template listing all the required roles, the overall number of days they need to work on the initiative, and their typical costs, as shown here:

Resource	Role Definition	Estimated FTE Cost	Project Cost	Day Rate	Effort (Days)
Project Manager	Status reporting, team co-ordination, plan management, issue and risk management	80,000	80,000	320	250
Data Quality Architect	Requirements gathering and definition, design of solution, management of developers and testers	80,000	93,440	320	292
Data Quality Developer(s)	Build of data quality rules, ETL processes and reports in chosen tool, testing, support of testing	50,000	137,400	200	687
Data Quality Tester(s)	Testing of the data quality rules and management of defects from business users.	40,000	60,000	160	375
Business Users	Active contribution to requirements, review of design, testing of data quality rules, sign offs.	65,000	116,740	260	449

Figure 3.4 – Details of the required roles, their expected effort, and costs

- Detailed assumptions for each role that helped to determine the FTE Effort Requirement:

Role	
Project Manager	Discovery phase: The discovery work is led by the data quality lead for the company and the PM is only needed one day per week (**0.2 FTE**) to create the high-level plan and start preparing for the planning phase.
	Planning and business case phase/design phase: These phases require preparation of a detailed plan and co-ordination of business resources and developers/architects so will require a full-time project manager (**1 FTE**)
	Development/test phases: The development phase requires less business and data quality team interaction and therefore less co-ordination work for the project manager, hence a reduction to 3 days per week (**0.6 FTE**). The test phases are overseen by the manager, with support from the tester(s) and again three days per week is sufficient (**0.6 FTE**).
	Go-live/embedding and remediation phases: These phases represent a hand-off of the project to business-as-usual resources and the project management role is gradually ramped down to two (**0.4 FTE**) and then one day per week (**0.2 FTE**).
Data Quality Architect	Discovery/planning and business case phases: This role is providing guidance and advice on data quality tools, required team members, and high-level design in these phases - one day per week is sufficient (**0.2 FTE**)
	Design, development, and test phases: This role is primarily responsible for the design and development phases and therefore is full time. The test phase is a busy period for this role as it manages resolution of all defects (**1 FTE**)
	Other phases: As the go-live occurs, the role starts to ramp down - providing intensive support while the business gets used to using the data quality rules. (**0.6 FTE** in Go Live, **0.2 FTE** during remediation phase)
Data Quality Developers	Managed by the data quality architect, these roles (two developers) are required to support the design process (**0.4 FTE**).
	After design, they ramp up to full time in the development and test phases (**2 FTE**). They will build data quality rules, ETL and reports, and resolve defects identified.
	A reduced version of the team will need to be present to manage support issues after go live (**1 FTE**).
Data Quality Tester	Managed by the data quality architect, these roles exist to find issues with the data quality rules prior to business users being are critical toward the end of the development phase (0.5 FTE) and ramp up significantly through the test phase (**1.5 FTE**).
	In the test phase, they will also train and support business users on how to use the data quality tool and how to test rules.
Business User	A variety of business users will need to be involved in the initiative at different phases. The FTE count is an amalgamation of the expected effort.
	Discovery phase: 3 different team members (each representing a department) for 2.5 days per week each (**1.5 FTE**).
	Planning and business case phase: 3 team members for ~1.5 days per week to help determine business benefits for the business case (**1 FTE**).
	Design phase: 3 team members totaling 2.5 days per week of effort to review and sign off the design (**0.5 FTE**).
	Delivery phase: Business users are not required in this phase except for small points of clarification (**0 FTE**).
	Test phase: Business users required to test in the second half of the phase. Each tester may need up to three days per week for two weeks, but are not required in the first half of the test phase, which is conducted internally by the team. (**1.5 FTE**).
	Other phases: During the go live and embedding and remediation phases, there is a significant effort required from business users to use the results of the data quality rules to make improvements to the data. This is a significant effort that should decrease over time as data reaches a higher standard and is maintained at this level (**1.5 FTE**).,

Figure 3.5 – Assumptions used to determine the FTE effort per phase

- A calculation of expected effort based on deliverables, as depicted here:

Rule Development Effort	Number of Rules	Effort Per Rule (Days)	Effort in Total (Days)
Low	75	2	150
Medium	60	3	180
High	25	6	150
Total Rule Development and Testing Effort			480

Other Cost Estimates	Effort (Man Days)
ETL Effort	240
Tool Setup Activities	100
Report Development	250
Total "Other Cost" Effort	590

Total Estimated Effort	1,070

Reconcile to Resource Estimates	
Developer Effort in Plan	687
Tester Effort in Plan	375
Total Effort Per Plan	1,062

Figure 3.6 – Effort estimate based on deliverables

Figures 3.4 and *3.5* are critical to identifying the costs in *Figure 3.3*. They are also critical to showing budget holders that the initiative has been well thought through and costs will be closely monitored.

Figure 3.6 is not strictly necessary to calculate the costs in *Figure 3.3*. However, it is a useful tool to sense-check the initiative costs. The *Figure 3.3* model is based on how much time the initiative is expected to take and sizing a team that should be able to deliver a broad set of data quality rules. It ignores the number of data quality rules that have been identified for implementation.

Figure 3.6 provides an estimate of the development and testing work required based on the number of rules. Some of the costs are relatively fixed and do not depend on the number of rules. These are as follows:

- It usually takes about 100 days of effort to set up and configure a data quality tool (in development, test, and production)
- Usually, a data quality initiative needs around 10 reports to be delivered with the effort per report at about 25 days (Further details on these reports will be covered in *Chapter 7* !)

The other costs involved in a data quality initiative depend on the number of rules and, therefore, are completely variable. These include the following:

- Usually, costs are driven by the number of data quality rules required. Rules can start extremely simple, but can sometimes be very complicated. Usually, rules are considered to be of low, medium, or high complexity, and a standard day estimate is applied to rules in each of these categories.

- The effort to ETL data for quality checks is based on the number of systems that need to be connected. (This example assumes three systems are connected for the first time, at a cost of 80 days of effort for each.)

In the example that forms the basis of *Figures 3.3, 3.4, 3.5*, and *3.6*, 150 rules have been identified, across data from three different source systems. The effort for developers/testers to achieve this (ignoring project management work, design documentation, and end user testing) is 1,070 days. Compare this to the effort in the *Figure 3.3* plan of 1,062 days. These numbers are very close, which suggests that the planning and estimates are sound. If there were large differences between these two numbers, it would suggest that either the scope needs to be changed to fit the team size or the team size needs to be changed to fit the scope (resulting in a need for greater funding).

Every organization will be different when it comes to determining whether the people costs need to be budgeted with the initiative or not. Typically, organizations request that initiatives include the following items in their budget requests:

- The costs of incremental resources you need to add to the organization to complete the initiative

- Incremental costs plus the costs of the effort required from existing resources being re-deployed from their "day job"

Identify and document costs – non-people costs

The majority of a data quality initiative's costs will be made up of people costs. However, a business case will not be complete if it doesn't consider the *non-people costs*.

The typical items to obtain a cost estimate for are mentioned in the following table:

Area of Cost	Item	Details
Tools	Data quality tool	Software licenses for a tool, which allows developers/end users to provide business rules that data should be following and evaluate the data against the rules. Examples include Informatica Data Quality, SAP Information Steward, and Semarchy Data Quality.
Tools	ETL tool	A tool to extract data from source systems and transform it so that the data quality tool can assess the data against the business rules. Examples include Informatica iPaaS, SAP BusinessObjects Data Services, and MuleSoft.

Tools	Data visualization tools	Tools to take the results of the data quality tool and create easy-to-use reporting. This reporting is used to identify all the issues with data quality and quickly drill down to the individual failed records. Examples include Microsoft Power BI, Qlik Sense, Tableau, and Google Looker.
Infrastructure	Hardware/cloud vendor capacity	A new application or expansion of the role of an existing application may trigger additional costs for the organization. For example, a new data quality tool hosted on a cloud provider (such as AWS, Microsoft Azure, or Google Cloud Platform) may require additional server capacity to be added to existing contracts. This can attract costs.
Infrastructure	Network capacity	In some limited cases, moving data from a source into a new data quality tool can create new network pathways that did not previously exist. This may require investment in network infrastructure to allow the movement of data. Sometimes, additional capacity will need to be added to existing network capabilities.
Third-party support costs	Application support and maintenance	At the end of an initiative phase, any new software developments need to be handed over to a "business-as-usual" support team. Often, this can be a application development and maintenance supplier such as Capgemini, IBM, or Cognizant. These vendors may charge the organization more for the additional support and sometimes, these costs need to be included in the initiative's business case.

Table 3.2 – Areas of non-people costs in a data quality initiative

When considering tool costs, it is highly likely that the organization already has an ETL tool and a data visualization tool. It is important to speak to the owners of these tools internally to see whether they will require the initiative to pay for incremental license costs for these tools. If the tool is already in place for general use in the organization, then there may be no additional cost to use it in your initiative.

Data quality tools are rarely found in organizations. All the initiatives that I have been involved in at various organizations started with the procurement of a data quality tool that was new to the organization. Therefore, it is likely that license costs for this element of software will be required. Software vendors who already have a footprint in your organization often have a data quality tool as part of their portfolio, and it might be possible to acquire this at a reduced cost. The IT team in your organization will usually have an architecture team that maintains an up-to-date catalog of the tools internally and has an awareness of supplier capabilities that the organization does not yet have.

For example, SAP's data quality tool (SAP Information Steward) is part of their SAP Data Services Enterprise Edition product (which many organizations already have), and changing from one license type to another may be more cost-effective than starting a new license. It is worth investigating the portfolios of existing suppliers to look for these opportunities.

When the initiative has established both people and non-people costs, it is time to start looking at benefits.

Developing quantitative benefit estimates

As explained in *Chapter 1*, one of the most difficult challenges when getting a data quality initiative "off the ground" is quantifying the benefits. I have already said that it is not possible to identify a comprehensive set of benefits.

At the business case stage of an initiative, there are usually few (or no) data quality rules in place to measure a full population of data. This means the size of the problem is not known and therefore the benefits of fixing the problem are also not known.

On top of this, "fixing" the data quality issue does not in itself provide business benefits. The benefit is "one step removed" because the corrected data only provides benefit at the point that it is used in a successful business process or in a meeting where a better decision is made based on more complete reporting.

For anyone thinking that calculating the benefits of data quality improvement cannot be as hard as I am making it sound, here is an example of the difficulties that can be encountered.

Example – the difficulty of calculating quantitative benefits

In one business I worked with, remittance advice email addresses were missing from the supplier master data. This field was used to send a notice to the suppliers that they were soon going to receive a payment.

The finance team raised concerns after being overwhelmed with supplier questions about when their invoices would be paid. The finance team believed that the ERP system was "broken" because it was not sending remittance advice. In reality, the ERP system was fine, but the data was missing.

Obtaining and entering the missing data would not deliver any benefit in itself. The benefit would come from a reduction in effort for the finance team to resolve supplier payment queries. To assess this, we would need to know how long an average request takes to resolve and predict the request volume reduction. This prediction is hard to produce. Here are the steps that would produce an accurate prediction:

- Identify the historic number of invoices raised against suppliers with no remittance advice email address and estimate the future invoice volumes

- Identify the historic number of payment queries received from these suppliers

- Identify the number of email addresses that would be added
- Assume that these suppliers would raise 80% fewer payment queries
- Calculate the historic number of queries per invoice and apply the assumed 80% reduction of queries to the future invoice volume
- Multiply this by the average time taken to resolve the query

This is a relatively simple calculation, but it just gives us the business benefit of remediating the data for a single data quality rule. Given that most data quality initiatives include 100 or more rules, it would often be more effort to calculate accurate expected business benefits than to deliver the data quality initiative itself!

Strategies for quantification

If benefits quantification is difficult in data quality initiatives, then what are the possible approaches we can take?

This section outlines the approaches that I have used until now and discusses the pros and cons of each.

Approach 1 – calculating sufficient benefits to pay back the cost

In the *Activities, components, and costs* section, we showed an approach to calculating cost.

Once an estimated cost is available, one approach to quantification is to follow the standard business case approach – identifying and quantifying sufficient benefits to cover the cost. Here are more details on this approach:

1. Prioritize the key examples of known data quality challenges identified in the discovery phase and calculate the potential benefits of each as accurately as possible – from highest to lowest priority.

2. Continue to do this until the benefits that have been identified are sufficient to pay back the costs within a relatively short period – for example, 2 years.

Here's a working example of this approach:

Detailed Calculation	Result	Calculation	Supporting Information
Typical Rate of Remittance Queries Per Invoice	5%	6,000/120,000	- 6,000 remittance queries were raised in the last quarter against 120,000 supplier invoices (5%).
Expected Number of Remittance Queries Next Quarter	7,500	5% * 150,000	- The number of invoices for the next quarter is expected to be 150,000.
Effort to Resolve Remittance Queries Next Quarter (Days)	166.7	7500*10 / (60*7.5)	- Each query takes 10 minutes to resolve on average. Each working day is 7.5 hours.
Annual Effort to Resolve Remittance Queries (Days)	666.7	166.7*4	-Number of invoices and query percentage remain flat across the year if no action is taken.
Cost of this Effort Annually	125,000	45000/240 * 666.7	-Annual cost of FTE in this role is 45,000, assuming 240 working days per year.

Figure 3.7 – Detailed calculation of benefits for a single rule

Assuming that 80% of the suppliers can provide a remittance advice email address and that this reduces the query levels by 80%, we can expect to save up to $96k from our data quality initiative for this rule. This already repays 20% of the $487k expected cost of the initiative.

The next step would be to continue to identify business rules that would contribute benefits. The best examples to look for come from the following:

- Master data issues that can affect many transactions – for example, customer master data issues that affect thousands or millions of invoices.

- Data issues that can impact revenue. For example, issues are known to trigger customer complaints, which then affect order volumes from those customers.

- Data issues that might delay a critical product launch or project completion. Often, a business case already exists for the product launch or project completion and the delay in those benefits can be easily quantified.

- Tightly regulated areas of the organization where data quality issues could lead to fines or negative press.

The benefits that are identified can be built up until they reach a reasonable payback period and then presented. This is a very standard practice in business case development.

> **Note**
>
> An explanation of the payback period from `https://www.accountingtools.com/articles/payback-method-payback-period-formula` states that the payback method is widely used due to its simplicity.

The only real difference to a standard business case approach is that we are not attempting to identify all of the benefits. We are using a limited set of examples to build up sufficient benefits. If you use this method, it is crucial to emphasize that there is a high probability of underestimating the benefits. Organizations with a lot of cost pressure will often only take on projects with very short payback periods (1 year or less), but it is often not possible to find this from data quality initiatives.

Evaluation of this approach

The "pro" of this approach is that it is a very standard practice that most project management offices and senior leaders will recognize. It will fit within most organizations' decision-making methodologies and templates.

The "cons" of this approach are as follows:

- It will not necessarily mean that your data quality initiative business case stands out against other more traditional initiatives. The payback period may be longer, and for smaller organizations, it may be very hard to identify sufficient benefits to cover the costs. The reason that this impacts smaller organizations more is that the number of transactions is relatively small, so a minor master data issue will not impact the thousands (or even millions!) of transactions that it would for a larger organization.

- This approach is the most time-consuming because you have to work very hard to deep dive into the effect that identifying and resolving the data quality issue would have. The work on each rule must be robust enough that it is hard to challenge the benefit.

Approach 2 – calculating limited benefits and extrapolate

This approach is very similar to approach 1. The key difference is that you deliberately do not attempt to get the benefits to cover the cost in a short payback period. You spend less time on the benefits identification and quantification work and demonstrate that the benefits will scale differently.

In more depth, the approach is as follows:

1. Choose the two to three data quality issues that stand out the most during the discovery phase to "deep dive" into.
2. Calculate the potential benefits of each as accurately as possible.
3. Extrapolate the benefits across the remaining population of known issues/rules.

One important tip here is to ensure that you record how long it takes to calculate the benefits in Step 2. It is expected that there will be an investment of "days of effort" into this, and by recording this effort, you can easily explain to senior leaders why the business case benefits are not as comprehensive as they might be used to.

For example, if calculating the benefits from three potential data quality rules takes one person 2 weeks, and there are potentially going to be 150 data quality rules, the full benefits calculation would take one person 100 weeks! This is not at all palatable in business case preparation.

The approach to calculating the benefits would be very similar to that shown in *Figure 2.7*, but the assumptions made need to be even more robust because they will be extrapolated over a larger population. You would not make any attempt to fully cover the costs of the initiative. You may stop calculating benefits even when you have only identified benefits adding up to 20% of the costs. You would then move on to the extrapolation process.

This process treats the cost number as a "target" and states assumptions to meet that cost that are hard to challenge. Take the following example:

- The cost is US $487k

- The benefits on three example issues are calculated to be US $150k (31%) over 2 years

- 30 other probable data quality issues have been identified in the discovery phase

- Even if on average, each of these rules only provided US $11,250 of benefit over 2 years, the cost would be paid back in those 2 years

This assumption feels hard to challenge. The "best" three issues have identified US $50k of benefit each over this period – almost five times what is needed from the other 30 rules. It is also likely that further rules will be identified and bring additional benefits. Usually, a data quality initiative starts with a small number of rules, and more are identified all the time.

Evaluation of this approach

The main "pro" of this approach is that it is much less time-consuming than approach 1 but the individual benefits calculations are still very robust. It may be possible to start with this approach and then switch to approach 1 if this does not get successfully approved.

The main "con" of this approach is that it does not fit with traditional business case methodology and is more easily challenged than approach 1.

This approach works well in smaller organizations where there may be more flexibility in business case presentations to allow different approaches. Larger organizations with very formal project management offices may insist that the business case follows an approach similar to approach 1.

Approach 3 — a top-down benefits calculation

This approach is very different to both approaches 1 and 2. It is about looking at metrics within your organization and benchmarking them against similar organizations to detect where you could be underperforming.

You would then estimate the benefit of reaching the benchmark and identify how much of that benefit could be attributed to the resolution of data quality issues. It does not focus on the details of data quality issues themselves.

Further breaking this down, we have the following table and examples:

Step	Detail	Example
Analyzing metrics versus benchmarks	Discovery phase workshops should identify areas of the business suffering from the most significant data quality challenges Benchmarking data is obtained (for example, from an organization such as Gartner or The Hackett Group). The benchmarks will be tailored to the size and industry of your business.	If supplier and purchase order data is identified as a potential issue, benchmarking would be obtained for **procure-to-pay** (**P2P**) processes. These would include on-time payment rates, invoice processing times, and cost per invoice (of the P2P team).
Estimating benefits	The gap between current organizational performance and the appropriate benchmark can be analyzed, and a benefit can be determined if the organization reaches the benchmark.	If the cost per invoice were reduced from US $35 to US $15, the benefit would be US $20 multiplied by the forecast number of invoices.
Attributing benefits to data quality issue resolution	This step requires surveying the operatives in the target process. Ideally, all operatives should receive a survey that allows them to allocate a percentage of the problems they experience to various levers – such as data quality, system issues, and process design.	The P2P operatives who take part in the invoice processing activity are briefed on the definition of data quality, system, and process issues and are then asked to allocate a percentage of the issues they experience to each. The results might be as follows: • Data quality issues – 20% • System issues – 40% • Process design issues – 30% • Other – 10% The benefit calculated in the "estimating benefits" step would then be reduced to 20% so that it can be included in the data quality business case benefits.

Table 3.3 – How to estimate benefits using approach 3

> **Note**
>
> More details about Gartner and its benchmarking services can be found here: `https://www.gartner.co.uk/en/insights/benchmarking`.
>
> More details about Hackett and its benchmarking services can be found here: `https://www.thehackettgroup.com/best-practices-benchmarking/`.

This approach tends to work best in an organization where you know that you already have significant backing from senior leaders. This is typically where data quality is known to be a major issue for the organization and leaders are keen to move quickly to action.

Evaluation of this approach

The pros of this approach are as follows:

- It often links directly to the strategy and objectives of business leaders – who typically want to improve benchmarks against similar organizations
- It is a relatively efficient way of quickly producing business benefit estimates

The cons of this approach are as follows:

- It can be quite political. Often, benchmarking leads to a reduction in the workforce. For example, in the P2P cost per invoice metric, reducing this usually means that you can process the same number of invoices with a smaller workforce. Process leaders may feel their team is being "targeted" and you could lose engagement.
- The fact that there is a reduced level of detailed analysis often means that estimates can be challenged more easily. Probing inquiries from leaders can make the business case appear insufficiently thorough.

We have now discussed three potential approaches to business case benefits calculation and evaluated them. We've learned that approach 1 is the most standard and will be what your organization usually expects from a business case. However, it can be inefficient to prepare. The other approaches (particularly approach 3) are more innovative and efficient, but very formal organizations that have clearly defined and inflexible ways of working may not accept them.

In all cases, it is important to create a rounded set of business cases by considering other broader benefits. The next section will explain this in detail.

Developing qualitative benefits

Qualitative benefits are intangible and cannot be quantified with sufficient certainty to be included as quantitative benefits.

Most qualitative benefits relate to the avoidance of different types of risk. They cannot be easily quantified because they are only a probable risk rather than past events where the impact can be accurately measured. Here are some typical data quality risk examples:

- Impact on compliance risk.

- Reputational risk – including the perception of the brand and damage to your reputation in terms of customers, suppliers, and employees. Employee dissatisfaction, in particular, can lead to impacts on efficiency in general, and staff retention.

- Risk of challenges to the delivery of future projects/activities.

This final example could be quantified project by project, and where this is possible, the benefits can be included in the quantified benefits area of the business case. In general, though, the final category covers the fact that every future project (even those not on any plan at present) will be delivered more easily after the qualitative benefit has been delivered. Referring back to the e-invoicing example in the *Quantifying the impact of bad data* section in *Chapter 1* – if a data quality initiative had already been delivered before that program, 3 months of consultant costs would have been saved (assuming the VAT and email address fields had been in the scope of the data quality initiative!).

It is important to dedicate appropriate time to the qualitative element of your business case. Many people make the mistake of simply listing categories of benefits and providing a few sentences of "backup" information to support each one. This information is often ignored by stakeholders because it is too generic and unsupported.

To avoid this mistake, I recommend using various tools and techniques to obtain detailed information from stakeholders. Gathering this detailed information starts with surveys and focus groups.

Surveys and focus groups

A useful approach is to try to add an element of quantification to the qualitative benefits. Similar to the last part of approach 3 in the *Developing quantitative benefit estimates* section, this involves using surveys and discussion groups to obtain and document opinions.

For example, you may run a survey as follows (this survey was created for free using Momentive.ai's SurveyMonkey: `https://www.surveymonkey.com/`):

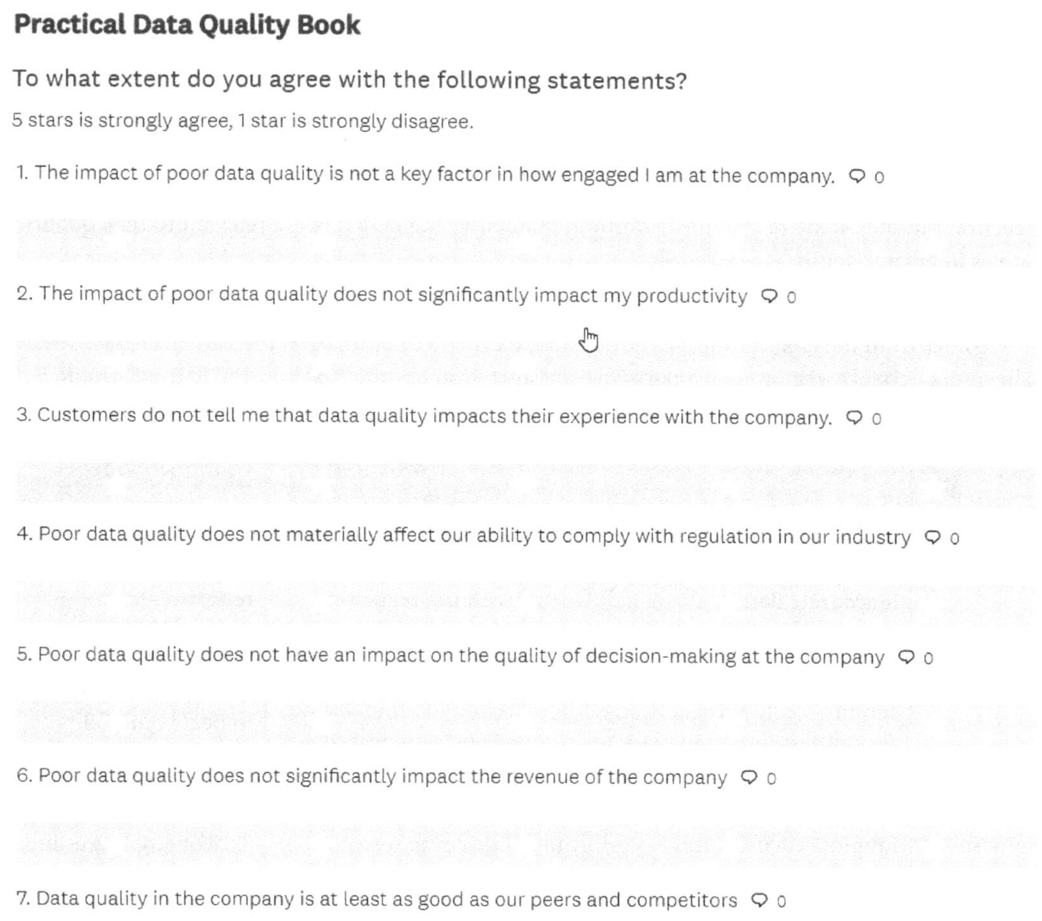

Practical Data Quality Book

To what extent do you agree with the following statements?

5 stars is strongly agree, 1 star is strongly disagree.

1. The impact of poor data quality is not a key factor in how engaged I am at the company. ♀ 0

2. The impact of poor data quality does not significantly impact my productivity ♀ 0

3. Customers do not tell me that data quality impacts their experience with the company. ♀ 0

4. Poor data quality does not materially affect our ability to comply with regulation in our industry ♀ 0

5. Poor data quality does not have an impact on the quality of decision-making at the company ♀ 0

6. Poor data quality does not significantly impact the revenue of the company ♀ 0

7. Data quality in the company is at least as good as our peers and competitors ♀ 0

Figure 3.8 – A typical survey used in qualitative benefits research

Questions such as these would also be asked in focus groups, where people can provide detailed reasons for their answers. Sample answers would be recorded and included as "soundbites" in the business case. These can be beneficial to repeat later on after data quality issues have been detected and resolved through remediation (see *Chapter 8*). Comparison of the "before" and "after" view of survey results can help illustrate the benefit that you have managed to deliver.

Ideally, survey and focus group results are grouped by function, seniority, and any other relevant dimensions. The benefit of this can be a "reality check" for a senior leader of a function. In a project decision board, a leader may be resisting approval of the data quality initiative because they do not believe there is a problem in their area. If survey results in their function show a disconnect between senior leadership opinion and operational-level opinion, this can be a useful talking point to influence this leader.

Once the surveys and focus groups have concluded, the findings can be discussed in more detail with the participants. It is important to ensure that the results are documented in sufficient depth to engage with decision-makers.

Outlining data quality qualitative risks in depth

This section outlines some of the most common qualitative benefits that are relevant to data quality initiatives in greater depth.

The following table shows the key categories of risk-related issues. The information in the **Detail** column comes from the focus groups and the example evidence comes from the survey results. These have been deliberately written with a particular organization in mind to show the level of specificity that is required to influence stakeholders:

Area	Detail	Expected Benefit of DQ Improvement	Example Evidence
Compliance risk	Regulatory submissions regularly include missing or inaccurate data. The regulator contacts the chief data officer after each data submission to raise concerns about the controls in place for data quality.	Improvement in the relationship with the regulator and an increase in regulator confidence. Avoidance of the risk of costly increased regulatory engagement in the future.	A survey of the regulatory reporting team showed that 76% felt that poor data quality materially impacts our ability to be compliant with regulation.
Employee engagement risk	Employee frustration is significant in the P2P process area because of workarounds required due to data quality issues. Workarounds mean that the team spends much more time than expected on detailed manual work and receives system error messages in the majority of transactions. They are not able to perform value-added activities such as supplier performance management or supplier consolidation and spending analysis. Employee churn in P2P is up 47% from the prior year.	Employee retention would improve and employees would be able to perform broader higher-level value-added activities.	82% of employees in P2P report that poor data quality has a significant impact on their engagement at the company.

Risk of poor decision-making	Data used in reporting is often incomplete or inaccurate, leading to an inability to trust the data for decision-making. Users of reports either disregard them and produce their own analyses directly from source systems or use the reports and subsequently learn that decisions were flawed. A large customer contract was recently signed based on a flawed forecasted raw materials cost. Once the raw materials cost was corrected, the contract (which was slightly positive in terms of margin) became loss-making. It was intended to be priced aggressively to engage the customer, but certainly, a loss-making contract would not have been approved.	Decision-making would be more in line with the company strategy, and onerous contracts such as the one with this customer would very rarely be signed.	43% of senior leaders report that they believe poor data quality has a significant impact on the quality of decision-making. When looking at operations and commerce, this number increases to 72%.
Reputational risk	Customers are directly impacted by data quality issues. Customer surveys have indicated that the company is considered "hard to do business with" and the examples given are mostly related to data quality – for example, shipping addresses that were not updated, leading to cold chain products being delivered to the wrong location. The third largest customer stated that if another transaction with these kinds of issues occurs, they will switch to a competitor, even though they prefer our product.	Customer retention and acquisition would improve and relationships would deepen with retained customers.	The brand team reports that the **net promoter score (NPS)** is weakening (from 20 to -10 in the last year) and customer brand surveys reveal concerns about operational procedures and data. 64% of the customer services team state that customers regularly tell them that data issues are impacting their experience with the company.

Risk to future projects	Our business strategy outlines a major transformation in the finance area, with several new systems planned for implementation. These include financial consolidation systems, financial planning systems, and a new finance-focused data warehouse and visualization tool. While the detailed data requirements for this area are not yet known, so the risks cannot be quantified, it is widely known that data quality issues around the chart of accounts and cost center structures are poor and will not support projects of this magnitude.	The likelihood of finance projects running on time and to budget is significantly higher if a data quality initiative with a financial focus is approved before these projects commence.	The finance team, which manages the chart of accounts and cost center data, reports a particularly poor score on the survey question about data quality impacting productivity (91%).

Table 3.4 – Typical risks to data quality, which form qualitative analysis

If you put effort into research and add some quantitative detail, such as survey results, qualitative analysis like this becomes much more impactful.

It is often really important to have the messages from the qualitative research delivered with support from colleagues in the organization. For example, it is a lot more powerful to have one of the operational or commercial leaders (from the 72% mentioned in *Table 3.4*) give examples of where they felt data caused them challenges with decision-making.

So far in this chapter, we have outlined how to create the key components of the business case – the detailed costs, the quantified benefits, and the supporting qualitative information. With this, you can produce a compelling business case that is ready to be presented.

Anticipating leadership challenges

The time has come to present your business case to a board – a set of senior leaders who have a limited budget and what they feel is a "never-ending" set of projects trying to take up that budget.

It is a hard position for them to be in. They have to disappoint some of the presenters and deny their requests, and they know that people have worked extremely hard in most cases to produce a strong business case.

To make quality decisions and accept the projects and initiatives that will have the greatest impact on the organization, leaders have to ask challenging questions. They have to ensure assumptions are truly valid and do not "fall apart" under the slightest exploration.

This means that any presenter must expect challenges. Our intention in this section is to prepare you as well as possible for these challenges and give you the best chance of approval. We will cover the most common challenges to a data quality initiative and the best responses.

The "Excel will do the job" challenge

Many times, when presenting the implementation of a data quality tool, I have heard the same challenge – that it would be easy to write a data quality rule in a tool such as Microsoft Excel.

This is when a stakeholder takes one of the rules that you have measured the benefits for and provocatively states that they could do the following:

1. Download the data from the source system into Excel.
2. Create an Excel formula to validate which rows were correct and which rows were not correct.
3. Produce a list of records that need cleansing.

They typically state they could do this in 30 minutes or less.

It is hard to argue against this at a single-rule level. What they propose in Excel is usually possible (except for truly complex rules).

The response to this should be the following:

- This is not about a single rule measured at a single point in time – this is about creating a portfolio of rules that highlights holistically where our data is strong and where it is weak.

- It is about doing this analysis automatically, refreshing it daily, and showing trends in data quality. Doing this once on a given day does not sustainably lead to data quality improvement. At best, there would be a short-term improvement. Adding the 30 minutes of Excel analysis per day to your business-as-usual processes would eventually add up to a significant resource investment and the nature of the work would be repetitive for the employees involved.

- Holding data in Excel is not practical for all types of data. For example, employee data is protected by GDPR and having this in Excel spreadsheet format is a compliance risk. It is also common for organizations to experience the impacts of corruption of data through processing errors made in Excel.

- It is about providing people with bespoke views of the failed data so that they can act quickly and effectively. For example, a data quality failed data report will not only show which supplier is missing a telephone number, but it will also provide the email address field (if completed) for that supplier so that the telephone number can be requested.

The effort to reproduce what a data quality initiative can do in Excel (daily analysis of 100+ rules) would be unmanageable. It is also unlikely that a person would be given enough access to a source system to be able to download the wide "cuts" of data that would be needed for many data quality rules. Sharing these Excel spreadsheets would leave the data uncontrolled from an access management perspective.

Ownership of ongoing costs challenge

The next most common challenge is around what happens to the costs after the initiative phase is completed.

Usually, initiatives such as this one will create the following:

- A tool that needs to be maintained – because data quality rules change over time, and source system structures change as well. Upgrades to the software itself will be required.

- License costs, which will typically be charged annually for the tool.

- A set of reports that will show "bad data." These need to be reviewed and "acted upon" by team members across the functions. In some organizations, this may result in the creation of a specific data governance team to operate the reports day to day.

Senior leaders will want to know that there is a clear "home" for these costs in the future organizational budget. This can be a very difficult question to answer. Does a single function pay for the data quality "function" in the future as a service to the rest of the organization? Or does each function contribute a piece of the costs in their budget?

My experience is that the latter approach never really works. It just takes a single function to change their position and the agreement loses traction. My experience is that it is critical, when going into a business case discussion, to have agreed with a single functional leader that they will budget for the tool in their normal operational budget after it is live. The candidate functions are as follows:

- A data office (that is, a dedicated function of the chief data officer) – if one exists

- IT (if the IT function owns data)

- Another function where the data quality lead resides (this is quite often finance)

It can be possible to provoke this discussion at the board to try to get an agreement in place, but this should be a last resort because it will almost certainly lead to an action to discuss it outside of the approval meeting. This can be the right way forward when no function will agree in advance to owning data quality, but every function is generally supportive. In this situation, it brings the decision to a head, and usually, a single cross-functional leader will push for a clear outcome. In these circumstances, it is best to raise this proactively rather than wait for the question to show clearly that this has been considered and you are now asking for help.

The excessive cost challenge

Another very common challenge is that the initiative is too expensive. This is often combined with the "I could do this in Excel" argument in a "two-pronged" attack!

Leaders who raise this challenge will often choose one part of the plan and attack the cost. For example, in our cost template in the *Activities, components, and costs* section, the test phase is the most expensive. A typical question would be "*Why is testing so expensive? You can build the rules for less than it costs to test them.*"

My typical preparation for this kind of challenge is as follows:

- Spend time considering each aspect of the cost calculation and thinking about the challenges that could be raised. Document a suitable answer to each challenge. For example, the answer to the question about testing would include the fact that there are two different phases of testing (one involving end users) and that an element of defect correction is included in testing – which is essentially further development work.

- Be prepared with a reduced-scope version of the initiative that costs less – for example, take on one process area initially rather than two, or one data object instead of two.

- Explain that the first data quality initiative is much more expensive than subsequent work. There are fixed setup costs, such as software and hardware licenses, training documentation, design documentation (which will just be iterated in later development), and ETL processes for new sources.

- Finally, it is often worth exploring the cost to the organization of not completing the data quality initiative. At one organization, an initiative was approved after examples were given of the capabilities that were missing because of data issues. For example, the asset register was critical for this organization, and the data quality in this register was so poor that it was not possible to determine which items were still in use.

The "Why do we need a data quality tool?" challenge

Often delivered alongside the cost challenge, this challenge tends to come from functions where technology plays a less significant role.

Often, the license costs for data quality tools can appear relatively expensive compared to other tools in the data area. Microsoft Power BI (for data visualization) costs only US $9.99 per user per month for a Pro account. Data quality tools are often much more expensive and this can surprise stakeholders to the point that they raise this challenge.

I firmly believe that data quality tools are critical in the long term for success. They provide the most efficient way of automatically and regularly monitoring data quality.

A good approach to answer this question is to have reference calls with fellow customers of data quality tool suppliers and ask them to articulate the benefits they have achieved and their view on the necessity of data quality tooling. Often, external opinions can shift internal opinions in organizations.

Another approach that can be taken is to start without a dedicated data quality tool and gradually produce benefits that can be used to fund the dedicated tool. While we do believe a tool is a necessity, there are "workaround" options. For example, a data visualization tool can be used to connect to data sources and logic can be added that classifies data into "failed" and "passed."

It will not take long for this approach to cost more because the effort in the data visualization tool will include reproducing standard data quality tool functionality. It is also less robust and often starts to fail when a particular developer moves on from their role. It is possible to get started in this way, though.

My overall recommendation relating to data quality tooling is that it is possible to get started without a recognized data quality tool to show the potential value of what you are doing, but it is not possible to maximize the overall value of your work without this investment. It is important to choose a purpose-built data quality tool rather than trying to stretch the use of a tool designed for a complementary purpose (for example, a master data management or data visualization tool).

Summary

Data quality business cases are a very challenging area – and as many initiatives will fail at this stage as those that will succeed.

This chapter gave a clear message: that it is critical to be well-prepared. It is typically really important to share that preparation with the members of an approval board in advance. As mentioned previously, data quality business cases often differ significantly from what people are accustomed to seeing, and at first glance, they may not seem as competitive as others.

If you can explain one-on-one (or in small groups), you often have the chance to answer challenging questions before the decision-making session and get stakeholders to give a fair hearing to your initiative.

A lot of effort will go into the process of getting the approval that you need. As soon as that approval is given, the initiative will begin. Sometimes people spend so much energy in the preparation of the business case that they are not ready to start the initiative as soon as budget is available. The few weeks after approval of a business case are so critical that is important not to lose time. The next chapter outlines those weeks and how to set up your initiative for success.

4

Getting Started with a Data Quality Initiative

One of the most stressful points of a data quality initiative for those involved is the immediate few weeks following the approval of the business case. The approval is the starting gun for the delivery of the first set of data quality rules. There will be a clear commitment to a deadline – and meeting the deadline will be essential to keeping within the agreed budget.

Every week of delay will lead to a significant additional cost and the risk of having to go back to the approval group to request more budget.

This chapter outlines everything that will be on the agenda in those first few weeks and gives some guidance on how to keep all the "plates spinning." It will help you to identify the various workstreams of activity that need to be put in place and the types of people that you need to find to staff those workstreams.

Therefore, in this chapter, we will cover the following topics:

- The first few weeks after budget approval
- Understanding data quality workstreams
- Identifying the right people for your team

The first few weeks after budget approval

In *Chapter 2*, the data quality improvement cycle outlined the activities that were then costed and planned in *Chapter 3*. For simplicity, the cycle and the example project plans in those chapters show each of the activities happening in a sequence – generally starting only after another has been completed.

The reality is somewhat different though, for example:

- While working on data discovery work (covered in *Chapter 5*), you will inevitably uncover some live and critical data quality issues that cannot wait until the remediation phase to be addressed.

- Typically, the phase where data quality rules are built by developers will start while design work is still going on. Usually, groups of data quality rules that were agreed upon at the start of the design phase are released to developers to work on in parallel to the design work – to extend the development phase and to allow for some refinement/clarification of the rules without affecting the project timelines. For example, it gives the developer the opportunity to go back to the project team during the design phase if any of the rules need further clarification once they come to translate them into technical code and once they see the data.

- Testing requires significant effort in terms of data quality and often needs to begin while developers are still building additional rules.

In fact, you would be forgiven for thinking that everything happens all at the same time in a data quality initiative! The following section will outline the key activities in those first few weeks, and that are essential to start.

Key activities in those early weeks

Up until the business case phase, usually only a very small amount of budget will have been made available to the initiative. This budget will have been used to pay for people to help get a plan created, an initial scope defined, and the costs and benefits identified. This means that there are already people engaged in the initiative who can hopefully continue their work, funded by the approved business case budget.

However, the small business case team will now need to be augmented by the full project team. There are a variety of ways to find the required individuals, but the most common of these is to use a third-party consultancy. Therefore, one of the key activities is the selection of a supplier for these resources.

Supplier selection

Firstly, it is important to explain that the use of a third-party supplier is not essential. Other options include the following:

- **Using the contract market**: Identifying a number of data quality professionals working in an independent capacity.

- **Using internal resources**: It may be possible to bring a number of people into the initiative from around the organization that you work for, through the creation of new roles or secondments, for example.

In the long term, a data quality initiative requires resourcing from a range of different resources. Usually, a third-party supplier makes sense for the intensive phases when data quality rules are being designed, built, and tested, but in the longer term, internal resources are essential. The activities outlined in *Chapter 9* are best carried out by internal resources.

For the purposes of this section, the assumption is that a third-party supplier will provide the majority of resources – because this is the most common resourcing model. There are advantages to this model:

- The supplier has the responsibility to provide a complete and coherent team with the appropriate set of skills

- The supplier often performs other project or support work in your organization and the data quality team can connect with other members of the organization in those teams – for example, infrastructure engineers can support the data quality team in requesting firewall changes to support connections to a cloud data quality tool

- Some suppliers will engage in a fixed-price contract – meaning that if there are delays, the supplier bears more risk than the contracting organization

When selecting a supplier for a data quality initiative, there may be a clear starting point in your organization. There may already be an incumbent supplier that provides resources for the majority of projects. You may have already selected a supplier to provide the business case resources. If that goes well, you may decide to proceed with that supplier.

However, usually, there will be some kind of selection process, if only to ensure that pricing is competitive. In larger organizations, this may be managed by a procurement team via a **request for proposal** (**RFP**) process. I do not intend to explain an RFP process in depth here – I am sure that there are excellent procurement books available that would do this much better than I could. For this section, I will explain the factors that I have used to make decisions about data quality resource providers in the past.

Depth of data quality resources

It is easy to assume that the largest, household-name suppliers in the consulting world have a depth of resources in every discipline. At one organization I worked with, the incumbent supplier did have fantastic depth and a great track record in data quality and did an amazing job. At another organization, the incumbent supplier had a surprising lack of depth in this area.

The signs of this were as follows:

- They did not have data quality resources in the home country of the project. Team members were asked to travel on a weekly basis.

- They advertised additional contract roles to support our project.

- Key resources could only be provided in an advisory capacity one day per week, supporting less experienced members of staff.

That particular organization, at the time, only had around 25 people globally who had direct data quality experience. The experience that those 25 people had was relatively limited (most team members had experience from only 1-2 projects).

In that particular case, the large supplier was bidding against a small, niche data governance consultancy. That small organization (with only 150 people employed in total) had more data quality experts available than the large household name. They were able to show their depth of expertise in their bid. The average day rate was much higher, but the total cost was lower because they were able to provide a lean but very productive team – getting the work right the first time.

It is important to ask questions such as the following:

- What is the total size of your data quality practice globally and in the country (or at least the time zone) that the project will be based in?
- What is the average number of months of direct data quality experience of the proposed team?
- How many of the team are experienced in the technology that we have selected for our initiative?

The experience of the team is the key driver of success or failure in your initiative, and therefore ascertaining the depth of experience you will get from the supplier is key.

Cost

Clearly, cost is a key driver of any supplier selection decision. At this point, there is an agreed budget. This should have been based on research into the expected number of days of effort and daily rates of the potential suppliers.

If costs are estimated by suppliers as higher than the business case submission, it is better at this point to reduce the scope of the initiative than to immediately return to the approval group to request additional funding. Often, a competitive process can get the costs to the appropriate level. If a supplier is aware that they are the only organization in the running, there is no pressure on their price.

Cost estimates must be properly compared to ensure that they are "like for like." For example, if one supplier includes an assumption that they will handle up to 50 defects, but another supplier does not place a limit on the number of defects, then the second proposal is of greater value.

Another important area of consideration is the type of resources that the supplier proposes assigning to the work. A bidding supplier may offer a lower price by using more junior resources with a less expensive daily rate. This may appear attractive initially, but the resources have to be experienced enough to meet the requirements. Another supplier with higher rates and a higher price might actually be more appropriate where the complexity is high.

Given a similar overall price, the higher rate card is usually a better option because you get senior resources who deliver correctly the first time and can guide you as a client to give them what they need to succeed. The overriding message here is that it is important to make sure a complete cost breakdown of resources and scope is provided in response to tenders from all suppliers so that detailed comparisons can be made.

Ideas and accelerators

Many organizations working in data quality will have developed their own approaches, ideas, and accelerators for the work that they do. An accelerator in this context is a generic piece of work that can easily be brought to a new client and will be relevant to that new client. For example, one supplier I worked with had a well-developed methodology to detect inactive supplier data in an SAP ERP system. They knew which tables of data needed to be checked for activity, and they knew specifically what to look for. All they needed from us as the client was a time period after which we would consider a supplier to be inactive. This saved the initiative as a whole 5-10 days of effort.

A good supplier will also be able to look at a sample set of data quality rules and comment on them. They will be able to assess the level of effort to build these data quality rules and to identify any ambiguity in the rules that will need to be resolved before any development can take place. They may also be able to suggest additional rules that may not have been considered so far.

Industry knowledge

In some industries, it is important that suppliers have some industry experience. This is most relevant for highly regulated industries such as pharmaceuticals or banking. An organization with no experience in pharmaceuticals, for example, may not accurately estimate the effort to design and build data quality rules.

Pharmaceutical companies have to operate under a higher level of governance where there is any relevance at all to patient safety. If you work in an industry like this, it is important to explore your suppliers' experience and "pressure test" their estimates to ensure they include adequate time for the additional governance.

Track record

As with any procurement activity, it is important to ask for references from other previous and current customers. Most prospective suppliers will agree to arrange a call with the customer to discuss their experience of working with the supplier. In the data quality area, it is important to ensure that references are appropriate as a comparison. A reference should meet the following requirements:

- Ideally, it should be from a customer who has worked with key members of your proposed project team

- It should be from someone who uses a consistent technology set to you (for example, similar source systems and a similar data quality tool

- It should be from an organization at a similar level in terms of data governance maturity – a data quality activity in an organization that has been working on improving data governance for years is very different from a brand-new initiative in a company that is starting out

After consideration of these key drivers, a decision can be made, and the focus moves to bringing resources from the supplier to the initiative. This can sometimes be a frustrating phase as contracts must be signed, the budget must be drawn down, supplier master data must be created, and then purchase orders are created and approved. It can take several weeks for this to happen and, in my experience, it is critical to be aware of the status of each step in the process and ensure progress is as expected. Usually, any delay at this point pushes the end date of the initiative beyond what you originally planned.

Now that we have outlined factors that are important for supplier selection, it is time to consider the selection of a data quality tool.

Tool selection

The selection of a data quality tool should be one of the earliest decisions made. In the preceding *Supplier selection* section, there were several references to checking that the supplier is experienced in the selected tool. It stands to reason then that tool selection should take place before supplier selection. There should be a clear shortlist (of no more than three tools) in place prior to the business case being finalized, and if the cost varies significantly between tools, then the highest cost of the shortlisted tools should be in the business case.

The typical approach to assemble a shortlist is to use the following resources:

- **An IT benchmarking organization**: These organizations (which include Gartner and Forrester) undertake independent research into comparable tools and provide a review and a ranking.
- **Discussion with the architecture team**: Most organizations have an architecture team who are able to offer advice on tools that fit the organization most appropriately. For example, if there is a large investment in SAP tools already, then a SAP tool may have an integration advantage over tools from another supplier.

A short list can be rapidly assembled through the use of these resources. Organizations will use IT benchmarks to find the best-in-class tools and use architecture teams to work out which of these are the best fit for their particular IT landscape.

The next step is to engage with the supplier of each shortlisted tool to get an understanding of the costs involved in investment in their tool. Each tool will have a different licensing model and different drivers of cost (some charge by processing power, some charge by number of users, and so on). Some tools may be immediately eliminated because the cost does not match the available budget.

Once the shortlist is assembled, the following factors must be taken into account when making the decision:

Factor	Relevance
Capabilities of the tool	Ideally, this should be the most heavily weighted factor in your decision-making. The capabilities of the tool are paramount to your success. Again, IT benchmarking organizations can be of great assistance here.
Cost	The cost of the tool has to be in line with the business case submission that you have made. If two tools are equally capable, clearly cost is going to be a key deciding factor.
Fit with any other data management tools	Data management tools are often sold in a "suite." For example, master data management tools, metadata management tools, and data quality tools in a single package. If the organization already has other parts of the data management suite of a particular software supplier, then it might be more cost-effective to invest in the related data quality tool. This can be more cost-effective but can also deliver a more usable, integrated solution. For example, the data quality scores would be tightly integrated with the data catalog, so that users can see the level of quality as they search through the catalog.
Fit with other system architecture	Some organizations make a deliberate decision to choose the products of a single software supplier. For example, an organization might describe itself as a "Microsoft shop" or an "SAP shop." Organizations decide on this strategy for a number of reasons – for example, a better overall commercial deal with the supplier, a close integration with the supplier to ensure the success of implementation, compatibility of all the tools, and so on.

In organizations like this, the architecture team may suggest that the first option evaluated should be the tool of this one particular organization. Care should be taken to review IT benchmarks to ensure that the tool of that supplier is a leading tool. It is relatively common for large suppliers to have amazing tools in the ERP or CRM domain, but not have the same strength in data management software. Data management software can be a niche area.

Note: Although SAP and Microsoft are both mentioned in this row of the table, I am not implying that either of them lacks strength in data management software.

Organizations must also review the technical requirements of the tool and check that these are within agreed standards and policies. For example, does the tool require a particular web browser or some software installed on users' machines? Does it require any network settings that are not conformant with security policies? |

Sustainability of the tool	There are often new entrants into the data governance software market. It is important to evaluate the company that is providing the software to analyze its sustainability. If the company were to fold, then the investment in the tool could be lost.
	Having said this, in some circumstances, it can be really valuable to work with a small but growing software provider. If you are an important "trail-blazing" customer for them, they will provide the highest quality of support and may even shape the product with your input and guidance.
Fit of licensing model to budget	Different suppliers offer different licensing models. For example, one supplier might offer a one-off investment with an annual maintenance fee (usually about 20% of the initial investment). This is usually considered to be a capital purchase (known as a capex purchase)– meaning that the license is placed as an asset on your balance sheet and the cost is spread over a number of years.
	Other suppliers may offer only an annual fee where the price is the same every year that you use the product. Accounting rules do not allow this kind of investment to be treated as an asset and the budget does not come from the capex budget of your organization (it comes instead from operating expenses (known as opex)).
	If your organization has a capex budget available, but a minimal opex budget, then you might need to find a supplier who can offer an asset-based model.
	This model is actually becoming less prevalent in software. As the **software-as-a-service (SaaS)** model has grown, most license charges are annual fees and are treated as part of the opex budget.
Fit of licensing model to ways of working	Some organizations make a decision early on that they would like every employee to be able to see the data quality tool (or at least every employee in a head office role).
	Other organizations would limit this to only data stewards and owners.
	Some software suppliers charge by the number of licenses and the license costs can become infeasible for organizations that want to have a large number of people using the tool. Another supplier offering a capacity-based model might be more appropriate for these organizations.

Table 4.1 – Factors to consider when selecting a data quality tool

Typically, suppliers will present their product to the organization, covering their company, their customers, and the benefits of their tool before presenting a live demo. These sessions are a good opportunity to ask about the factors outlined earlier and record the results for each tool.

Prior to these presentations, a list of people who need to contribute to the tool selection process must be agreed upon. This might include the following:

- Data quality lead

- Data governance lead

- A selection of data owners (or stewards if the owners choose to delegate)

- A representative of the architecture team

- Individuals involved in compliance (most applicable to organizations in highly regulated industries)

It is a good idea to work with your procurement team to devise a scoring mechanism for supplier selection. Scores can be provided by each internal participant and compiled by the procurement team to try to reduce the level of subjectivity involved.

Once the decision has been made, a contract must be signed and purchase orders raised and approved. It is important to factor the time that this takes into your planning.

This section has focused so far on the selection of suppliers to provide the external resources and tools that you need to be successful. We will now move on to the internally focused activities that must be conducted in these first few weeks. The first of these is detailed planning for the next phase.

Planning the data discovery phase

The first formal phase of activity after the business case is agreed upon and the budget is available is the data discovery phase. The data discovery phase is covered in depth in *Chapter 5*, but for context in this section, this phase is about understanding the strategy of the business as a starting point and using it to work out the required scope for the data quality initiative and to determine data quality rules.

This phase requires the organization of a set of meetings, which start with very senior stakeholders. It takes time to get slots in the diaries of these stakeholders, and there must be good preparation for the meetings to ensure that they go well.

The planning of business meetings and IT activities for the data discovery phase must be started immediately when the business case has been approved – or even before the approval when there appears to be a strong prospect of success.

At the end of the data discovery process, the data quality tool is used for data profiling activity. This requires the data quality tool to be set up, and ideally to be linked to databases of data from within the organization. This usually requires some activities to take place in advance:

- Approval for the tool from an architectural review board in IT. This approval will usually bring together architects, IT security experts, infrastructure experts, and IT leaders to ensure that they are comfortable with the selected tool and how it is intended to be implemented.

- Discussion with infrastructure experts on how to integrate the tool:

  - If it is a SaaS tool, it will be hosted by a third party in a cloud. In this scenario, the infrastructure teams need to help to integrate this new cloud tool into the existing architecture, through changes to the firewall, the addition of the tool to ticketing systems (for example, ServiceNow), and so on.

  - If it is not a SaaS tool, then new hardware (typically, virtual machines) will need to be added by the infrastructure teams, and the data quality software will need to be installed. (This is rarely the case in 2023 – most data quality tools come with a SaaS option and are in a cloud.)

- Training for the project team might need to be arranged so that they are ready for data profiling activities.

These IT-related activities typically take place over 4-6 weeks and can take 2-3 weeks to organize.

Hiring

Earlier in the chapter, we talked about the process of bringing in resources from a third-party supplier and how to select the right supplier. Usually, some of the resources for the initiative will be hired into permanent internal roles in the organization. The hiring process for these roles must begin as early as possible after the business case approval. With so much activity starting in parallel, the small team that is responsible for the business case can be easily overwhelmed and will need support. A good way to bring resources in quickly is to look at secondments or internal transfers. It is possible, in some cases, to identify people who have an interest in data quality early on and engage with them and their current team so that they can join very quickly after a successful business case approval.

Later in the chapter, I will outline in depth the roles you will need in the initiative and the profiles of individuals who might successfully fill them.

Communication

As soon as the business case has been approved and the initiative is formally started, it is imperative to communicate with the stakeholders that you will need to engage with. The first communication should ideally come from the most senior person involved (for example, the **Chief Data Officer (CDO)**) and engage at least the following stakeholders:

Stakeholder Group	Communication Content	Communication from
Data owners/stewards	Explanation of the broad scope of the initiative and an outline of what data owners, stewards, and their teams are expected to contribute.	CDO

IT leaders	Explanation of the broad scope of the initiative and an outline of what support IT will need to provide – for example, IT security review of how any sensitive data will be managed in the data quality tool, or infrastructure changes as outlined previously.	CDO
Functional leaders	An outline of what a data quality initiative is and how it should help functions to improve, with examples of what is going wrong today. Advance warning of the data discovery phase and a request that their teams are prepared to talk about their strategy and impediments to achieving the strategy.	CDO
Process/system owners	The same information as was provided to the functional leaders, but also a detailed explanation of what is required from each role. For example, process owners will be expected to outline where the challenges outlined by functional leaders occur in the processes they own and where data plays a role. System owners will be asked to be prepared to provide subject matter experts to explain how specific fields are used in processes and analytics. They may also be asked to provide access to their systems for data profiling and eventually data quality rule checks.	Data governance lead

Table 4.2 – Typical early communications in the organization after business case approval

In addition to the stakeholders identified in *Table 4.2*, it might be appropriate to engage with a training and communications team in the organization. Larger organizations have very supportive teams in this field who will help standardize the initiative's communications approach and make it consistent with other messaging.

Starting the communication process early lays a foundation for the required engagement in those early weeks after the business case approval. Senior business and IT leaders should cascade the messaging via their teams, preparing them to expect the initiative to make requests of them. Ideally, teams should appoint single points of contact that the initiative can work directly with and bring into status meetings.

In this section, we have covered a significant number of different parallel activities that will need to be managed in the early stages of a data quality initiative. In the next section, we will outline how to organize these activities into workstreams so that they can be assigned to different groups of people.

After this, we will talk about the team you will need around you to staff these workstreams and make this overwhelming period feel productive and valuable.

Understanding data quality workstreams

In the previous section, I outlined the following activities, which all need to be started in the first few weeks after the business case is approved:

- Supplier selection for initiative resources, such as data quality rule developers
- Data quality tool selection
- Detailed planning for the data discovery phase, including engagement with IT to get the data quality tool ready for profiling work
- Internal hiring
- Communication

In addition to this, it is highly likely that, in the first data discovery sessions, there will be immediate reports of known data quality issues that are causing significant or even severe impacts on the effectiveness of the organization. For example, at one organization, where my team had committed to work on HR data quality, the very first data discovery meeting uncovered that the data required for the calculation of the annual employee bonus was not of a high enough quality. The bonus calculation was due to be presented to the board within four weeks of the first discovery meeting.

The initiative was then faced with an immediate piece of work to help the HR team with remediation activities, while also trying to identify and document data quality rules for development. Although this remediation was not in scope for the early phase of activity, it would not have been sensible to refuse to help the HR team with this work. They were going to be a stakeholder in (and were partly funding) an initiative to improve their master data and this was clearly a great opportunity to start doing that at a time of great need. In this case, working side by side on the remediation effort early on meant that we built a supportive relationship from the start with that team.

If this happens in your initiative, then there is yet another item of work to juggle in those early stages.

This section is about organizing this work into workstreams and will start to indicate the skills required in each workstream.

Workstreams required early on

The activities outlined in the previous section can be easily organized in the following groupings, which I refer to as workstreams:

Workstream	Activities	Participants	Future of the workstream
Supplier and tool selection	Selection of the supplier for implementation work Selection of the data quality tool	Data quality lead Data governance lead IT Third-party suppliers	This workstream ends when the supplier and tool are selected.
Planning and initiative management	Detailed planning for the data discovery phase and beyond. This includes the plan for the supplier and tool selection activity. Planning of any remediation activities picked up by the initiative in early data discovery meetings. Communications from the initiative to stakeholders at various levels.	Data quality lead Project manager (if available)	This workstream continues throughout – focusing on different phases.
Early remediation	Where data quality issues are identified from early stakeholder conversations (potentially, months before the remediation phase), a workstream will be required to ensure these get appropriately focused attention.	Data quality lead Project manager (if available)	This workstream eventually becomes the workstream which will manage the main remediation activity covered in Chapter 8. This will be the main focus after the initiative has developed and released data quality rules and reports. Other team members will finish their work on their workstreams and join this one.

| Data discovery | The data discovery process is where the initiative meets with stakeholders to understand which data is most critical to the organization and starts to identify rules that the data might need to adhere to.

Over time, once the rules have been defined and the initiative scope is fully agreed, this workstream changes its role. | Data quality lead

Data architect (once available)

Data stewards | Once the discovery element is complete, the workstream changes focus to work on the design of the data quality solution (rules and reports) and then drives the business-led testing activities. |
| Data quality tool implementation | This workstream starts by establishing the data quality tool in the organization. It will cover the activities outlined earlier in the chapter, such as working with the infrastructure teams to establish the appropriate firewall settings. | Data quality architect

Data quality developer

IT | Just as for the data discovery workstream, this workstream changes focus over time and morphs into the build workstream. |

Table 4.3 – Required early data quality initiative workstreams

Table 4.3 summarizes the various workstreams and also indicates which continue throughout the initiative, and which come to a natural conclusion.

The value of workstreams is the ability to assign different people to a defined and manageable scope of work. Each workstream has clear objectives and can make progress against those objectives on a weekly basis. This helps with the motivation of the team.

Previous sections in this chapter have already covered all the workstream activities in detail, with the exception of the early remediation workstream. The following section outlines how to manage this challenging workstream in more depth.

The early remediation workstream

The early remediation workstream is a difficult one to manage. Immediately after business case approval, the initiative should be very focused on gathering requirements, designing and building data quality rules, and designing reports showing the data quality position. It can be a distraction when you identify a data quality issue that requires immediate attention, and therefore it is important to separate this into a distinct workstream with a carefully agreed scope. However, as I will explain later in this section, the role of the core data quality initiative team should be strictly limited to co-ordination and subject matter expertise on how to approach the remediation of data.

This workstream can be thought of as a *quick-wins* workstream. The ultimate goal of any data quality initiative is to improve business outcomes through improvement of data quality. Therefore any improvements that can be made before a tool is even established are in the interests of the initiative and the organization. However, the scope must be carefully controlled because this work can become very time-consuming. The following example illustrates this effectively.

During an HR data quality initiative, as part of the benefits calculation in the business case, data was extracted from the system of record and a subject matter expert identified a significant issue. The organization was subject to cost challenges and was working on a board-level review of the headcount. The headcount reporting was not working as expected for the following reasons:

- Employees were not allocated to the correct organizational units in all cases. Many employees were still allocated to old, defunct organizational units following a re-organization.

- Different types of workers were not correctly classified as consultants, contractors, or employees. It was difficult to ascertain how much of the workforce was permanent and how much was contingent labor.

Getting the data extracted for the data quality business case required significant effort because data came from various tables and had to be connected in a model for analysis. Once it was realized that the business case work could immediately be used to correct the data, the data quality and HR teams started to use this as a "to-do" list for the data that needed correction.

This worked really well and helped HR achieve its objective, but it was a significant effort for the data quality team. The extraction of the data had to be repeated on a regular basis to ascertain the progress being made. Essentially, people had to do the job that the data quality tool would do after the implementation of data quality rules! This work led to a delay in the final implementation of the data quality rules.

In hindsight, it was still a good idea to get involved in this because it solved a real business issue and strengthened the relationship between the data quality initiative and the HR team. It also led to greater belief in the initiative from the HR leadership team. However, I feel that the split of activity could have been different between the HR and data quality teams. The HR team could have been shown how to extract and connect the data on a regular basis and the data quality team could have focused more on the rule implementation work and delivered on time. This is what I mean by carefully controlling the scope.

To summarize this workstream, I would say the following:

- It is not sensible to "stick your head in the sand" and ignore early data quality issues that need remediation before you would ideally be ready. It is very important to support your stakeholders at any point and you will get their support if you do so.

- The workstream should ideally be mainly about co-ordination, communication, and data quality subject matter expertise, with activities in this area such as:

  - The workstream should identify people within the affected function who can spend some of their time working on the issue.

- The workstream should work with the team to agree on an approach to correcting the data (for example, emailing line managers to collect missing employee data) and then co-ordinate and communicate as this approach is implemented.

- If it is managed in this way, the workstream can usually be a relatively small effort for the members of the data quality initiative. It can be managed by a single person, and depending on the scope of the issues, it can be part-time.

It is a difficult workstream to plan for because when the data quality initiative begins, the number of issues that will be taken on is unknown. It is a good idea to build some contingency into resource estimates in the business case to ensure there is capacity for this.

The skills required for this workstream are a combination of those found in a project manager and a data quality analyst. The project management skills required include the ability to organize and influence people who do not report to you, planning, co-ordination, and communication (for status reporting). The data quality analyst skills required include data extraction and analysis and the ability to identify appropriate solutions to data quality issues.

Interactions between workstreams

The idea of the workstreams is to try to define the scope and expectations of each stream clearly. Separating these activities helps to "break down" the initiative and make it easier to drive progress. Having said this, it is clearly very important for the workstreams to interact. Many of the interactions are obvious – for example, all of the workstreams will depend on the planning and initiative management workstream to understand their scope and objectives for a given period of time. This section will outline some of the less obvious interactions between the workstreams:

Source Workstream	Target Workstream	Interaction
Early remediation	Data discovery	Early remediation gives an opportunity to get a deep understanding of the data early on. Conversations in this workstream will usually lead to data quality rules being identified or refined. The two workstreams should meet weekly to share what they have learned and the possible implications. For example, during the correction of the HR headcount issue outlined earlier, several other rules were identified: • Consultants should always have the name of their organization correctly maintained • Active organizational units should always have an active employee or contractor as their owner

Data discovery	Data quality tool implementation	The data quality tool implementation involves connecting the tool to the appropriate sources of data. The data discovery workstream establishes which data is most impactful on the organization. The tool implementation is heavily reliant on the data discovery workstream finding out early on what the key sources of data will be. This does not need to be specific tables and fields this early on, but ideally, the most likely source systems should be identified. This should be relatively easy to achieve. If a particular function has been identified as "in scope," then the main sources will be obvious. For example, a focus on HR always means that the system that holds employee data must be included.
Data discovery	Planning and initiative management	In the early stages of the initiative, the scope can move quite quickly. The work done to prepare the business case will have suggested an appropriate scope of the initiative, but detailed data discovery conversations can quickly change this. For example, in one organization I worked with, the supply chain and commercial teams worked very closely together. The company was unusual in that it could only produce a limited amount of a product for a given period – which would always sell out. This meant that the commercial team made commitments to customers based on what the supply chain team estimated manufacturing levels to be. The initial business case assumed a focus on supply chain data, but data discovery conversations revealed that the most significant challenges were in the commercial data. This affected timescales and scope and the planning workstream had to react accordingly.

Table 4.4 – The interactions between workstreams

This section has explored the various workstreams required in the early weeks of a data quality initiative and how they might interact with one another.

The rest of the chapter will focus on the most important aspect of a data quality initiative – the team.

Identifying the right people for your team

Just like any other initiative in the workplace, the success or failure of data quality work depends on the people on the team. It depends on their skills, knowledge, motivation, and their ability to work as a team. With the growth of the data governance discipline over the last 20 years, there are now many skilled individuals in the marketplace. The challenge is bringing people together who have the right mix of these skills and properly supporting and motivating them.

A data quality initiative usually has an enhanced team (in terms of size) for the implementation phase, which requires the entry of people into the organization. When the implementation phase settles into business as usual, members of the team who are employed on a contingent basis (either as contractors or consultants) usually leave, or move on to the next initiative. It is therefore key to ensure that the people who are brought into longer-term roles are given the appropriate opportunities to learn any skills that the contingent team has that they do not, and also that they are given a strong transfer of knowledge on the work that they were not directly involved in.

In *Chapter 3*, I outlined the various types of resources required for the data quality initiative as part of the business case. In the next section, we will explore these roles in more depth together.

Mapping resources to the workstreams

This section aims to explain the key skills required for this early stage of the initiative, how these map to the workstreams, and where the resources may be sourced from.

In *Chapter 3*, we outlined the different roles that might need to be paid for in the business case. These were as follows:

- Project manager
- Data quality architect
- Data quality developer
- Data quality tester
- Business user

These should not be confused with the data governance roles outlined in *Chapter 2*. The following table explains how the two sets of roles relate to one another:

Business Case Role	Data Governance Role	Explanation
Project manager	Data quality lead	At the beginning of a data quality initiative, when a project manager has not yet been recruited, the data quality lead may have to step into this role. In some smaller initiatives, the data quality lead might have to hold this role throughout. Once a project manager has been recruited, the data quality lead returns to an overall leadership role. The project manager will report status, risks, and issues, and direct key decisions to the data quality lead. The data quality lead will provide support, direction, and guidance to the project manager. The project manager may be a contingent resource (from the consultant or contract market) or they may be from a pool of project managers that the organization assigns to in-flight initiatives.
Business user	Data owner Data steward Data champion Data producer Data consumer	In order to keep the business case simple, the five different types of spoke roles are summarized in the simple term "business user." For a more detailed explanation of spoke roles, please see the *Stakeholders in data quality initiatives* section in *Chapter 2*.
Data quality architect	This is not a permanent data governance role	This role only exists during a data quality initiative. This is a good example of a role that usually comes into the team as contingent labor (through the consultant or contract market).
Data quality developer	As above	As above. A small development team may need to be retained when the initiative is over to keep rules up to date. This is explained in detail in *Chapter 9*, in the *Strategies to identify rule changes* section. These resources often form part of a managed services team – where day-to-day application maintenance and support is managed by a supplier for a range of IT systems.

| Data quality tester | As above | Again, this is a role that only exists during a data quality initiative and comes through the contingent labor route. |

Table 4.5 – Mapping of business case and data governance roles

This table shows the difference between the roles that are typically permanent (data quality lead and the various business user roles) and those that are contingent (data quality architect, developer, and tester roles). For each of these roles, we will now consider the attributes of the people who will make the role a success.

Data quality lead

The data quality lead is the most important role of all. They set the tone and direction of the initiative on a day-to-day basis. The key attributes required for success in this role are as follows:

- **Experience leading and influencing** a team that does not report to them directly. It is often really challenging to get time from the business user roles in a data quality initiative and the lead needs to be able to excite people about the benefits of the work so that they prioritize it above other pressing activities.

- **Subject matter expertise** in the data quality and the wider data governance area. The person in this role ideally needs to have been involved in data quality initiatives previously. Personally, I feel that two years is sufficient experience for a high performer to lead an initiative as long as they are well supported by the data governance lead and CDO.

- **Strong business acumen** to enable them to have meaningful conversations with business leaders about strategy and about which issues are more or less important than others. I personally found that my experience as a chartered accountant was critical in my ability to influence senior leaders. I had seen a range of different businesses of my clients' work and was well placed to spot the most critical issues.

- **Project management experience** can be critical for this role, at least initially. Although, ideally, there is a project manager in place once the business case is signed off, there is a lot of project management work required before that point. As mentioned in *Table 4.5*, all too often, there is no project manager at all.

- **Experience managing supplier relationships** is a critical attribute for the data quality lead. They will need to ensure that the supplier is delivering on time, on budget, and with the right level of quality. Where this is not the case, they will need to liaise with the data quality architect to try to improve performance and understand any support that the supplier needs.

Data quality architect

The data quality architect is an important partner for the data quality lead. The data quality lead does not necessarily have to bring technical expertise in the selected data quality tool (although this does help!). They will rely heavily on the data quality architect for that. As such, the data quality architect should possess the following key attributes:

- **Data quality tool experience**: The data quality architect should ideally be selected after the tool selection process has been completed because they need to be experienced in the specifically selected tool. They need to be able to hold their developers directly to account, making sure that effort estimates are robust and the solution developed is ready for the business to test and easy to support. They need to be able to work with IT teams to ensure the conditions are right for the data quality tool to work effectively.

- **Leadership and communication skills**: The architect leads all the technical resources on the initiative. Sometimes the technical resources will be based in a different location and time zone to the architect. They need to be able to form strong working relationships with their team despite these challenges. They need to be able to detect technical issues (for example, a data quality rule that is too complex to build or difficulties in ingesting important data) and communicate these clearly to the data quality lead and project manager.

- **Data architecture**: The data quality architect needs to insert the data quality tool into what is usually a complex set of system architecture in the organization. They need to understand how to integrate the tool with all the sources of data that it needs to connect to and to use existing tools in the organization (for example, **Extract, Transform, and Load** (ETL) tools or data visualization tools) where possible.

- **Business acumen**: Just as with the data quality lead, the architect needs to be able to have conversations with senior leaders. In the early stages of the initiative, they will be a key part of the design process and they need to be able to translate business rules into technical language that the developers can work with.

Data quality developers

The data quality developers will be the ones who complete the hands-on work in terms of creating the following:

- ETL jobs to bring in the source data
- Data quality rules
- Data quality reports

As a result, they need to have the following attributes:

- **Data quality tool experience**: The data quality developer, again, must be experienced in the specifically selected tool. They need to be able to interpret the rules communicated to them in the design process and ascertain the tables and fields of data they will need access to in order to develop the required rules.

- **Business acumen**: Data quality developers do not need the same level of business acumen as the architect, but it is still helpful to have some. For example, when developing a rule, they should be able to recognize when the number of records does not look right. For example, in an organization with a revenue of $100 million, it would be highly unusual to have more than a few thousand suppliers. If the rule found 1 million suppliers, the developer should know that this is strange and ask appropriate questions about it.

- **Data visualization skills**: The data quality development team has to produce data quality reports as well as data quality rules. These reports are covered in detail in *Chapter 7*. The developers need to have sufficient skills to be able to build reports like those shown there. Sometimes this leads to two different profiles of developers. There might be a developer for the ETL work and rules with one skillset and a developer for reports with the corresponding skillset.

Data quality testers

The objective of the data quality tester's role is to check the rules before they are exposed to the business. At a later stage, business users themselves will test the rules. It is essentially a role to ensure that the development team is appropriately checking their own work before it is ready for business testing.

In smaller initiatives, the developer and tester roles may be merged. For example, if there are two developers, they may perform the tester role on one another's work.

The key attributes for the data quality tester role are as follows:

- **Business acumen**: This is clearly a common theme across all the roles! Testers require this to be at a greater level than the developers. They need to be able to understand different rule scopes (see *Chapter 6* for an explanation of rule scope) and to be able to check that the number of records being evaluated matches the rule scope. For example, if a rule only applies to employees on a fixed-term contract, and not to all employees, then the tester must understand (or find out) the approximate number of employees on a fixed-term contract and ensure the rule is only picking these up – and not all employees.

- **Attention to detail**: Rule testers need to be extremely thorough. They must be the kind of person who is not satisfied unless they have addressed every "nagging doubt" in their minds. For example, if they check 20 records, and just one has a slight difference from the source system, they need to be the kind of person who does not want to move on until they have understood what happened with that one record. Sometimes, the single record difference can be a symptom of a much larger issue and the tester exists to find these before business stakeholders do.

- **Written and verbal communication skills**: Testers need to be very good at explaining any issues that they identify to the developers and the architect. They also need to be able to train the business users to use the tool and reports well enough to do their own testing.

Business users

The *Different stakeholders and their roles* section of *Chapter 2* explained the various business user spoke roles in detail, so I will not outline their attributes again in this chapter to avoid being repetitive. Each role would be heavily involved in these early workstreams in the data quality initiative.

Each role will be working across the data discovery workstream and helping to resolve any early remediation issues. This activity will be alongside their usual day-to-day responsibilities. They are partners in each phase but are also your customers to a certain extent. As such, it is important that the data quality team (the lead, the architect, the developers, and the testers) are aligned in their communications with the business users.

In this section, we have outlined the key roles required in the team from the start of a data quality initiative. The intention is to help you better understand what people you need on your team, and to be able to articulate to any third-party consulting organizations what you will need from them.

Summary

This chapter has focused heavily on the difficult first weeks after the approval of a data quality initiative business case. In every data quality initiative I've been involved in, those early weeks have not been as productive as I had hoped.

Choosing your third-party partners (both for resources and tools) and hiring the right people in your team will define the success and failure of your initiative. This chapter has outlined what to look for in team members and will hopefully help you to get the right team in place.

We also discussed how to break down the initiative into manageable chunks and to ensure that most, if not all, of the workstreams progress at the right speed.

If the early weeks are successful, the initiative will be well set up to deliver a successful data discovery phase. That is the subject of *Chapter 5*.

Part 2 – Understanding and Monitoring the Data That Matters

Organizations have a vast quantity of data – and data volumes are growing all the time. A key part of a data quality initiative is understanding which data is worth your time and effort and provides the greatest benefit. To understand this, data quality professionals need to start with all the different stakeholders connected to the data and establish what they all need.

Once this is understood, stakeholders can communicate their business strategy and how it links to data and surface the challenges that data issues cause them. Data quality rules can thus be derived so that bad data can finally be identified.

Once you have completed this part of the book, you will understand how to optimize engagement with stakeholders so that the right rules are identified, and a suite of data quality reports accurately reflects the data quality position and trends over time.

This part comprises the following chapters:

- *Chapter 5, Data Discovery*
- *Chapter 6, Data Quality Rules*
- *Chapter 7, Monitoring Data Against Rules*

5
Data Discovery

Regularly in my data quality career, customers and stakeholders have told me that they know their data "inside out". However, from my experience, the application of data profiling will surprise even these stakeholders. For example, at one organization, the procure to pay process owner assured me that no suppliers were on "pay immediately" terms (meaning that invoices would be paid as soon as they were issued). Data profiling revealed that in fact, 40 suppliers were set to these terms, with a total spend of several million dollars being paid immediately instead of accruing interest for the organization.

Data profiling helps to identify the data quality rules that organizations would like their data to comply with by pointing out the "extremities" of the data. Often, these extremities are examples of something that has gone wrong with the data and needs to be corrected.

To detect these extremities, a tool typically evaluates all the records in a dataset and provides basic information about each column of data within it. Data profiling, however, is only a part of the process of discovering data quality rules. This chapter will walk through this data discovery process and the best ways of applying data profiling at this early stage of a data quality initiative.

The topics we will cover in this chapter are as follows:

- An overview of the data discovery process
- Understanding business strategy, objectives, and challenges
- The hierarchy of strategy, objectives, processes, analytics, and data
- Identifying data quality issues through data profiling

An overview of the data discovery process

Data discovery is the process where an organization obtains an understanding of which data matters the most and identifies challenges with that data. The outcome of data discovery is that the scope of a data quality initiative should be clear and data quality rules can be defined.

This starts with understanding the strategy of your organization, the objectives of key stakeholders, and crucially, what is getting in the way of fulfilling these. It is important to ask stakeholders to talk about this holistically and not to filter their answers, based on what they think might be data quality related. It is very common for issues to appear to have little to do with data, but when an investigation takes place, a link to data quality is uncovered. Clearly, not every problem will have a data quality root cause, but it is important to have the chance to form your own expert opinion.

Once the strategy and objectives are well understood, it is time to review the challenges in achieving these. The challenges themselves should then be linked to the processes, systems, and data that relate to them. See the following for an example:

- The strategy includes paying suppliers later (on average) to improve working capital management and cash flow.

- A challenge to that strategy is that many suppliers have a payment term set to "pay immediately".

- It would be important to link this challenge to the following:

  - The supplier creation and change process where these suppliers were assigned this payment term (to understand the root cause)

  - The system (for example, the ERP system) where data would need to be profiled, checked against defined data quality rules and then finally corrected

  - The data itself – for example, obtaining an understanding of the table and field that holds the supplier payment term

Once you have this level of specificity, the areas to which data profiling techniques should be applied becomes much clearer. These techniques should lead to the key data quality rules that you need to implement for your organization to improve its data.

The discovery process, end to end, involves the following steps:

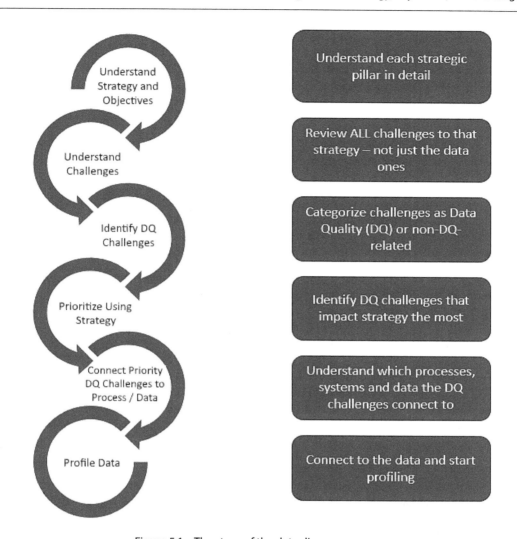

Figure 5.1 – The steps of the data discovery process

Understanding business strategy, objectives, and challenges

The biggest mistake that can be made in a data quality initiative is focusing on the wrong data. If you fix data that does not impact a critical business process or drive important decisions, your initiative simply will not make the difference that you want it to. It could lead to the end of your work before it has had the chance to mature. Senior stakeholders have a lot of proposals competing for budget, and it is common for initiatives that do not make the right impact to lose their funding.

Focusing on the wrong data often happens when the person instigating the data quality initiative or sponsoring it has a particular background. One organization I worked with had a new data quality manager with a purchasing background. They came from a large organization with a manufacturing element, where the efficient purchasing of raw materials was *make or break* in terms of margin. Suppliers were managed really effectively, and associated suppliers were grouped together for spend analysis in order to negotiate better deals.

The manager then joined a services organization, where purchasing was still important, but it was no longer make or break. At that organization, client experience differentiation was the way to succeed in the marketplace, and as such, client data was the priority.

The data quality manager put their initial focus into improving supplier data. The difference they made in that area was exemplary, but it was not well recognized as a success in the organization. There were much more important data quality issues to resolve, such as duplicate client accounts that led to confusing communication when invoicing and trying to collect cash.

This section is about taking the time to understand organizational strategy and objectives in order to make sure the focus of your initiative is right. This starts with identifying the right stakeholders to liaise with.

Approaches to stakeholder identification

It can be very challenging to find the right stakeholders to explain an organizational strategy at the right level of depth. Most organizations will communicate their vision and strategy *loudly and clearly* to their employees. This is a key part of creating a cohesive organization because people can use the strategy as a framework to make decisions (for example, *we shouldn't do this because it doesn't seem to contribute to any of the strategic pillars*).

Objective setting for every employee should ideally be tailored to the strategy. The ultimate goal of this is to ensure that every employee can understand how they individually contribute to the delivery of the strategy so that they feel accountable for successes and motivated to resolve challenges. Organizations that do this can progress delivery of their strategy more rapidly because they can delegate more effectively internally, and decision-making is shared through the hierarchy of people.

Despite this broad understanding of strategy that many organizations strive to give to their employees, finding those who can give greater detail (beyond that which has been broadly communicated) can take time.

I have identified the common approaches to stakeholder identification that worked across the organizations I have supported. These approaches are mentioned in the following table:

Approach	Detail
Consult a central strategy team	Many organizations have a central strategy team that owns the development and communication of the strategy. They may be able to share more detail on the strategy than is available to employees generally, and they can usually point you toward the people from the top down who are accountable for each pillar of a strategy.
Leverage a Data Governance Council	Some organizations will have a Data Governance Council and a list of data owners or stewards to consult (as mentioned in *Chapter 4*). It is really valuable to have this because it gives you a clear set of stakeholders to consult with at a range of different hierarchical levels. The stakeholders are usually embedded in most business functions you need to engage with and are predisposed to expect and support data quality-related conversations.
Review the organizational structure	The organizational structure of a company is generally easily available. It can help you to find departmental leadership and try to arrange meetings with key executives. In a smaller organization, it may be possible to start with C-Suite executives (for example, a **Chief Financial Officer (CFO)** or **Chief Operating Officer (COO)**). In larger operations, a mid-management level might be more appropriate (titles such as director, VP, and so on). For larger organizations, if you start at a lower level, there will almost certainly be a longer list of people to meet with than you have time for.
Engage other parts of the data and analytics team	Other members of the data and analytics team of your organization can often provide great insight into strategic pillars.
	For example, the BI/analytics and data science teams will be able to explain the key reports that their stakeholders use, who uses them, and which parts of the organizational strategy they support.
	This should be a mandatory part of your approach. If you are part of the same wider team, you should glean all the information you can before approaching the stakeholders. If you do not do this, you risk duplication in conversations and frustration from the stakeholders.

Table 5.1 – Common approaches to stakeholder identification

The following section has some examples of applying these approaches from my experience.

Examples

One organization that I worked with had a central strategy team, and I asked for their help to better understand a strategic pillar related to supply chain optimization. This pillar was about ensuring the following:

- Products were manufactured as close to the eventual customer base as possible to reduce logistics cost

- Production schedules were optimized so that no capacity was wasted

- Processes were harmonized across the globe

Discussion with the strategy team led to connections with the leader of the supply chain organization and his leaders. These connections were the obvious ones for the strategy team to make because supply chain was the main contributor to this part of the strategy. However, the strategy team also suggested discussions with commercial leadership, who provided input into the planning process to get goods to customers. This process defines which customers need which products, and when.

The strategy team identified additional stakeholders who would be able to help. For example, the team had discussions with the quality team (who would need to change documented processes to support the changes made through the strategic pillar) and the operational excellence team. The input of these teams was critical to the identification of the appropriate data to profile and to the eventual set of rules that we designed. Without the strategy team, it is doubtful that these crucial yet less obvious discussions would have taken place.

In another organization, the central analytics and data science teams were very helpful to the understanding of the strategy and how it linked to datasets.

They explained a report they designed to support the objective of making inventory management more efficient in the organization's warehouses. The report looked at the rate of inventory turnover (usage) in different locations and contrasted this with the average time it took to load/unload to/from the location. The aim was to look for the inventory that moved quickly but was put into a difficult location (from an access perspective – such as one requiring a cherry picker to reach it). The **data lineage** of this report (a diagram showing the flow of data, typically available in most business intelligence tools) helped the team to find the datasets that supported inventory and warehousing in general at the organization. The team was then able to link objectives tied to this area of the company (and the challenges they were experiencing in meeting these) to the underlying data.

> **Note**
> Data lineage refers to documenting the movement of data from its source through to a report, including the transformations made along the way – for example, the table name in the data source, the **extract, transform, and load** (ETL) program that moves the data from the source to the data warehouse, and the report that the data is displayed in.

All the conversations described take a lot of time – both yours and also the time of the stakeholders. Sometimes, it can be challenging to get the time that you need from stakeholders.

Difficulty in engagement

If you are struggling to get into the diary of a key stakeholder (particularly a senior one such as a C-level executive or senior VP), my recommendation is to do the following:

- Include in your initial email a meaningful example of a data quality issue that may be occurring in their area and connects clearly to their business strategy and objectives

- Have the email sent by the most senior person in your department– for example, if you are in a data organization, the email should ideally come from the **Chief Data Officer (CDO)**

- Make it clear that this first conversation is to give context and to be *signposted* to the right people in their leadership team – that is, you do not intend to take up a large amount of their time and need them primarily to direct you to others within their leadership teams

The key to success is to tailor communication to each individual so they can see clearly that they can add value through having the conversation.

Once the stakeholders have been identified, sessions can be arranged, and time can be allocated to prepare the content of the conversations.

Content of stakeholder conversations

In most data quality discovery exercises, there will need to be more than one conversation with each stakeholder. Clearly, these conversations will differ according to the personalities involved. The following sections aim to help you structure each of the conversations to achieve the outcomes required.

Initial conversations

The initial conversations should focus on the following:

- The context and desired outcome of the initiative

- An overview of the business area from the person you are talking with

- Relevant strategic pillars and the role of that function in the delivering work that contributes to one or more pillars

- Current and expected future challenges that could impact the ability to deliver one or more pillars of the strategy

As already mentioned, the conversation should not be restricted to just known data challenges.

In one such conversation, a senior HR leader explained that they were unable to meet their objective to make the annual bonus calculation process more streamlined (reduced from three months to a target of just one month). They explained that the line managers were taking longer than desired to enter bonus proposals for team members. The intention was to replace the system used by line managers to do this to make it easier and more efficient. The stakeholder remarked at the time that this issue was "nothing to do with the data."

On exploring the issue with the data stewards in HR, it became clear that this was very much a data issue. A high percentage (more than 10%) of line managers had to raise tickets to the HR helpdesk because of data issues that they observed. These issues included the following:

- Duplicate data (duplicate employee records)
- Missing mandatory fields for their employees (for example, their hierarchical level)

The system where bonuses were entered showed an error when they tried to submit their bonus recommendations.

The issues became part of the scope of the data quality initiative, and when the data improved, the process speed also improved in line with the ambitious target of one month. There was no need to invest in a new system – simply to improve the data. Had we just asked the stakeholder for the "data issues", we would not have been informed of and resolved this challenge.

As in this example, following the initial conversations, the challenges outlined by senior leaders must be followed up with operational-level members of the team (such as data producers and data consumers), who are "on the frontline" and use data every day. They are the ones who can help to translate strategic challenges and blockers into either data issues or other issues.

Here is an example of one of these conversations, showing the topic, the typical presentation materials, and the expected outcomes.

Agenda item	Presenter	Typical materials	Expected outcomes
Initiative context	DQ lead	A high-level plan, explaining phases. Anecdotal evidence of data quality issues. An example data quality profile/scorecard (showing the end product they might receive).	The stakeholder understands the purpose of the discovery phase in an overall project context.

| An overview of the business area | Business stakeholder | An overview of the responsibilities of each element of their organization and the key priorities of the function. | The DQ team understands how this part of the organization fits into the overall picture.

Identification of additional stakeholders to speak with. |
| The role of the function that the stakeholder owns in delivering strategic pillars | Business stakeholder | Organizational strategy slides, highlighting those that carry the most relevance for the stakeholder's function and the objectives that tie to them. | The DQ team understands key priorities for the stakeholder's area. |
| Function KPIs | Business stakeholder | Definitions of key performance indicators and how they tie into the relevant strategic pillars. | The DQ team understands empirically where the function achieves its objectives and where it is struggling to deliver due to challenges. |
| Challenges in pillar delivery | Business stakeholder | Articulates a list of current challenges, both short-term and long-term, to delivering a strategy.

Identifies those in their team currently managing those challenges. | The DQ team understands the key challenges of the team and who to explore them further with. |

Table 5.2 – The typical agenda and outcomes for the first stakeholder meeting

The last section (challenges in pillar delivery) is very important, and the next stage is to translate the list of challenges into a list of possible data quality implications to explore with the stakeholders.

Detailed conversations

Here is an example list of challenges from the initial conversations and what the data quality team might look to do with them. The list is based on a manufacturing team:

Challenge	Questions	Possible data quality implications
Unpredictable demand leads to unused capacity in manufacturing plants.	Why is demand unpredictable? What data would be required to make the demand more predictable? Which team is responsible for predicting demand? Is demand managed at a local level (for example, European demand in a European manufacturing plant, or US demand in a US plant)? If the data was available, could it be managed globally? Are there specific product lines where demand is less predictable?	Commercial sales forecasts may be incomplete or disconnected from the manufacturing data (for example, held in a file rather than a data platform). Data may be siloed so that global demand is not easily understood. Data may be incomplete or duplicated in one region. Particular product lines might lack reliable sales forecast data.
Quality control picks up manufacturing issues too late. A product is completed but then must be scrapped, causing increased costs.	Do quality control activities take place throughout the manufacturing process? Where is the data for these checks recorded?	Assuming quality control checks take place throughout the process, an issue with the data might prevent it from being available on a timely basis. Perhaps teams have to clean the quality control data before it can be used.
Raw material costs are excessively high and are impacting the profit margin.	What is driving increased materials costs? Are costs increasing for the whole industry or is the effect more pronounced for our organization? Who are the suppliers of the raw materials? Which purchasing teams are responsible for the procurement activities?	Supplier spend aggregation may be adversely affected by missing supplier hierarchy data. In other words, the organization may not realize it is spending a large amount with a single supplier group. Realizing this through improved data can lead to a stronger negotiation position and lower prices.

Table 5.3 – Sample questions and possible data quality implications of challenges

Many of these questions and data implications will not lead to anything useful. At this stage, it is important to be expansive in your thinking because many of these will be *dead ends*. Even if only 10% of the implications you identify are found to be valid data quality issues, it is likely that you will uncover enough to proceed with the next phase of activity.

The detailed conversations will involve exploring each of the questions and looking to prove or disprove the possible data quality implications identified from the initial conversations.

The detailed conversations will usually be with people at least one level down in the hierarchy from the stakeholder in the initial conversation. The conversation should cover the following:

Agenda item	Presenter	Typical materials	Expected outcomes
Initiative context	DQ lead	As before, but also an outline of the initial stakeholder input, and a list of challenges, questions, and data quality implications.	The stakeholder understands the purpose of the discovery phase and the view of their leadership team.
Their role and challenges	Business stakeholder	An overview of what they and their team do. An outline of the challenges as they see them.	Validation of the challenge articulated by their leader. New challenges they would like to add.
Detailed exploration of challenges	Business stakeholder, supported by the data quality team and system subject matter experts	A review of the challenge and the work done so far to overcome it.	Categorization of a challenge as data quality-related or not data quality-related. An understanding of the processes, systems and data involved in the challenge. An understanding of any new system changes or implementation work aimed at resolving the challenge.

Table 5.4 – Agenda and outcomes for detailed conversations

Once senior stakeholders have been consulted, it is important to identify a selection of people at lower levels of the organization and present the findings so far to them. Those who actually manage the impacts of the data *day to day* may give a reality check. They may identify a series of issues that have not yet been discussed, or they may identify misunderstandings in the issues identified so far. Sometimes, leaders do not have a realistic view of what is really going on at an operational level (usually, this suggests an issue with the organizational culture, which I will come back to as part of *Chapter 9* in the *Requirements for success* section) and this is a sensible precaution to identify these situations.

Finally, it is important at this early stage to start engaging with IT application leaders and system owners. This is for two reasons:

- The discovery phase may require system-specific knowledge from their teams
- Long-term correction of data quality issues may drive change to source systems – for example, where data validation can be added to a data capture form to present errors occurring in the first instance

As outlined so far in this section, the process of identifying and engaging with stakeholders can become complex and time-consuming. In some organizations, stakeholders want formal documentation of who is consulted and the role that they play.

In these cases, I would recommend two possible templates. A stakeholder map could be prepared to plot stakeholders against two variables – their level of interest and their level of influence. This would be used to identify stakeholders who must be managed most closely. To understand in more depth who is required to contribute time, an alternative to this would be to create a RACI matrix, documenting which roles are involved and their level of responsibility (**Responsible, Accountable, Consulted, or Informed**).

The outcomes of all the conversations so far are usually sufficiently detailed that you can start to act. A conversation may have identified a particular system of record that is tied to a challenge. You could start to explore the data in that system and try to identify data quality gaps.

Many data quality professionals will *jump to action* at this stage, but my recommendation is to pause and review your findings to ensure that your scope is carefully selected to focus on the issues that will drive the most value in the organization. The next section will talk about how to do that.

The hierarchy of strategy, objectives, processes, analytics, and data

If you have followed the process outlined in the *Understanding strategy, objectives, and challenges* section, you should have at this point a list of data quality-related challenges, as well as an idea of the systems and data involved in the challenge. It is likely at this stage that you identified more potential challenges than you can prioritize at this time.

The next step in the process is to review these holistically and select where to put your focus.

Prioritizing using strategy

Having gathered data quality challenges that impact various pillars of a strategy, it is time to take stock. This may involve going back to the strategy team to present your findings.

The following diagram illustrates the typical outcomes of the early discovery meetings.

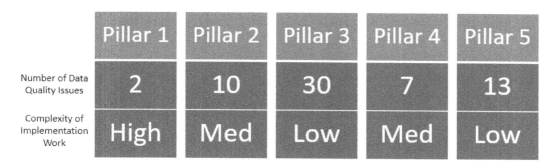

Figure 5.2 – Strategic pillars by the number of rules and complexity

There is often a particular strategic pillar where a significant number of data challenges are identified. This might be because this particular pillar is highly data-driven, or because the stakeholders in that area are particularly data-literate.

The complexity of implementation work refers to the level of effort that it might take to deliver data quality rules for a particular pillar. The complexity can be high for a number of reasons, including the following:

- The number of systems that the data spans (for example, data about the organization's staff may be spread across Workday, SAP Concur, SAP SuccessFactors, etc.)

- The complexity of the data quality rules that might be required

- A perceived lack of clarity from stakeholders that may require deeper investigation work

- Different parts of the organization operating in different ways, which would require separate data quality rules

If looking at *Figure 5.2* in isolation, it appears obvious that **Pillar 3** and **Pillar 5** would be prioritized. There is a lot to do, but the complexity of each issue is low, so the progress would be fast.

However, we need to bring another view to this analysis. It is highly likely that one element of the strategy brings greater benefit than another if fully delivered. It is also likely that there are dependencies between strategic pillars.

For example, **Pillar 1** may only have two data quality challenges, but it may be the fundamental strategic pillar upon which all the others depend. One organization I worked with had an aging product for which margins were eroding and sales quantities were falling. They had a new competitive and differentiated product ready for release, and this was the key pillar of their strategy at the time of the data quality initiative. The other pillars include enhancing their commercial operation with new systems, new teams, and new processes. The commercial pillar was worth very little without a successful new product launch. Therefore, all the initial data quality work was to support the new product launch. There were tangential benefits for the commercial pillar anyway because part of the work involved customer data cleansing.

One challenge arising from this approach is that one or more pillars may be eliminated from the early scope of the data quality initiative. They may have put a substantial effort into the discovery phase before seeing their requirements de-scoped.

It is very important to manage expectations on this in the discovery meetings. It should form part of the initial context provided in the meetings. Additionally, the outcomes of the strategy conversations should be presented to all the stakeholders engaged in the discovery phase, and scoping decisions should be discussed and approved by everyone.

Once the meetings have helped to refine the list of challenges to focus on, it is time to research each of the issues in detail and link them to the underlying business processes, data, and reporting.

Linking challenges to processes, data, and reporting

In order to properly understand the data quality challenge and how it impacts an organization, you must deep dive into each of the issues that are going to be in scope.

Typically, each challenge will warrant its own meeting or even several meetings. Ideally, these should be condensed into a relatively short period of time, to maintain stakeholder interest and keep the focus appropriately tight. Usually, representation will be needed from multiple functions and locations. Different functions will often have a different viewpoint, and sometimes even a conflicting view. These can actually be very challenging conversations. In one organization, separate meetings with the finance and procurement teams identified that each function felt the other was "to blame" for the data quality issues. The data quality team needed to broker a discussion between the two functions, where the facts were carefully analyzed and shared issues were identified. This is a relatively regular occurrence because data quality teams are very cross-functional in nature, whereas other functions (such as those in the preceding example) can sometimes focus only on their area – even if this is not best for the organization.

This is a particularly problematic area because data objects often have shared components. For example, supplier data can be considered to belong to procurement, but procurement only manages supplier selection, onboarding, and purchasing. It does not manage payments, which are the purview of finance. Finance relies on the procurement team to collect the bank details of the supplier, but procurement does not need this data to perform its primary role. Arguments can be made for either procurement or finance to own the supplier bank details, but in reality, cooperation is needed for the good of the organization as a whole, rather than success for procurement or finance. Procurement will not be successful if the organization gets a reputation for being poor at payment.

In these meetings, for each issue, the following information needs to be ascertained:

Information	Relevance	Example
Impacted end-to-end processes	An understanding of whether the challenge affects one process or many.	Procure to pay.
Which teams are involved in that process?	Identifies which teams need to be consulted or are impacted by the data quality challenge.	Procurement. Finance.
Which step(s) in the process is/are impacted?	Allows the data quality team to focus on a particular step or steps. The focus would then be on the input, output, systems, and activities involved in that step.	A supplier invoice posting against a purchase order. Supplier spend analysis and negotiation.
What would improve if the data quality challenge was resolved?	Understanding in more depth the impact of the issue.	Supplier invoices could be posted more rapidly. Supplier spend could be properly measured and negotiations would be improved.
What workaround(s) is/are being applied today because of the issue?	Understanding in more depth the impact of the issue.	Suppliers are manually consolidated in a spreadsheet on a weekly basis. Suppliers are also consolidated manually in the data warehouse by the data engineering team.
Which systems are involved in the process?	Data quality issues have to be resolved in the systems of record. Understanding the systems involved helps you to identify system owners. The system owners will need to provide access to the system so that the data quality tool can assess the data.	SAP Ariba
Which tables and fields are involved?	If table/field level information can be provided at this stage, it makes the data profiling step much more specific.	SAP – an LFA1 table.

Information	Relevance	Example
Which subsets of data are affected?	Allows the data profiling checks performed on the data to be more specific.	Only suppliers in the raw materials group
The source of the data	When the data needs to be corrected, where does it come from? Does it come directly from a business partner (for example, a supplier) or an external source?	Completed supplier registration form.
How can we identify which data is active?	Data quality checks are only valuable if they are against actively used data. Take for instance a data quality report showing that 1,000 records checked and there were 800 failures, this will only be of value if most of those 800 failed records are actively used. If, for example, only 300 of the records were actually in use, the report will show a large number of irrelevant failures and the stakeholder will not get value from the data.	Active suppliers are determined by the following: • The purchase order in the last 12 months • Open invoices unpaid or Purchase Orders unused • Whether they were created in the last six months
Is data duplication an issue? If so, how can duplicates be identified?	Duplication is a very specific type of data quality issue that typically requires a different approach, where different resources and costs may come into scope.	Duplication is an issue. Duplicate suppliers can be identified when the following details are the same: • DUNS number • Tax number • Address • Email address

Table 5.5 – Information required for each identified data quality challenge

The best-case scenario after a series of these meetings is that you will have a very specific dataset to investigate. With the information from the example column in *Table 4.5*, you will be able to connect to SAP and find the LFA1 table, filter it only for a specific material group, and profile that dataset.

The profile would then identify some potential data quality issues at the field level, which might lead to initial data quality rules.

For example, the profile might show that the DUNS number field is only 15% complete, and that the tax number field is only unique for 60% of the suppliers. This would imply two problems:

- There are many different supplier records that share the tax number, with at least 1 other supplier record. The implication of this is the following:

  - A finance person would need to choose one record to post an invoice against – sometimes, invoices would be posted to one account, and sometimes, they would be posted to another account

  - This would lead to a fragmented accounts payable list and no easy single source of truth for how much the company owes to the supplier

  - There is also the risk that the invoices on one account are settled on time but the invoices on another account are not settled on time, leading to supply issues

- The poor completeness of the DUNS number field would make it difficult to understand which suppliers are actually part of the same group. Imagine 10 suppliers, which in reality are all part of a group of companies. The total spend across the group might be $10 m, which might trigger a significant discount. If the organization does not connect these suppliers together as part of a single group using the DUNS number, then negotiations might only identify the spend against a single supplier – for example, $1m. This would be subject to a much smaller discount.

In *Chapter 6*, we will discuss how to use results like these from profiles and turn them into data quality rules that can be used to monitor and improve data quality.

Obviously, in any aspect of work, the best-case scenario is not always the outcome. Many of these discussions do not dive into the specifics of tables and fields. These discussions are with people in business roles (rather than data roles), and often, they do not discuss this kind of technical detail. This implies that there will often be another step in the process. The initial conversations may not produce suggestions of tables and fields to review in a system, but they will certainly be able to provide the names of the systems used and the forms that are completed in their processes. Usually, the next discussion will be with teams such as the following:

- **System center of excellence:** Most applications will have a center of excellence team who are responsible for the roadmap of a system and own the implementation of the business process in the system. For example, in one organization, there was a business systems team, with a SAP center of excellence. That center of excellence team was able to take the information provided by the business – the process step, the completed form, and so on – and translate it into relevant tables, fields, and filters.

- **Operational excellence or process governance**: Some organizations have teams who have a specific role to manage a wide set of business process designs. They may use tools such as ARIS (a popular business process mapping and documentation tool) to document process steps and understand the underlying data used in those processes.

- **Analytics teams**: In many organizations, the analytics teams have a strong understanding of the data dictionary in various systems of record. If a business person is talking about supplier data and purchase order data, the analytics teams (particularly the data engineers) will often know what that means in terms of tables and fields.

- **Colleagues in data governance**: More mature organizations may have implemented a metadata solution. Metadata solutions help to translate business concepts into underlying system tables and fields. For example, the business may define a "supplier group" field as a concept. The metadata solution may record that in SAP, the supplier group information is actually captured in the "material group" field on the supplier purchasing data table. In other words, the material group field is used for a purpose other than the one for which it was intended.

Before finally moving on to the data profiling process, it is important to spend some time thinking about the impact of the identified data quality challenges on reporting. This is important because, in the process so far, we have mainly considered the impact of data issues on business process effectiveness. Some data issues will not impact business processes at all. They will only impact the ability of an organization to make important decisions.

These decision-making challenges should hopefully have arisen through the process detailed in *Figure 5.1* already, but it is worth spending time with the reporting team to ensure that nothing major has been missed.

Specifically, it is important to talk about the following:

- Manual *workarounds*, which are managed by reporting and analytics teams to handle gaps in data. These can cause major inefficiencies in an organization and can make data very latent. The workaround can take so long to implement each period that the data is very out of date by the time it reaches the report stage. Manual workarounds are inherently risky because human error becomes a variable. A mistake in manual data manipulation can completely skew the outcome of reports.

- Any reporting requirements that could not be delivered because the data is simply not available or accurate enough.

- Reporting requirements that are delivered later than necessary for internal customers because of a high level of manual effort needed from busy team members.

Often, the manual workarounds list is very long and seriously impacts the ability of the reporting and analytics teams to be effective. One organization I worked with had made many attempts to create a single source of truth for their customer master data. This led to four different live repositories of customer data because not enough was done to decommission the older repositories before implementing a new one. There were overlaps of customers, and data was different across different sources. The analytics team had to decide which version of the customer to include in data warehouse tables, and where there were conflicts, they had to consult the customer services team. Another organization introduced a full-time data quality role into a data platform team of four, simply to correct data issues before they could negatively impact reporting each month.

These issues need to be surfaced so that they can be considered when prioritizing which data quality issues to tackle first.

Once all the different meetings have been conducted and there is a single agreed list of data quality priorities, it is time to start the technical activity of data profiling in order to start identifying the rules that data must be compliant with – that is, defining what good data looks like.

Basics of data profiling

Data profiling assesses a set of data and provides information on the values, the length of strings, the level of completeness, and the distribution patterns of each column. For example, for both values and string lengths, the minimum, maximum, mean, and median are provided to help identify outliers.

Most of you will have some experience in data profiling – even if you have not heard the term before. The first task that many people perform when looking at an unfamiliar set of data is to open it in a spreadsheet tool and apply a filter (the autofilter feature in Microsoft Excel, for example) to all the columns. They will check all values in each column, looking to see whether the column contains a couple of values that all the rows are associated with, or whether there are many. People look to see whether the data is a number, a date, text, and so on. It's quite common to look for the smallest and largest values. Even this basic action is an example of data profiling.

As an example, consider a spreadsheet containing a list of invoice postings against different customer accounts. If you place a filter on the amount column, you might expect to see only positive values. You might be surprised to see negative values, and you might see that another column contains "INV" for the positive values and "CRN" for the negative values. It is highly likely that the positive values are invoice postings and the negative values are credit notes, issued when a customer complains about a product not arriving, for example. By profiling the data, you might realize for the first time that the spreadsheet contains both invoices and credit notes, and you might ask a colleague to filter out the credit notes in the future, depending on the business need.

Data profiling in a data quality initiative is simply a more powerful version of this kind of analysis, often using tools that are specifically designed for this purpose.

There are a number of tools available in the marketplace specifically to help organizations manage data quality. All of these will have data profiling capabilities. The typical tools used in the marketplace are as follows:

- Informatica Data Quality, Informatica Intelligent Data Management Cloud, and Informatica Data as a Service
- Ataccama ONE Data Quality Suite
- IBM Watson Knowledge Catalog, IBM InfoSphere Quality Stage, IBM Match 360, and IBM InfoSphere Information Server
- SAP Information Steward, SAP Data Services, and SAP Data Intelligence Cloud
- Talend Data Fabric and Talend Data Catalog

I have knowledge of all the various tools from considering them in selection processes, but I only have specific experience implementing Informatica and SAP solutions.

I do not intend to focus on the capabilities of a particular tool. They all have their strengths and weaknesses, and I am not promoting one over the other. The decision will often depend on the organization buying the tool to some extent. For example, an organization implemented SAP, many of the systems holding key data were also from SAP, as well as their other data and analytics tools. For example, SAP Information Steward might be a good choice when an organization uses SAP ERP systems, SAP CRM systems, and SAP Master Data Governance for master data management processes.

The following section provides a guide to the basic capabilities that all data quality tools share when data profiling.

Typical tool data profiling capabilities

This section will explain in depth what a typical data profiling tool actually does and how to read the results.

Data profiling tools typically provide information on a whole dataset, covering the following:

- **String evaluation**: For each column, this is the minimum, maximum, mean, and median string lengths. For example, if a "title" field was being profiled for customer data, you would expect to see a minimum value of 2 (for Mr, Ms, or Dr) and a maximum value of 9 (for "Professor").
- **Field value evaluation**: For each column, this is the minimum, maximum, mean, and median field values. For example, for a numerical field such as "Order Value" on a sales order table for a company that has made 1,000 sales so far, the minimum might be "0000000001" and the maximum might be "0000001000".

- **Pattern matching**: For each column, the tool provides an analysis of the patterns of data within the field in terms of data types. For example, a postal code field for the UK might have the pattern XX11 1XX (where X = an alpha value and 1 = a numeric value). You would also see patterns such as XX1X 1XX for Central London postcodes. The number of records against each pattern is provided, along with the number of records that are null or blank.

- **Completeness**: For every column, the tool will provide the number of records that are blank, the number of records that are null, and the number of records that are zero.

  Null, blank, and zero are technically different. Null means that there is no value in the field at all. Blank applies to text fields, and it means that a user has deliberately selected blank – for example, perhaps a user is asked their age and told, "If you are not willing to provide this, leave it blank." Zero is the numerical equivalent of this. For example, where a company is dormant and the revenue for that year is zero, this is clearly different from null (where the revenue has not been entered at all yet).

- **Distinct**: For every column, the tool will provide the number of values that have at least one record associated with them. For example, a customer dataset with an age column in it with ranges 0–15, 16–30, 31–45, 45–60, and 60+ would return a distinct value of 5, as long as there was a customer registered in each of these different age ranges. If there were no customers aged 0–15, then the distinct count would be 4.

- **Uniqueness**: For every column, the tool will provide the number of values where there is only one record associated with it. For example, with the aforementioned customer dataset, if there is only one child customer (aged 10) and one customer over 60, but every other range has many different customers, then the uniqueness value for this column would be 2/5, or 40%.

It is important to say that it is possible to leverage many of the techniques described in this chapter without buying a data quality tool. It may take longer and cost more in people costs, but you can at least make progress and start to bring your organization on the journey with you. To give a simple example of this, a very commonly used data visualization tool (Microsoft Power BI) provides some great data profiling capabilities. Power BI is already embedded in many organizations, and the part of the application that provides these capabilities (Power BI Desktop) is available without license costs anyway.

When you connect to data in Power BI, you can use the **View** menu to see three options:

- **Column quality**
- **Column profile**
- **Column distribution**

Column quality provides an indication of whether the data in the column matches the expected data type and is complete. For example, it will note any text values in a numerical column as errors.

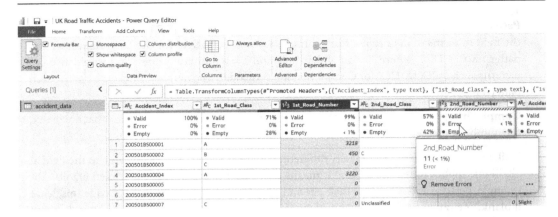

Figure 5.3 – The Power BI Column quality capability

Column profile provides a view of the uniqueness of the data and the distribution of the data across the different values.

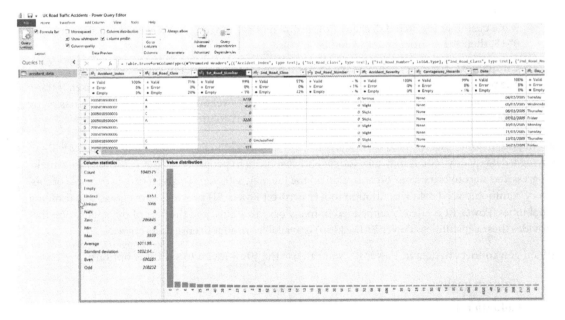

Figure 5.4 – The Power BI Column profile capability

Finally, **Column distribution** provides a view of the value distribution for all the columns at the same time.

Figure 5.5 – The Power BI Column distribution capability

These capabilities can be applied to the entire dataset instead of the default 1,000 rows, as follows:

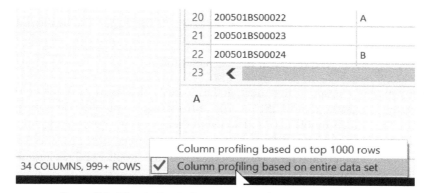

Figure 5.6 – The setting in Power BI to profile the entire dataset

Clearly, these capabilities are not a full replacement for a data quality tool, and they are not intended to be. However, they are certainly helpful in getting started and making the case for a data quality tool.

Once this case has been made and the data profiling capability is available, it is time to run profiles and use the capabilities to learn about data.

Using these capabilities

When I get data profiling results back from our data quality tool, what am I looking for? This section is intended to answer this question with as many practical examples as possible.

String and pattern evaluation

The idea of string evaluation is to identify where your data does not fit an expected pattern. Your expectation when looking at string length for a column might be that every record has a certain string length. For example, if you were looking at supplier VAT numbers in the UK, there is only one valid string length – 11 characters (UK VAT numbers have the GB123456789 format (two alpha and nine numerical characters)). The mean and median can give you a sense of whether most of the data matches an expected string length or not. For example, a mean of 13 with a maximum of 14 would suggest many records are 14 characters in length.

In a profile, it is very common to find in a column such as this that the minimum string length value is 9 and the maximum is 14. At first glance, it would appear that the profile has immediately uncovered *bad data* in this case. It would be tempting to simply delete these values from the dataset because they are *wrong*. However, consider this additional information:

- 5% of records have a string length of 9 – one procurement team has dropped the use of "GB" because all UK records are known to have "GB" at the start.

- 10% of records have a string length of 14 – all procurement teams enter "Not Registered" for suppliers that are too small to register for VAT.

- 1% of records have a string length of either 10, 12, or 13. These appear to be the result of poor data entry.

- The remaining 84% of records have a string length of 11.

In this example, it may be appropriate to remove all the records with a length of 10, 12, or 13. It would definitely not be appropriate to remove the records with a string length of 9. These are potentially correct VAT numbers, which simply need GB added to them. In fact, you could decide to remove GB from 84% of the correct records if that is faster for the procurement teams, and it still results in a full VAT number being printed on correspondence with the supplier and tax authorities if the correspondence is set up correctly.

Finally, the 10% of records with a string length of 14 could all be correct and appropriate.

From this, we can derive a data quality rule like this:

- For a VAT number string length, check the following:

  - The length should be 11 or 14 characters

  - For a string length of 11, the format must be GB111111111 (where each 1 represents any number between 1 and 9)

  - For a string length of 14, the value should be "Not Registered"

Pattern evaluation can provide us with even more intelligence about our data. We assumed earlier that all records with a string length of 11 or 14 are potentially correct. The pattern may show us otherwise. For example, for records with 11 characters, we might find the following:

- 86% have the AA111111111 pattern, which is correct

- 10% have the 11111111111 pattern, which is not correct

- 2% have the A11111111AA pattern, which is not correct

- 2% have the 111111111A1 pattern, which is not correct

For records with 14 characters, we might find something very similar:

- 90% have the XXX XXXXXXXXXX pattern, which is correct
- 10% have the 11111111111111 pattern, which is not correct

This can help us to make our data quality rule more specific. The rule can be coded to fail all records with an incorrect pattern and to accept all the correct patterns. For particularly urgent rules, we could proceed immediately to correct the data – for example, if we know that this causes issues with the tax authority on our VAT returns. Chapter 4 outlined the need for an early remediation workstream. This is an example of where data profiling can lead to immediate work for a workstream like this well before the official remediation phase has been reached.

The specificity of the profile is also very important. The profile for this column is really only valuable when it is filtered just to suppliers based in the UK. If we had run this profile for a global dataset, we would not be able to identify a single pattern that we would expect in terms of string length. For example, in South Africa, the VAT number format is a 10-digit number, always starting with a 4.

Pattern matching is very valuable when looking at the larger quantities of data that are typically found in "fact" tables. There are other techniques that are more suitable to analyze columns within "dimension" tables. Field value profiling is one of these techniques.

Field value evaluation

Field value profiling helps us to understand the "extremities" of the values found in a column. As mentioned previously, it is a little less useful than string length and pattern matching to examine "fact" tables. This is because only looking at the "extremities" of data values in large datasets often doesn't tell you much. Having said this, there is still value in using this element of the profile, as the following examples will show.

> **Note – facts and dimensions**
>
> Facts are the large tables of data that you want to analyze – for example, sales orders and their amounts. Dimensions are usually much smaller tables and are the information you want to "slice and dice" the data by. Examples of dimensions are countries, organizational units, and sales channels. You might want to report on the total value of sales orders (fact) by country and sales channel (dimensions).

The dataset used here is a list of all the road traffic accidents in the UK between 2005 and 2010. It contains information about the location and nature of each accident, as well as the weather at the time of the accident.

In this dataset, the number of the road that the accident occurred on is captured. In the UK, roads are typically numbered with an M (motorway), A (major road), or a B (minor road). From the field values, we can immediately notice some issues in the road number column. The following screenshot is from the Attacama DQ Analyzer tool, which is available for free via this link: `https://www.ataccama.com/download/dq-analyzer`:

Expression	Type	Domain	Non-null	Null	Unique	Distinct	Min	Median	Max
Accident_Index	STRING	pattern	1,048,575	0	670,991	671,340	2.0050...	200601TE002...	201091NM02142
_st_Road_Class	STRING	enum pattern	742,986	305,589	0	5	A	A	Motorway
_st_Road_Number	STRING	integer pattern	1,048,573	2	1,066	6,552	0	272	9999

Figure 5.7 – A profile of UK road numbers in Accident Data (UK Accident Data is from Kaggle (`https://www.kaggle.com/datasets/tsiaras/uk-road-safety-accidents-and-vehicles`) and was curated from publicly available information by Thanos Tsiaras)

From the preceding screenshot, we can see the following:

- The minimum value is 0, and the maximum value is 9,999. Neither of these values is a real road number in the UK.

- When looking at the frequency of these values occurring, we can see that 0 is a very common selection and that there are some null values:

Basic	Frequency	Domains	Mask	Quantiles	Groups

Frequency Analysis

Range: none

100 most common values:

Value	Count	%
NULL	2	0.00%
0	286,845	27.36%
1	13,835	1.32%
6	11,998	1.14%
4	9,889	0.94%
25	7,080	0.68%
5	7,018	0.67%
40	6,781	0.65%
38	6,401	0.61%
3	5,697	0.54%
23	4,892	0.47%
41	4,738	0.45%
2	4,488	0.43%
34	4,367	0.42%
62	4,147	0.40%
61	3,935	0.38%
27	3,831	0.37%
12	3,631	0.35%

Figure 5.8 – Frequency Analysis of the road number data

- The 0 value is assigned to 27% of the dataset, which implies that it probably has some meaning – for example, to signify a road with no number, such as a small residential road.

Immediately, this analysis gives us some questions to ask the people who know this dataset the best. The obvious next step would be to connect to an external data source with a correct list of UK road numbers, comparing the data in this dataset to it and identifying records in the dataset that do not appear in the external data source. For example, Wikipedia has a list of all UK A roads (`https://en.wikipedia.org/wiki/A_roads_in_Zone_1_of_the_Great_Britain_numbering_scheme`). However, as stated earlier, there is probably some meaning to the 0 value, and this may need to be taken into account.

Often in these situations, there will be a way to correlate two fields to get a better data quality result. For example, if there is a field in our accident data that tells us about the road in more detail, then it can be correlated with the road number.

The road types are as follows:

- Motorway/dual carriageway
- Main through road
- Side road/lane
- Residential cul-de-sac
- Industrial unit roadway
- Private land

Here is an example to further explain the road referencing nomenclature:

- An "A" road would have to be a "dual carriageway" or a "main through road"
- A "B" road would have to be a "side road/lane"
- A road with a "0" in the road number might be a "residential cul-de-sac," an "industrial unit roadway," or "private land"

Using this "mapping" will enable us to create a data quality rule to identify where "0" has been used in the road number, but the road type indicates that we should have captured a proper number.

Completeness

The most basic data profiling check is the completeness check. From our road traffic data, we can look at the **Weather Conditions** field. This is used to capture the weather at the time of the accident.

We can see from the basic analysis that there are 20,699 rows that are "null" – nearly 2% of the data.

However, when looking at the frequency analysis, there are other values that we might consider to be incomplete as well.

For example, "Other" does not provide any useful details about the weather. Beyond the main values, we can also see *nonsense* values, which appear to be times (for example, **17:00**). For a full completeness check, we can add up all the rows of data that are not in one of the useful values (the ones that are not highlighted in the following figure). Other fields in the dataset indicate that it would be possible to document the weather data – for example, there is a road conditions field where there are values such as "wet" or "damp."

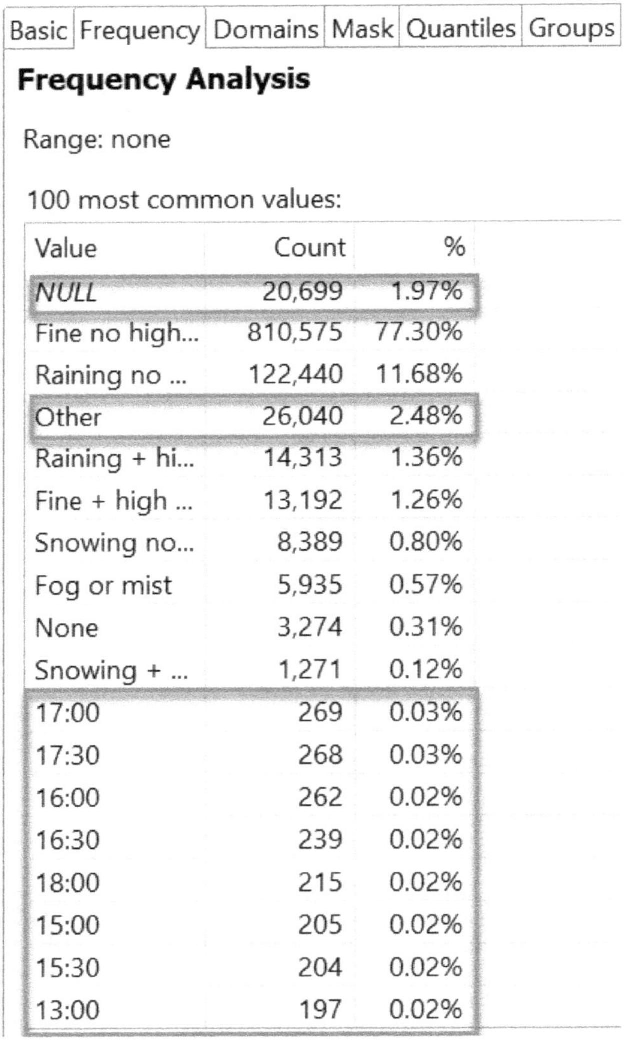

| Basic | Frequency | Domains | Mask | Quantiles | Groups |

Frequency Analysis

Range: none

100 most common values:

Value	Count	%
NULL	20,699	1.97%
Fine no high...	810,575	77.30%
Raining no ...	122,440	11.68%
Other	26,040	2.48%
Raining + hi...	14,313	1.36%
Fine + high ...	13,192	1.26%
Snowing no...	8,389	0.80%
Fog or mist	5,935	0.57%
None	3,274	0.31%
Snowing + ...	1,271	0.12%
17:00	269	0.03%
17:30	268	0.03%
16:00	262	0.02%
16:30	239	0.02%
18:00	215	0.02%
15:00	205	0.02%
15:30	204	0.02%
13:00	197	0.02%

Figure 5.9 – Value frequency analysis of the road traffic data weather column

A data profiling outcome such as this one might lead to a rule such as the following:

- A weather column must be one of the following values:

  - Fine with no high winds

  - Fine + high winds

  - Raining with no high winds

  - Raining + high winds

  - Snowing with no high winds

  - Snowing + high winds

  - Fog or mist

  - None

In this case, **None** is likely to indicate that there were no notable weather conditions affecting the likelihood of traffic accidents – this is different from "other."

Another key point is that completeness checks are only really useful when filtered to a subset of the data. Returning to the VAT number example from earlier, it is not really appropriate to apply the same expectation of VAT number completeness to large organizations as it is to small/medium and micro-sized entities (for example, small single-owner limited companies). For the population of small/medium entities and large entities, you might expect the VAT number field to be 90% or more complete. All these organizations will very likely be registered for VAT because it is usually better for them financially. For micro-sized organizations, the completeness level is more likely to be around 50%. Some of these entities will benefit from VAT registration, and some will not so not all will register.

Therefore, it makes sense to run the profile twice – once for the micro-entities and again for all other entities.

Uniqueness and distinct values

These are included in a single section because, typically, they are dealt with together.

There is a field in the road traffic accident dataset that contains the location of the accident, using a system called **Lower Layer Super Output Areas** (**LSOA**). The LSOA system is explained on the Census methodology page: `https://www.ons.gov.uk/methodology/geography/ukgeographies/censusgeographies/census2021geographies#lower-layer-super-output-areas-lsoas`. The LSOA is a code with the "E11111111" format. It always starts with "E" and then has eight numbers. It represents a relatively small geographic area. Our unique and distinct numbers in the profile provide some insight into the data:

Basic Analyses

Expression: LSOA_of_Accident_Location
Data type: STRING
Domain: pattern
Rows: 1,048,575

Counts

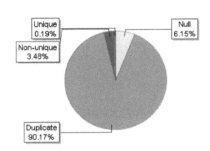

Type	Count	%
Null	64,528	6.15%
Non-null	984,047	93.85%
Duplicate	945,531	90.17%
Distinct	38,516	3.67%
Non-uni...	36,515	3.48%
Unique	2,001	0.19%

Statistics

Type	Value	Frequency
Minimum...	167040	1
Median v...	E010169...	72
Maximu...	W01001...	7

Type	Value
Minimum...	2
Median le...	9
Average l...	8.92
Maximu...	9

Figure 5.10 – Unique/distinct numbers for the LSOA column

From this analysis, we can see that there are **2,001** of these areas (the unique value) where only one accident happened during the period that the data spans. There are **38,516** (distinct) different LSOAs that experienced at least one accident. Most of these were **Non-unique**, meaning that they experienced two or more accidents during the period that the data spans.

This seems logically quite sensible and does not immediately imply a data quality rule.

However, when looking at the "Accident_Index" column, we can see clear problems. The "Accident_Index" should be a unique reference number that can be used to count the number of accidents in different areas. Each accident should have its own unique "Accident_Index".

Basic Analyses

Expression: Accident_Index
Data type: STRING
Domain: pattern
Rows: 1,048,575

Counts

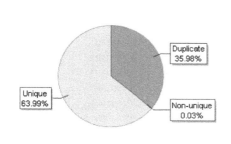

Type	Count	%
Null	0	0.00%
Non-null	1,048,575	100.00...
Duplicate	377,235	35.98%
Distinct	671,340	64.02%
Non-uni...	349	0.03%
Unique	670,991	63.99%

Statistics

Type	Value	Frequency
Minimum...	2.00503E...	1,900
Median v...	200601T...	1
Maximu...	201091N...	1

Type	Value
Minimum...	8
Median le...	13
Average l...	12.25
Maximu...	13

Figure 5.11 – Unique/distinct numbers for the Accident_Index column

This analysis does suggest a problem. There are a large number of duplicate values (nearly 36%). The duplicates are distributed across a small number of the actual values (349 of them). We can see this in the frequency analysis:

Frequency Analysis

Range: none

100 most common values:

Value	Count	%
2.00513E+12	7,277	0.69%
2.00613E+12	7,162	0.68%
2.00713E+12	6,867	0.65%
2.00813E+12	6,501	0.62%
2.00913E+12	6,255	0.60%
2.01013E+12	5,760	0.55%
2.00644E+12	5,578	0.53%
2.00744E+12	5,561	0.53%
2.00546E+12	5,519	0.53%
2.00746E+12	5,391	0.51%
2.00646E+12	5,368	0.51%
2.00552E+12	5,341	0.51%
2.00547E+12	5,219	0.50%
2.00846E+12	5,208	0.50%
2.00946E+12	5,158	0.49%
2.00747E+12	5,107	0.49%
2.00652E+12	5,082	0.48%
2.00647E+12	5,039	0.48%

100 least common values:

Value	Count	%
201091NJ1...	1	0.00%
201091NJ1...	1	0.00%
201091NJ1...	1	0.00%
201091NJ1...	1	0.00%
201091NJ1...	1	0.00%
201091NJ1...	1	0.00%
201091NJ1...	1	0.00%
201091NJ1...	1	0.00%
201091NJ1...	1	0.00%
201091NJ1...	1	0.00%
201091NJ1...	1	0.00%
201091NJ1...	1	0.00%
201091NJ1...	1	0.00%
201091NJ1...	1	0.00%
201091NJ1...	1	0.00%
201091NJ1...	1	0.00%
201091NJ1...	1	0.00%
201091NJ1...	1	0.00%

Figure 5.12 – Frequency analysis on the Accident Index column

We can see that there are some values in the index column that have more than 7,000 rows of data associated with them. When reviewing the many rows of data for the first index on the list, it is possible to see that not every column of data is the same. For example, there are different road IDs and different locations for the different rows, even though the accident reference is the same. Essentially, the data tells us that the same accident occurred in many different locations!

This indicates a significant issue with the data quality of the index column. It appears that the same index value has been written to distinctly different records by mistake.

Usually in this kind of situation, there would be a need to return to the source data to find out the root cause and potentially re-profile the data.

From the various examples, I hope that you can see how valuable a data profiling exercise can be. It is a great way to encourage discussion about what the data actually looks like, compared to how we want it to look.

Having explained the benefits of profiling, the remainder of the chapter explains how to approach connecting a data profiling tool to the systems which contain the data.

Connecting to data

A significant part of the challenge when profiling data is connecting to it. In the preceding examples, an Excel file was uploaded to the Attacama data profiling tool. This tool (and the others mentioned earlier in the chapter) can also be connected directly to databases.

The advantages of connecting to a database

It is usually better to connect to a database. This is simply because you have the control to quickly and easily re-profile data with different parameters once you have established a connection to the data.

For example, if your first profile analysis suggests that you actually need to split data geographically and run one profile per continent, you can do this quickly and easily. If you need to obtain another file extract of data (or many file extracts), this can depend on another team and may take time.

Another aspect is that it is good to be as close to the source of data as possible to avoid any changes in it being made by extraction, transform, and load programs. For example, I have been asked in the past to connect to data via an API for data profiling. While this is very efficient, in those cases, the API already contained an element of data transformation, which meant that our profiling didn't reflect the reality of the database data that needed to be improved.

Finally, getting a connection to a database in place is going to be necessary for the full data quality initiative when you start to create and monitor data against rules, so getting this done now is a positive step forward.

Before connecting to a database, it is important to take into account the considerations explained in the following section.

Other considerations

If you are connecting to a database, it is important to consider the following:

- Will the owner of the database provide permission to connect to it?

- What impact (if any) will the data profiling have on the performance of the database? Will there be any impact on the other activities required from the database?

- Does the database contain data that it is appropriate for you to have access to? Are there any data privacy considerations?

The owner of the database can usually provide answers to these questions. In some data quality initiatives, it was agreed to create an ETL program to extract data (usually outside of business hours) for profiling to a dedicated database for analytical processing (an **Online Analytical Processing (OLAP)** database). This separated the potential performance implications of data profiling work from the database that contains live data.

Sometimes, connecting to the database can take longer than you have time for in the discovery phase. It is important to identify non-live systems (for example, test systems) to connect to because user access to these is usually subject to lower levels of governance. However, the data in the test system must be representative of the live system.

There can be multiple approvals required to get a connection in place. In these situations, it may be appropriate to extract a file of data, and in cases where you have access to do this within your team, it may be the fastest way to progress. If you do use file extracts, it is important to discuss this with data security teams before proceeding.

Summary

The early part of this chapter outlined how to properly understand the business strategy of a business. If this element goes well and has the right support, an organization will feel that the data quality initiative truly understands the priorities of the business. This breeds confidence that the work done on data quality will be focused on the right aspects.

The chapter also outlined how to use the information from this discovery phase to properly research the root cause of challenges that impact the strategy. It also outlined how to link these challenges to processes, analytics, and data.

All of this has informed which data to profile. The chapter covered the main outputs that profiling provides and the potential data quality rules it can generate. This is likely to have revealed some surprises about data, even to those who use it every day. The maturity of the data conversation has now reached the point where data quality rules can be fully developed.

Following the data quality improvement cycle to this point has prepared you to start identifying rules, refining them, and getting them ready for implementation. This is the subject of the next chapter.

6

Data Quality Rules

The chapters so far have been about understanding how to shape your data quality initiative – who should be consulted, how to win their support, and how to ensure you focus on the right areas.

Having used data discovery techniques in the previous chapter to identify critical data and identify its flaws, it is now time to define data quality rules. This moves the work into a critical phase, as the rules lead to a data quality score that, ultimately, people will judge an organization's data against.

This chapter will help you write a clearly understandable business definition of a rule, which can then be converted into a programmatic check of data with a data quality tool. We will explore all the different features of a rule, such as rule thresholds, how they are assigned to data quality dimensions, assigning a monetary value to a rule failure, and weighting important rules over others.

In this chapter, we will cover the following topics:

- An introduction to data quality rules
- The key features of data quality rules
- Implementation of data quality rules

An introduction to data quality rules

A data quality rule is logic that is applied to each row of a dataset, which can determine whether the row of data is correct or incorrect. Correct data is deemed to have passed the rule, and incorrect data is deemed to have failed the rule – hence, the term *failed data*, which is used heavily in *Chapter 7*.

Data quality rules always give a Boolean output – in other words, a row of data always passes or fails.

The following table provides a few (purposefully very simple) examples:

Business logic	Passed row example	Failed row example
The VAT number must be complete for all suppliers.	Any row with any character in this field would pass.	Any row which is "null" or "blank" would fail.
The VAT number must be in the format AA111111111, where A = a non-numerical character and 1 = a numerical character.	GB123456789	12GB3456789
Suppliers in the "Services" category (Supplier Group 1-1) must have a payment term of 30 days or more.	60 days	Pay immediately

Table 6.1 – Examples of data quality rules

The power of these rules is not in each one individually; it is in the amalgamation of the individual results of each rule into a broad picture of the data quality position, and also in the provision of a clear list of failed records that can be corrected.

The simple examples in *Table 6.1* provide an understanding of the concept of a rule, but they lack one critical element – a rule scope.

Rule scope

Rules often lack impact when they are as generic as the first two examples in *Table 6.1*. What usually increases the impact of a rule is to make it specific – in other words, defining a scope for the rule. The final rule in *Table 6.1* already does this. The scope of the rule is specific to the "Services" category of suppliers. This means that other types of suppliers, such as government, intercompany entities (companies that are part of the same group), and utilities will not be subject to this rule. That might be appropriate because perhaps these suppliers need to be paid immediately. If the rule has been applied generically to all these suppliers, then many "false positives" would be generated, which would reduce trust in the rule from end users.

A rule scope also needs to be applied to the other rules in the preceding table, as shown in *Table 6.2*:

Amended rule definition	Rule scope	Importance of the scope
The VAT number must be complete for UK and **European Union (EU)** suppliers with a turnover greater than the minimum requirement for each country (for example, £80,000 in the UK).	The suppliers table will include a field to capture supplier total turnover and a field for the region of the supplier. All suppliers with a region equal to the EU and turnover in excess of the minimum for VAT registration in each country will be included in the rule scope. For example, all UK companies will be included if their turnover is greater than £80,000.	VAT is a UK and European concept primarily, and therefore, suppliers from outside these regions are not expected to have a VAT number (there are some exceptions to this, but I will ignore these to keep this example simple). If "micro" suppliers (suppliers with a very small turnover) were included, they would be asked for a VAT number, and many would not have one.
Suppliers in the UK must have a VAT number in the format AA111111111, where A = a non-numerical character and 1 = a numerical character.	This rule applies to only UK suppliers. The format in other European countries is different. In reality, there would be many subtly different sub-rules that would be grouped together into an "invalid VAT numbers" rule. The complexity of EU VAT number formats is shown in this article from the UK government: `https://www.gov.uk/guidance/vat-eu-country-codes-vat-numbers-and-vat-in-other-languages.`	If the rule provided in *Table 6.1* was not made specific to the UK suppliers, it would identify all suppliers from outside the UK as failed data because their VAT number formats differ.

Table 6.2 – Amended rules with an appropriate scope applied

When asking business users for data quality rules in design workshops, often they will provide rules like those listed in *Table 6.1*, without a clearly defined scope. It is important to challenge these and see whether there is some missing scope information. Final rules usually read more like those listed in *Table 6.2*.

If you are unable to get this level of detail from your stakeholders, the rule will be built without the appropriate scope and will identify false positives. These false positives will help to identify where a rule scope needs to be more tailored. This, in turn, will allow you to iterate the rule to a new version that only returns truly incorrect data. Clearly, it is more efficient to identify the correct scope from the beginning, but in reality, some iteration always happens.

The differences in scope between rules lead to different numbers of records being assessed. Consider a case where an organization has 3,000 employees and writes data quality rules to assess the quality of the employee master data. Some of the rules may apply to all 3,000 employees, but some may apply only to a subset of these records, as shown in the following table:

Rule	Total records assessed	Comment
All employees must have a social security number.	3,000	Although social security number types will vary by country (for example, it is called a National Insurance number in the UK), this is usually a universal requirement in countries where large organizations operate.
All employees must have a first and last name.	3,000	Again, this is a universal requirement that will apply to everyone, irrespective of employee type or location.
All employees must have an email address.	3,000	Almost everyone in employment will have an email address in the modern world.
Employees of type contractor must have an end date within 18 months of today's date.	400	Organizations will need to capture different information about contractors – for example, end dates, daily rates of pay, and agency names. This will not apply to permanent employees.
Employees of type permanent should have a value between A and G in the banding field.	2,600	The reverse is also true – some information about permanent employees (for example, their level in a hierarchy or their years of service) is not required for contractors.
Employees with at least one direct report in the organization structure should be included in the "people managers" Azure Active Directory group.	1,100	A subset of people in your organization will have people management responsibility. These people usually need specific communications. This rule would be used to ensure they are included in these communications. In this specific example, the communications are sent to everyone in a specific security group in the Microsoft ecosystem (called an Azure Active Directory group).

Table 6.3 – An example of different rule scopes impacting how many records are assessed

Often, the differences in the number of records assessed can be confusing to people who access the data quality reporting for the first time. It is important, therefore, to explain this clearly in the rule definitions that business users see. We will return to this concept later in the chapter.

Having explained what a rule is and introduced the fundamental concept of a rule scope, the next section will examine the other important features of rules that data quality initiatives must take into consideration.

The key features of data quality rules

Now that data quality rules have been introduced, we will focus on the key features that must be taken into consideration when developing rules for the first time. The following diagram summarizes each of these features:

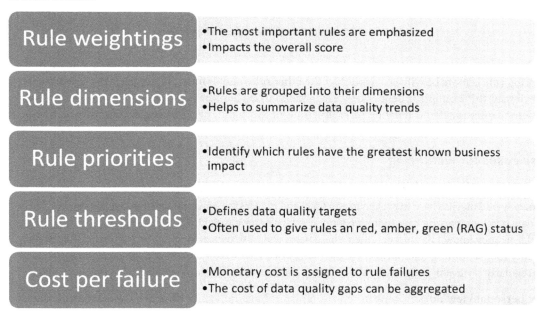

Figure 6.1 – A reference diagram for the key features of data quality rules

Each of these concepts needs to be considered when designing a data quality rule. It is important to understand the concepts well before starting the design process to avoid having to revisit every rule and retrofit them later on.

The remainder of this section will explain these concepts in depth and provide examples.

Rule weightings

Rule weightings are used to assign greater or lesser importance to certain rules. Greater weighting will be placed on critical rules. A data quality tool will use the provided weightings when calculating an overall data quality score, such as the following:

Rule ID	Unweighted score	Weighting	Weighted score
1	60	1	60
2	60	1	60
3	60	1	60
4	90	1.5	135
Average	67.5		78.75

Table 6.4 – An illustration of the impact of weighting

Table 6.4 shows the impact that weighting can have on an overall data quality score. The highest-scoring rule is more heavily weighted than the other rules and dramatically impacts the overall score. Obviously, this example is deliberately exaggerated to explain the concept, but weighting does have a significant impact and must be carefully thought through. The following section provides some guidance on when weighting should and should not be used.

Use cases for weighting

I will start this section by saying that I am not a significant user of weightings for data quality rules. I generally find that it is hard to explain to end users and reduces the transparency of data quality scores. Users of data quality reporting have to understand which rules have weightings, why they have the weightings, and how they impact the scores. Often, these users will raise concerns about the robustness of the data quality tool, assuming that the average has simply been incorrectly calculated. The weightings have to be regularly reviewed, and frankly, they are "yet another thing" to think about during the design phase.

My personal view does not mean that weightings have no value. Here are two scenarios where weightings might be useful.

A distinct group of rules determines whether a dataset can be used successfully or not

In this scenario, there might be a significant number of rules overall, but only a very small subset of these actually impacts the main usage of the data, such as the following:

- An employee and employee rating dataset is to be used to calculate an annual bonus
- Five rules are deemed critical for this:
  - The employee has a rating between 1 and 4 (1 being the top level of performance)
  - The employee has a start date (to see whether the bonus must be pro-rated)

- The employee has a salary (the bonus is calculated based on a percentage of the annual salary)

- The employee has a hierarchical level maintained (the annual bonus scheme percentages differ for different levels of employee)

- The employee has a number of contractual weekly working hours maintained (to determine part-time or full-time employment)

- There are also rules that check the following:

  - Employee names and address completeness

  - Employee contact details (email addresses and telephone numbers)

  - Employee line manager details are present

- These additional rules are used to ensure that the bonus letter to the employee is correct and looks professional – for example, it uses the correct name and address and comes from the correct line manager

In this example, the bonus letter is important for the perception of the organization by the employee, but the critical outcome is a correctly calculated bonus. Clearly, the employee's well-being will be more heavily impacted by an incorrect or missing bonus than by an incorrect letter.

In a scenario like this, it might make sense to increase the weighting of the earlier five rules above the others. It might give a truer picture of the data quality for this intended purpose to the leaders of the organization, who will assign resources to correct the data before the bonus payment. If the data quality for the five critical rules was low but the name, contact details, and line manager data quality was very high, the perception of the size of the problem could be skewed. Increasing the weighting for these five critical rules would show that this area needed urgent attention.

A heavily regulated industry has to prioritize rules for compliance

In regulated industries such as banking and pharmaceuticals, it is commonplace for businesses to submit data to a regulatory body. For example, in the banking sector, regulatory submissions will provide the regulator with data about the financial position of the institution and the level of risk it is currently exposed to. Regulators will also look at how a financial services organization has conducted itself in its interactions with individual consumers. In the pharmaceutical sector, a regulatory submission is required for each new product. Regulatory inspectors will also request data about adverse events (for example, a reaction from a patient to a medicine) and deviations from agreed signed-off procedures in manufacturing products. The data that contributes to these submissions is routinely checked by data quality rules at organizations in these sectors. These organizations will also use data quality rules to manage other data, such as supplier, employee, or customer data. If an organization had a single overall data quality **key performance indicator** (**KPI**), then it might be appropriate to put a greater weighting on those rules which would impact regulatory compliance. A lack of regulatory compliance is a risk to the very existence of organizations like these, and therefore, a greater weighting might be needed.

However, in this example, it is worth remembering that data quality reporting can be split into different subject areas. The data relevant to compliance could simply be separated into a dedicated report so that it was visible. This would be an alternative solution to weighting.

As already stated, I am not a proponent of weighting. I include it in this chapter because it can help certain organizations move forward, and sometimes, using it can be the difference between persuading a stakeholder to support or detract from your efforts. The next key feature of data quality rules is more generally accepted – in fact, I have never seen an organization decide not to group rules into data quality dimensions.

Rule dimensions

I introduced data quality dimensions back in *Chapter 3*. This section will explain how rules are attached to the dimensions and the impact that this has.

Essentially, data quality dimensions encourage stakeholders to have a simple conversation about the current state of data within an organization. By attaching rules to dimensions, hundreds of rules can be added into any one of six groups (*completeness, uniqueness, timeliness, accuracy, validity,* and *consistency*), which can be easily discussed.

For example, there might be 200 rules about product data in total. It is hard to have a leadership-level discussion without grouping these in some way. You can highlight the most critical rules or the worst results, but dimensions can also be helpful. It is quite informative for senior leaders to hear an explanation such as "*Product data completeness is currently at a score of 64% for Q2, worsening from the Q1 score of 70%.*" This statement can be followed up with a description of precisely which rules have driven this trend and the business impact of this decrease in data quality. Presenting the information in this way allows leaders to consider how it might impact their objectives. The detailed evidence about which rules drove the trend is still important because it lends the statement a degree of credibility. If you move directly to the detailed evidence, it is likely that the message will be lost – particularly when talking to senior leaders who are used to receiving "big picture" information.

Data quality dimensions are a useful way to analyze data quality scores, but they should not be the sole focus. Going back to the employee bonus example in the rule weightings section, from the critical five rules, four of them would be mapped to the completeness dimension and the other would be mapped to validity. However, it does not make sense to separate these rules into their dimensions for analysis. It would be better to analyze these together as a strategic theme. Each rule can be assigned to a theme and analyzed holistically. This is in recognition of the fact that senior leaders will just want to know whether an organization is on track to calculate an accurate bonus for their employees or not, rather than understanding how completeness and validity apply in this scenario.

Rule priorities

When gathering rule requirements from business stakeholders, it is typical to find that some of the requirements are business-critical and some are less important. Usually, the most important "X" rules will be prioritized – "X" meaning the number of rules you can include with the resource and budget available to your team.

This will naturally mean that the lowest priority rules are dropped from the scope of the initiative. However, there will still be variation in the criticality of rules between the first and most important rules and the ones that only just crept into scope.

It is a good practice to assign a priority to these rules so that users of your reporting (as described in *Chapter 7*) are able to filter to only the business-critical priorities.

Deciding on priorities

Having decided that rules should receive a priority rating, the next step is to decide on a logical framework to determine the appropriate priority. This will vary from organization to organization, but this section provides an example as a starting point:

Priority level	Identifying characteristic
Critical	• Avoidable data quality rule failures in this category can only be tolerated for a maximum of one month • The sum of all failures has a direct and quantifiable impact of $100,000 or more on revenue or costs • Failures can lead to an immediate risk of being non-compliant with local laws or regulation • Failures will lead to a breakdown of important business partner relationships – such as the loss of a major customer • Failures may lead to irreparable damage to an organization's reputation in the marketplace
High	• Avoidable data quality rule failures in this category can be tolerated for up to two months • The sum of all failures has a direct and quantifiable impact of $50,000 or more on revenue or costs • Failures carry an increased risk of non-compliance with local laws or regulation • Failures may damage important business partner relationships – for example, leading to reduced trade with a major customer in the future • Failures may lead to significant damage to an organization's reputation in the marketplace

Moderate	• Avoidable data quality rule failures in this category can be tolerated for up to six months
	• The sum of all failures has a direct and quantifiable impact of $10,000 or more on revenue or costs
	• The data quality impacts to the performance of the organization causes its relationship with business partners to be impacted negatively
Low	• Other issues that do not fit in with the previous criticality levels
	• Note that judgment can be applied to increase criticality where an issue is considered critical for a different reason than those listed

Table 6.5 – Example criteria used to determine rule criticality

Rule thresholds

Of all the key features of rules described in this section, this is the one that I consider to be the most critical. Rule thresholds are about "setting the bar" that you expect data quality to reach before it no longer meets the definition of bad data from *Chapter 1*. For example, **Social Security Number (SSN)** completeness for employees should reach a threshold of 99%. This means that only 1% of the records can fail the rule.

Here is another table that illustrates this, which also includes a rule that has not reached this threshold:

Rule	Total records assessed	Total passed	Total failed	Data quality score	Threshold reached?
SSN completeness	3,000	2,970	30	99%	Yes
SSN validity	3,000	2,910	90	97%	No

Table 6.6 – An illustration of data quality rules with a simple threshold defined

There are some key considerations when developing rule thresholds, which we will look at now.

Low, medium, and high thresholds

In the examples so far in this section, only a single threshold has been defined. However, it is actually more common to define two thresholds. The following bullet points describe the meaning of scores in relation to these thresholds:

- **Scores below the lower threshold**: Scores below the lower thresholds are considered critically poor – in other words, well below an acceptable standard. If a **red, amber, and green (RAG)** color scheme was being used, scores below this threshold would be red.

- **Scores between the lower and higher threshold**: Scores between the lower and higher threshold are considered to be moderately below the expected standard – in other words, in a RAG color scheme, they would be amber.

- **Scores above the higher threshold**: Scores equal to or above the higher threshold are considered to be at the expected standard – in other words, green. The implication is that no special effort is needed to continue to improve the score.

In *Chapter 1*, we talked about the effort to get to perfect data often being greater than the benefit that might be achieved. The higher threshold is essentially a recognition of this. Once we are above the higher threshold, it is arguably not worth expending special effort to improve further. There will almost always be another rule that is still at the red or amber level to spend your time on!

Here is another table of data quality thresholds, this time with two thresholds included:

Rule	Data quality score	Lower threshold	Higher threshold	Threshold reached (RAG)
SSN completeness	99%	95%	99%	Higher (green)
SSN validity	97%	95%	99%	Between lower and higher (amber)
Employee email address validity	87%	90%	95%	Lower (red)

Table 6.7 –An illustration of data quality rules with two thresholds defined

Setting and tailoring thresholds

The key decision that must be made for each rule is the threshold levels that should be set for it. It is almost never appropriate to set the same thresholds for every rule. Each rule has its own nuances, and the different rule failures have diverse impacts on an organization.

Some rules will be set to have almost zero tolerance for failures – in other words, the high threshold would be set to 99%. Other rules will have a greater tolerance – for example, a high threshold of 80%. This is best explained through examples.

Zero tolerance – employee payroll example

A data quality issue that could prevent an employee from being paid on time would usually receive a higher threshold of 100%. There is zero tolerance because no organization wants to be in a position where employees are paid late, or not at all. An example of this kind of rule would be *"Employee bank details (bank key, account number, and account name fields) must be complete."*

Critically, the rule scope must be limited to only those employees who started employment before the payroll cutoff date for that month. If the payroll cutoff for August 2023 was August, 15, with a payment on August, 28, any staff who started between August, 15 and August, 28 would only be paid for the first time in the September payroll. This would be understood by the employee. Therefore, these employees must be filtered out to avoid false positives. When a zero-tolerance threshold is set, there cannot be false positives.

Lower tolerance – consumer email addresses

A data quality issue that might allow a lower tolerance would be the completeness of consumer email addresses. In the EU and the UK (and in more and more countries around the world through legislation similar to the GDPR), consumers can opt out of receiving marketing information from businesses they buy from.

The business selling to the consumer would benefit from having the email address, and they will encourage the consumer to set up an account and consent to marketing emails in their e-commerce process. However, the consumer is entitled to opt out and purchase as a guest. In this case, the business cannot retain the email address beyond the completion of the sale and delivery of the product. The business may set a lower threshold of 60% and a higher threshold of 80%, but a higher threshold higher than this would not be appropriate, as there is no way to predict which consumers will provide their email addresses and which will not.

If this rule showed a score below the lower threshold, the business might need to reconsider the benefits of setting up an account to make this more appealing to the consumer.

Reflections on lower-tolerance levels

In reality, I am not a believer in setting up rules like consumer email address rule in the preceding section. I generally recommend higher thresholds. The rule I have described is arguably not a good rule. It might be better to filter the rule scope to exclude all customers who opted out of creating an account, applying this rule to only check the validity of email addresses for customers with accounts. The percentage of consumers who sign up for an account would be a key performance indicator in analytics, and it would be used by the online product owner to inform changes to the web experience to encourage greater sign-ups.

However, there are times when setting the lower and higher thresholds to a lower level does make sense. It is widely recognized that good targets should be difficult to achieve but not impossible. If the starting score is very poor for a rule (for example, 30%, with 500,000 failed records), setting the thresholds to 90% and 95% is unlikely to motivate those who are involved in remediation. It might be more appropriate to set thresholds to 50% and 70% for the remediation cycle and re-evaluate this later on. However, moving the threshold is not always the best way to handle this. It can be better to set the proper thresholds from the start because, otherwise, you need to explain why something that was green has now become amber or red again. In the earlier example, employees could be incentivized to improve the quality from 30 to 60% in the first remediation cycle. This would still be red but would still provide the employee with appropriate recognition and reward. However, this is most definitely a gray area. Many well-run data quality initiatives will adjust thresholds in consultation with stakeholders until there is a level of comfort for all involved.

Overall data quality thresholds

So far, this section has described thresholds at an individual rule level. In *Chapter 7*, we will show how individual rules results are grouped together by various dimensions, such as the following:

- Data quality dimensions, such as completeness

- Business units

- Regions or countries

When these groupings are made, there may also be an overall RAG status at each level. This means that you need to define thresholds for the aggregations as well as the individual rules. The following table (which is a repeat of *Table 6.6* but with two aggregated rows) illustrates this:

Rule	Data quality score	Lower threshold	Higher threshold	Threshold reached (RAG)
SSN completeness	99%	95%	99%	Higher (green)
SSN validity	97%	95%	99%	Between lower and higher (amber)
Employee email address validity	87%	90%	95%	Lower (red)
Completeness score (overall)	99%	90%	95%	Higher (green)
Validity score (overall)	92%	95%	99%	Lower (red)

Table 6.8 – Thresholds for aggregated data quality scores

When setting the aggregated thresholds, the main consideration is the action that you want to drive to the stakeholders who will review the scores at that level. For example, for a threshold that is defined at a business unit level, the threshold level sends a clear message to that business unit leader. If the threshold is set above the current scores, the message will be that the data for the unit is poor. If the threshold is set lower, then the message might be that data is at the expected standard. The overall message should, of course, reflect the data quality rules applied to that business unit. If they mostly have relatively high thresholds, then it is sensible to make the business unit thresholds similarly high.

Some organizations take a different approach to this. One organization I worked with used the following logic:

- Any score below the lower threshold for any critical priority rule would trigger the overall RAG status to become red

- If more than 20% of the high-priority rules had a red RAG status, the overall score would also have a red RAG status

This was also applied at the business unit and regional aggregations. This approach worked well at this organization because they had done a thorough job of prioritizing rules. If a critical rule had a red RAG status, the business impact would be significant enough that senior leaders would recognize its severity, and therefore, the aggregated RAG statuses were understood and appreciated.

Having considered setting thresholds for data quality rules, the final feature we will cover is the ability to set the cost of each rule failure.

Cost per failure

Some organizations focus heavily on quantifying the impact of data quality failures. As mentioned in both *Chapters 1* and *3*, this is really difficult to do, particularly before an initiative has begun. Where an organization has had success in doing this, it can be reflected in data quality reporting.

For example, if a single failure of a rule is assigned a cost of $100, then clearly 50,000 failures would be expected to cost the organization $5m.

It is very tempting to try to assign a cost per failure to every rule. This kind of information really gets the attention of stakeholders. In a perfect world where the information was completely accurate, these numbers would help us get better support for remediation, and we would have stakeholders "queuing up" to start a data quality initiative in their area.

In reality, this has to be done very judiciously. Where the cost per failure value is speculative in any way, it will be quickly discredited by scrutiny, which can undermine what you try to do. When you report on the quality of data in an organization, your own data must stand resolute against scrutiny!

Here is an example that shows how quickly speculative cost-per-record numbers can be discredited:

- A rule identifies where a supplier does not have a valid DUNS number.

- The DUNS number is used to identify where a supplier is part of a group.

- Discounts are negotiated when the organization realizes that it trades with two different companies within a group. Discounts can range between 1 and 2% of total spending with that supplier group.

- The cost per failure has been calculated by finding the spending with each supplier in the prior 12 months and applying the lower range of 1%.

Senior management sees the cost per record information and asks the following questions:

- Are we sure we will spend with all these suppliers in the next 12 months?

- Are we sure that each of these suppliers is part of a group of companies?

- Are we sure that we trade with other members of this group?

There are unlikely to be any answers to these questions because it takes a long time to gather this kind of information, and that time would be better spent correcting the data. Therefore, it is likely that the cost per failure in this case will be discredited.

Examples of the valid use of cost per failure

Having explained where cost per failure can do more harm than good, it is time to provide some examples of where it can be helpful.

Cost per failure is most valuable where there is little or no subjectivity involved in the estimate. Here are some examples:

- A set of data quality rules checks whether all data required to activate the IT account of new starters (both contractors and permanent employees) is in place and is valid prior to the start date. The average cost of a worker is $400 per day, and they cannot be onboarded until this data is in place.

- A data quality rule checks that all professionals working for an organization have a valid license for their activities. The regulator fines $1,000 for every missing license ID.

In both these cases, the cost per failure stands up to scrutiny. When this is done well, the cost per failure can contribute to other aspects of this section. The cost per failure can inform the criticality level and the thresholds you define. For example, if each failure costs an organization $50k from a turnover of $12m, the higher threshold would be set very close to 100%.

We have now described all the key features of data quality rules. Remember that it is not mandatory to apply all of these concepts to your rules. The next section will describe how to go about implementing rules in a data quality tool.

Implementing data quality rules

The remainder of this chapter describes the end-to-end process of implementing data quality rules. This process is similar to any other IT implementation in that it has a design stage, a build stage, and a testing stage.

What is unique to data quality implementation work is the need to be ready to iterate. When a design is documented, you can feel that you have full confidence it is completely correct, and then in the build and test phases, you will find that the data requires additional subtleties in the rules that were previously unanticipated.

We will describe the implementation work in the following three sections.

Designing rules

The process of designing a data quality rule starts with the data discovery process outlined in *Chapter 5*. By the end of *Chapter 5*, we understood the business strategy and successfully linked it to the data that mattered. We profiled that data and learned about its values and patterns. The rule design phase of a data quality initiative is the next logical step from this point. The first step in this activity is to gather business descriptions of the rules.

Rule descriptions in business language

Gathering rule descriptions involves holding workshops with the business stakeholders. The workshops allow the data quality team to show stakeholders the profile results and conclusions before documenting a set of rule descriptions in business language.

The conversations should go along these lines:

- We all agree that our conversation needs to focus on a key element of product data.
- The selected element of product data contains three key fields.
- Here are the profile results for these fields. Do you see any values or patterns that do not fit your expectations?
- For these fields, can you describe what good looks like? Can you give some examples of values that would not be appropriate?

These conversations will result in a series of statements that should be sufficiently detailed to transform into data quality rules.

Here is an example from a manufacturing organization:

- The product weight for products in category X must be between 0.10 kg and 0.20 kg

This is an interesting example because it was intended to identify a common mistake that people made when creating product master data. The mistake was that operatives entered the weight for a standard-sized package (which contained 100 units of a product). The field in the **Enterprise Resource Planning (ERP)** system was intended to hold a "per unit" weight. This resulted in confusion and challenges in the logistics department when working out the appropriate full load of a delivery vehicle.

This additional detail was useful in this case because the data profile showed similarly large inconsistencies in another category of product. This category was overlooked because it was an intermediate state of the product that was being shipped between manufacturing plants for finishing. This category was then added to the rule.

The lesson from this example is that statements should be accompanied by a business reason to implement the rule. This offers the reviewers of the design the opportunity to add additional ideas that might have been otherwise overlooked.

To summarize, the rule description should include the following:

- The rule scope (in other words, any limitations on which products, suppliers, employees, and so on should be in scope)

- A constraint (for example, the lower and upper limit, or the pattern that the data in the field should follow)

- Any dependencies on other fields (for example, this field should contain value X when field A contains value Y)

Separately, a business reason to impose the rule and the impact if the rule is not followed should be documented. Having obtained the business description of the rules, the workshops should move toward classifying the rules.

Additional rule information

The business description is the most important part of our rule-capture process, but as I outlined earlier in the chapter, we also need to capture additional information. The following outlines this additional information:

- Any weighting associated with the rule – in other words, should this rule contribute more to the overall data quality score than other rules?

- The rule thresholds that will define the RAG status (the lower and higher thresholds).

- The data quality dimension (or dimensions) to which the rule should be assigned – for example, the rule on product weight would be classified as a validity rule.

- The priority of the rule (defined using criteria such as that outlined in *Table 6.5*).

- Any cost per failure associated with the rule.

- Technical information associated with the rule – for example, *product category* might be the business term used to group products together, but in a system of record such as SAP ERP, this field would be the *material type* or the *material group*. A precise field name ideally should be obtained from conversations or the profile.

This information should be sufficient for the business element of the rule design.

Technical rule design

Once the business design information is in place, typically a more technical team member (for example, the solution architect role outlined in *Chapter 3*) will translate this into information that a developer can use to code appropriately. The following table provides an example of this:

Rule	Relevant field	Table	Field	Code considerations
The product weight for products in category X and category Y must be between 0.10 kg and 0.20 kg.	Product weight (the net weight in SAP)	MARA	NTGEW	Mark records as passed if the NTGEW value >= 0.1 and the NTGEW value <= 0.2. If this condition is not met, mark it as failed data.
As above.	Product category (material group in SAP)	MARA	MATKL	Filter the MARA table for only products (materials) with MARA-MATKL = A101 and A102.

Table 6.9 – An example of the translation of a business description into technical details

Table 6.9 translates business terminology into system terminology, as follows:

- MARA is the main products table in SAP

- *Products* are called *Materials* in SAP

- The technical field names are provided (NTGEW for the product weight and MATKL for the product category)

- Categories *X* and *Y* are translated to the SAP product category (or *material group*) values A101 and A102

This is information a developer will understand and be able to use to build rules with code.

At this point, a solution architect should be able to assess the full complexity of rule development and provide an estimate of the effort to develop all the rules. This usually leads to a final scoping session where rules are selected and deselected until the scope fits the available budget and time.

Once the scope is final, this level of design information can be used by developers to start the build process.

Building data quality rules

This book is not intended to reach the level of detail that will teach prospective developers how to code data quality rules. This will, therefore, be a relatively brief section, aimed at ensuring that data quality team members and leaders adequately understand what is involved in the build process so that they can properly support developers.

These are the key stages of the development process for developers and the support they might need:

Stage of build	Detail	Support needed
Connecting to sources	The first stage is for developers to be able to connect to the source systems that data needs to be checked in. New background (technical) user accounts will need to be created to read data from these systems.	Leaders might be required to support the case for access to be provided or to work with security team leaders to ensure that work is prioritized.
Developing **Extract, Transform, and Load (ETL)** jobs	Once developers have successfully connected to the source systems, they will need to start extracting data from all the fields that they need to develop rules. These will need to be transformed into a format and structure that can be easily used by the selected data quality tool. Developers will need to combine data from multiple source systems into a single model. Jobs will need to be set up on a schedule to ensure that the data refreshes on the cadence that is required (for example, daily or weekly).	Relatively minimal support should be required at this stage from leaders. This is the most technical stage of the work.
Developing rules	Once the data has been loaded to the relevant data quality tool, developers can start to build rules. Some data quality tools allow developers to start with the data profile and create rules directly from that. This can save time because developers can select a set of values from the profile and indicate that only those are acceptable. The tool will then create the appropriate code for this. More complex data quality rules will need to be built without this support – in other words "from scratch."	Developers will uncover instances where the rule design is ambiguous, or where the data may suggest that the design should change. Leaders need to react quickly to these questions and get answers to ensure that no delay is introduced into the plan.

Integrating into data quality reporting	*Chapter 7* will cover data quality reporting in depth, but incorporating rules into these reports (and building the reports themselves) is a key part of the design and build process.	Leaders will need to support developers on which failed data reports the rules should map to, as described in *Chapter 7*. The design of the reports may evolve during the build phase, and leaders need to be prepared to bring stakeholders together to review prototypes and make comments.
Moving development work into test systems	Prior to the testing activity, developers will need to move the work that they have done from a development environment to a test environment.	Often, this requires change boards and other IT approvals to be in place. Leaders should be prepared to support development teams to get these approvals.

Table 6.10 – The stages of rule development and how leaders can support developers

This table will need to be adapted for different circumstances (different data quality tools or different source systems), but fundamentally, the point is that the support needed by developers should be understood early on, and leaders should be present in the build cycle. Leaders and stakeholders should also get early access to development work, as described in the next section.

Early build visibility

Early visibility of development work is critical to success. If a development phase will take eight weeks, it is important to make sure that the data quality team can see the work of the developers at least every two weeks. This is to ensure that the rule designs are correctly interpreted and errors are found early enough to be corrected prior to testing.

If you use third-party organizations, it is important to build these checkpoints into your contract. Some providers will only allow you to observe the build at the end of the build cycle. This can result in initiative delays and additional costs.

Representative data

A common problem in the build phase of data quality initiatives is that the data used for development work is not representative of real data.

Often, developers have to connect to a development system at this stage when there is also a test system and a production system. Usually, development systems have fewer server resources so are limited in their data volumes. They often have 5% of the data that is available in a live system.

This can often mean that developers cannot find the passed data or failed data they expect a rule to uncover. For example, our product weight rule might not find any products at all between the weight of 0.1 kg and 0.2 kg. This makes it hard for developers to test that their code is correct.

It is a good practice to agree early on in an initiative that a good copy of live data will be made available in the development environment. It is important to ensure that the sensitivity of data is appropriately considered when doing this. Some data may need to be scrambled so that personal information cannot be identified.

Once the development phase has been completed, it is time to test that the data quality rules return the expected passed and failed records.

Testing data quality rules

This book is not intended to be a manual on IT testing best practices. Therefore, this section does not aim to be an exhaustive guide to setting up a successful test cycle. Instead, it will cover the best practices specific to data quality rule testing.

Firstly, the overall testing process for data quality work is usually somewhat different from the kind of testing that might be completed for other types of systems. I recommend a two-phase test process:

1. Testing individual rules.
2. Testing the overall rule results in the data quality reports outlined in *Chapter 7*.

Usually, the testing of individual rules would be completed by people who are assigned fully to the data quality initiative. This might be called an **integration test phase** or **product testing phase**. This phase is intended to check that the data quality rules work as expected before taking up the time of end users in a later test cycle.

The second phase of testing is much more akin to the way that end users use rules in the real world after they go live. Therefore, this is best considered as a user acceptance test and should involve end users who will actually use the product, such as data stewards. These end users must be properly trained in the use of the data quality tool and related reports so that they can focus on their testing work. If they lack familiarity with the tools, it is likely that they will miss the defects that the initiative needs them to identify. It is also likely that their test execution will be much slower than the plan demands.

The most difficult phase is the testing of individual rules. For this work, the following best practices can help.

Setting up data sheets

When testing data quality rules, it can be very difficult to assess whether a rule has identified all the passed and failed data. The tester can quite easily see whether individual records have been correctly marked as passed or failed, but it is hard to see whether the overall number of passed and failed records looks appropriate.

For example, if I am presented with the following table for our product weight example, I can see that these records have been appropriately treated by the rule:

Record weight	Rule result
0.12 kg	Passed
0.19 kg	Passed
0.08 kg	Failed
0.21 kg	Failed

Table 6.11 – An example of rule results during testing

However, if I am presented with this information, it is much harder to verify:

Total records assessed	Passed records	Failed records
5,000	1,529	3,471

Table 6.12 – An example of aggregate rule level results in testing

It is critical that this aggregate information is validated as part of the testing because this is the level that senior leaders will examine. The use of data sheets can help with this and keep the test activity efficient.

A data sheet, in this context, is a simple Microsoft Excel spreadsheet that has been prepared in advance by a business analyst by taking data from the system to be used for testing.

In our product example, a business analyst would log in to SAP and access the MARA table. They would filter this table for just the records in material groups A101 and A102. They would then filter to the list of records that are within the 0.1 kg and 0.2 kg range, and those which are outside of this range. They would save this Excel spreadsheet in a location that the tester can access.

The tester can then compare the total results from the data quality tool to the data quality results prepared by the business analyst. The business analyst can complete this preparation work for testing during the rule development phase.

Although this can feel like a lot of work (we essentially build the rules in Excel as well as in our data quality tool), in my experience, it creates a very efficient and effective test cycle.

One key prerequisite of using this approach is that the data in the test system must be unchanged for the period between the preparation of the test sheets and the test activity taking place.

Even with this best practice, it can be difficult for testers to detect issues with the rules, so another recommendation that can help is to incorporate multiple levels of review.

Multiple levels of review

The role of a tester in any testing activity is to look for issues with the development work that might affect users after the product goes live. My experience is that testers often miss defects during the rule-testing phase. This is for a couple of reasons:

- The testers may not know the full business context of data. For example, there may be 100,000 products in a company, and a rule may have a wide scope that intends to check them all. The rule may show that 80,000 products were checked, and the tester may not realize that this is fewer than expected.

- The work is very detailed and can be monotonous. Testers eventually find their concentration waning, and defects get missed.

In one heavily regulated organization I worked with, screenshots of testing had to be taken at each step and attached to a test management system. Each test had to be reviewed by a reviewer. In this case, I was the subject matter expert, and I had a lot of experience with the organization and knew the approximate data volumes of each different type of data.

During the testing work, the testers themselves found around 20 defects on 200 rules. With my subject matter knowledge and access to the screenshots, I was able to find a further 40 defects. In previous (less regulated) organizations, this review would not have taken place, and the product would have gone live with 40 undetected defects.

It is critical to avoid defects as much as possible in a data quality tool. Once the tool has a reputation for having incorrectly built data quality rules, it is very hard to get stakeholders to take the results that it produces seriously. It is not like an ERP system that has to be used to run production or sales. A data quality tool can just be ignored if stakeholders do not find it useful.

Therefore, a key best practice that I now recommend is to find an experienced subject matter expert and ask them to review all the rule testing work. They will uncover defects that were missed, and then they can be resolved prior to going live to enhance the reputation of your work.

In this section, we have outlined the process of implementing data quality rules from start to finish. There are a lot of similarities to other software implementation processes, but there are also many aspects that are unique to data quality work. I would particularly emphasize the need for representative data and to review test results carefully to ensure defects are not missed. A high number of defects in a live data quality tool will quickly undermine all the hard work you have done so far.

Summary

In this chapter, we covered how to define useful data quality rules, with a tightly defined scope to avoid false positives. We also outlined all the key features of data quality rules in order to explain what information must be captured to document a useful data quality rule design.

We now understand the process that is required to design, develop, and test data quality rules and how good leadership can make a real difference in these technical phases of our work.

Now that we understand the end-to-end process of creating data quality rules, it is time to move on to how the results that these rules produce are presented to stakeholders.

7
Monitoring Data Against Rules

After all the hard work prioritizing and collecting data quality rules, monitoring starts to provide the desired payoff.

Monitoring is about organizing the rules you have developed into a set of reports and dashboards that help an organization take action.

Until this point, you have probably only seen your data quality rules in action against test data. This is the point where you will finally judge your data against the rules that you have established and you will see for the first time where the gaps are.

This can bring up conflicted feelings. As a data quality professional, you are hoping that there will be gaps in the data identified by the rules. If you do all this hard work and then find there are few or only inconsequential gaps, then you will have some explaining to do (this has never happened in all my experience!). However, if you are invested in the organization, seeing these gaps can be quite worrying. What is important to remember is this: it is *not possible* to start to improve the data until you have a clear and stark picture of what the gaps really are. This is what you have achieved through all your hard work. It is time to present this picture to your stakeholders in the best possible way and (as *Chapter 8* will explain) time to start planning the remediation process.

This chapter will cover the following topics:

- Introduction to data quality reporting
- Designing a high-level data quality dashboard
- Designing a detailed data quality report (called the Rule Results Report)
- Designing reports for failed data
- Managing inactive and duplicate data
- Trending data quality scores over time

Introduction to data quality reporting

Data quality reporting should provide an entire hierarchy of reporting – from a high-level summary, down to the individual rows of failed data. These different levels of reporting are aimed at different stakeholders of varied seniority.

This is to cover the diverse requirements of different users of the reporting. For example, a list of failed records is very useful for an operational person who has been asked to make corrections, but would not serve a Chief Data Officer very well. A level of aggregation is required for a senior stakeholder so that they can see an overall picture of the data in the area(s) that they are responsible for.

This section will outline the types of reporting required, who they are aimed at, and how they might look.

Different levels of reporting

In my experience, there are three main levels of reporting required in a data quality initiative. These are mentioned in the following table:

Report type	Main users	Aim
High-level data quality dashboard	Senior stakeholders – for example, data owners	Observe the progress in their area on data quality and allocate resources appropriately To help leaders to ensure that data quality is highest in areas that have known links to important business focus areas
Detailed data quality reporting (called a Rule Results Report)	Data stewards	Review the list of rules in a single view, noting the lowest scores, and prioritizing the remediation of data
Failed Data Reporting	Data producers	Act on a to-do list of records that are to be corrected

Table 7.1 – Report types, their users, and their aims

Although these reports are aimed at different users, people will often traverse all three levels of the hierarchy, as shown in the following:

Figure 7.1 – Data quality reporting hierarchy

The data owners may start at **Data Quality Dashboard** to see the performance of their business unit, but they will almost certainly drillthrough to the Rule Results Report for the next level of detail. For example, the dashboard may tell the procurement data owner that supplier master data has an overall score of 75%, up from 72% the month before. It may tell the data owner that the improvement has come from the *completeness* of the data. The data owner will probably want to know specifically which rules were improved. The rule results will allow them to see all the rules that make up *completeness* for suppliers and they will be able to see the trend from last month to this month.

They might then reach out to the team that made the improvement and congratulate them, or they might feel that progress is not fast enough and consider bringing in additional support for one of their teams to improve progress.

A data owner is unlikely to drill down to the individual failed records. They typically have broad responsibilities, with data ownership as one relatively modest component. They do not usually have the time to get into this level of detail. This is where the data stewards and data producers would spend most of their time.

Similarly, for **Rule Results Report**, the data steward will spend most of their time there, but will also look at **High-Level Dashboard** so they are aware of what their data owner is seeing. They will also drill down into **Failed Data Reporting** to get an idea of the time it will take the data producers to remediate the data.

There are usually multiple instances of Failed Data Reports. I will cover this in more detail later, but for now, it is important to say that Failed Data Reports must give the appropriate context. For example, if you need to collect missing supplier email addresses, the Failed Data Report needs to provide alternative contact details, such as a telephone number, so the data producer can contact the supplier to obtain the missing information. Depending on which rule failed, a different context is needed.

Lastly, *Figure 7.1* shows the **Inactive Report** and **Duplication Report**. These are separate from the rest of the hierarchy, but their results are used to filter the reports in the hierarchy. The **Inactive Report** (for example) identifies data that has not been used recently by the organization – and this can be filtered out of the other reports to avoid spending time on inactive records. As mentioned in previous chapters, if the failed data includes irrelevant records, our data stewards and producers may start to disengage from using the reporting and taking action. I will cover these reports in further depth in the *Managing inactive and duplicate data* section.

Together, this suite of reports should provide everything that the varied stakeholders require and should ensure that only relevant (active) data is focused on.

As already explained, some stakeholders require row-level detail. Row-level detail brings with it data security considerations because it can expose personal data protected by legislation such as the GDPR.

Data security considerations

Just as with any **Business Intelligence** (**BI**) solution, data quality reports must have a suitable security model set up.

As you will see later in this chapter, the data quality reporting gets down to the field-by-field detail of failed records. Where this data is sensitive, it is very important to protect it appropriately. At one organization, the data quality team assessed HR data and had been given special permission to pull in employee records. Although the Failed Data Reports did not include this field, the underlying dataset used was found to include salary information. This element of the data was later removed because it was not relevant to any data quality rule, but it is a good example of where security issues can impact a data quality initiative.

It is important to conduct a review of all the data that will be integrated into your data quality tool and identify the sensitive fields appropriately. This review would include the subject-matter experts (for example, HR professionals for the employee record), GDPR experts (if subject to the GDPR), and IT security professionals. The review would be looking for **Personal Identifiable Information** (**PII**), protected characteristics (such as gender, race, and religion), and confidential information (such as date of birth, salary, etc.). Once the sensitive fields are known, the appropriate protections can be added to the data quality solution data via a security model.

In addition to this, it might be necessary to exclude certain rows of data from data quality reporting analysis completely. Some organizations will have VIP customers for which the customer account details (including their address and contact details) should only be visible to a very small number of trusted operatives. This might extend to VIP employees (for example, C-level executives) in your organization.

Usually, a security model is created that will ensure that the right people see the right data quality reporting. This may be segregated by function, location, or a combination of both. For example, a product data steward in Germany might only see the records for supply chain-related rules for the country of Germany.

My recommendation is to try to leave the reporting as open as possible in terms of security and only hide the truly sensitive data – such as the HR data mentioned earlier. The value of leaving the data relatively open is to promote healthy competition. If the data steward in Germany can see that they have lower data quality scores than a colleague in another country in their region, they may want to change that position. This competition can lead to rapid improvement of data. At one organization I worked with, Spain and Portugal were particularly competitive. They started at the lower end of the *league table* of data quality and, by competing with one another, both became the leading countries in the organization.

Once an appropriate agreement has been reached on the security model for data quality reporting, the design of the dashboards and reports can begin.

Designing a high-level data quality dashboard

Every data quality initiative is different, and senior stakeholders at different organizations will have different needs. The example developed for this book is an amalgamation of various concepts successfully applied at different organizations. The figures in this section can be used as a starting point for discussions, but it is critical to get stakeholders involved in the design process.

This section explains the typical design of the various Data Quality Dashboards and reports. It should be possible to apply organizational differences to this typical approach to make it work for your organization.

Dimensions and filters

The high-level Data Quality Dashboard for the senior stakeholder is typically a simple data visualization aimed at showing a data quality summary for the following displayed dimensions:

- Each process area
- Each data object
- Each business unit
- Each region

The report is typically kept simple in recognition of the fact that this should be viewed by some of the most senior leaders of the organization – who will only have limited time to read and digest the information. The report will clearly display links to business **key performance indicators** (**KPIs**). For example, the supplier *paid on time* KPI would be linked to all rules relating to correct and complete bank details on the supplier record.

These are the typical dimensions used to *slice* the data quality results, but others can easily be incorporated. For example, if your organization is highly product-centric, adding *product* as a dimension might be more meaningful than a business unit. An organization that makes both food products and cleaning products in the same business unit (but operates both activities separately) might need to introduce *product* (or *product type*) as a dimension. Another example of this is where an organization has different physical factories – the quality of the data supporting one factory might be quite different from the quality of data in another factory. The factories might be headed by different leaders as well.

The data is always also trended over time. There is no restriction on how long the trending goes back, but usually, in the world of data quality, 18 months is sufficient. It is a good idea to clearly define how long you want to retain the data quality history, bearing in mind that there are usually quite high volumes of failed data, and storing data does lead to cost.

The data can also be filtered in several ways. This varies for each organization, but here is a typical list of filters that a data owner might request:

Filter	Relevance
Person responsible	Some organizations define an owner at the rule level. This can be used to see which of the team members are getting the most positive data quality result. Note: I do not necessarily recommend this because the analysis can be too simplistic and can drive a negative culture (a culture of blame).
Subprocess area	Often, data owners want to break their area down into subprocesses (for example, supplier master data creation, purchase order creation, and invoice management, within procure-to-pay). Data owners often wish to see this view.
Country-level results	The standard reporting might provide regional breakdowns, but often, data owners want to see the country level or compare two or more countries in a table.
Source system	If a stakeholder has a specific responsibility around a system (for example, an SAP ERP system owner), they might want a system-centric view of the data.
Data object-specific attributes (for example, material type or supplier type)	Some stakeholders focus much more on different types of data objects. For example, a product (material) in SAP can be a spare part for a machine or a critical component used in production. The data quality for one might be more important than for another. A second example might be supplier types. Suppliers may include intercompany and employees (to pay expenses), and the data quality results for these might be considered more or less important than for external suppliers.

Date range	In order to compare data quality from one period to another, the report would usually contain a date filter. For example, the stakeholder may want to see the improvement over a 3-month period and also over a 3-year period.
Data quality dimension	It is quite common for users to filter on rules that tie to a particular data quality dimension; for example, showing all rules related to the completeness of data, rather than rules on the validity of data.

Table 7.2 – Typical filters for a high-level data quality summary

Any of these filters can be added to the standard displayed dimensions (for example, process area or data object).

I have created a summary dashboard similar to those that have been successful during previous data quality initiatives. The following figures were constructed with Microsoft Power BI, but could easily be produced from any data visualization tool.

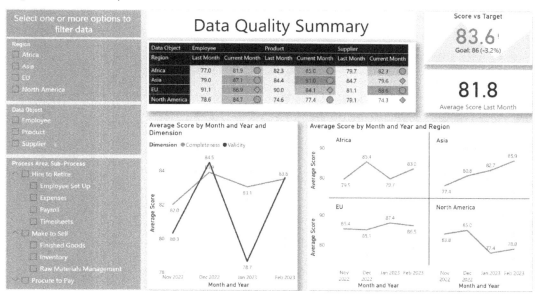

Figure 7.2 – A typical high-level data quality summary report

The report sample in *Figure 7.2* includes a number of key elements that I have found consistently useful across the various organizations I have worked with, notably the following:

- A summary matrix, showing the average data quality score for each data object, and by region. This includes a color highlight that makes the highest scores in the matrix most visible. It also includes icons to show whether the score improved from the prior month or not.

- A high-level summary of the current score (showing **83.6**) versus an overall target, including a trend.

- A line chart showing how the data quality score has changed over time for each data quality dimension (completeness and validity are shown).

- Four line charts comparing the data quality scores over time for each region.

These visuals can all be filtered by the slicers on the left-hand side of *Figure 7.2*. For example, applying a single region value in the first slicer has the following effect:

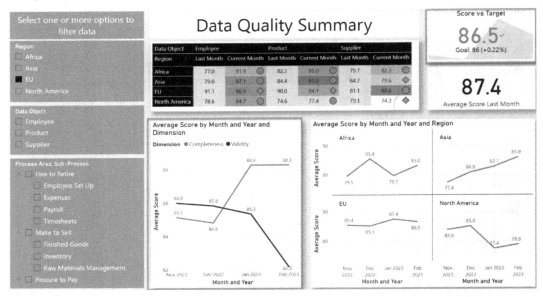

Figure 7.3 – High-level summary filtered to one region

The filter has affected the elements of the report highlighted in *Figure 7.3*. The score versus target provides an **EU**-specific view of the current score against an agreed target. The chart at the bottom shows an **EU** view of performance against the validity and completeness dimensions.

Note that using the filters does not impact all the visualizations. The summary matrix and the score by region are unaffected. This is simply because there is no value in filtering these views by region – because they are already broken down by region. If the subprocess filter was applied, then these visualizations would react.

Analyzing the results

Overall, the EU is ahead of target (the only region that is), but there are some warning signs. The overall score has decreased from the prior month, with substantial falls in both employee and product data.

The overall completeness metric has reached quite a high level over the last few months, but the validity metric is starting to fall away. People understand quickly that certain fields should not be left blank, and when measured on this, completion rapidly improves. However, it can take longer for people to change behaviors and take the time to find high-quality data. This is actually very common when organizations first drive their people to resolve data quality issues. There is always a balance to be found between the *quantity* of data added to systems and the *quality* of data being added. It is important to have an appropriate balance of data quality rules across these dimensions. If the data shows completeness improving but at the cost of validity, then communications can start to focus on redressing this balance.

This illustrates the type of analysis (and resultant discussion) that the Data Quality Dashboard can support. Senior leaders can use this dashboard to identify questions that they want to ask the data owners and stewards, which should lead to positive action on data quality.

Once some initial analysis is complete, it is likely that some (or all) report users will want to see a greater level of detail. The report includes a **Drill through** capability to support that.

Drill through capability

One of the most important features of this report is the ability to **Drill through** to the next level of detail—the rule summary report.

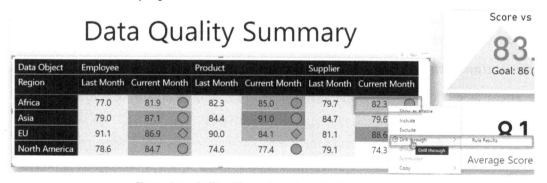

Figure 7.4 – Drilling Through to the Rule Results Report

Any number in the summary table (or line in other visuals) can be linked using the **Drill through** functionality to the **Rule Results Report**, as shown. This retains the applied filters for the selected data point – in this case, the following:

- Supplier **Data Object**
- The **Africa** region
- **Current Month**

The whole suite of data quality reports is designed to allow any user to start at the overview level and drill down to a more detailed view. In this case, we are traveling from an overall score and trend level for all rules, down to a view of each individual rule. This next view is designed to enable users to understand which rules are most and least adhered to by the organization, with the aim of targeting where improvement is most required.

In the figures in the next sections, you will see that these filters are applied to the Rule Results Report.

Designing a Rule Results Report

The Rule Results Report helps an organization move from a high-level aggregated trend to a more specific list of data quality issues. The report allows conclusions to be reached. For example, if there is a large backlog of supplier payments in a particular country, and all the bank-related data quality rules for that country show low scores, then the issues can be easily explained, and an action plan put in place to get to a resolution.

As with the data quality summary, it is important to take examples of report layouts to the data stewards and ask for their input. Your particular organization may have different needs, and to ensure good engagement, these must be taken into account.

This section provides a view of the features that have been commonly required for the Rule Results Report at a range of different organizations across different industries.

Typical features of the Rule Results Report

The overall objective for this report is to be able to quickly pick out the data quality issues at the rule level and put an action plan in place. This section outlines the features recommended to support this objective.

Information in the report

The report shows the results of each individual rule, providing the following information in a tabular format:

- Rule name
- Region and dimension
- Passed, failed, and total records assessed
- Scores (last month and this month)
- The trend (whether the score is improving or worsening between the current and previous month)

This is the basic information required to quickly identify the rules that require the most attention from data stewards and owners covered in Chapter 6 in the *Key features of data quality rules* section..

Color-coding

The current month's scores are color-coded. This shows whether the current score is above or below lower and higher data quality thresholds.

These thresholds are set individually for each rule and indicate what the data quality requirement is. Each rule has a lower and higher threshold. If the current score is below the *lower* threshold, it is considered to be at a very low level of quality. If it is between the low and high thresholds, it is considered to be at a moderate level of quality. If it is above the high threshold, then it is considered to have reached the target level of quality. In these cases, further improvement can often be made, but it might not be a priority.

These thresholds are shown in our reports using color-coding (red, amber, and green), but this can be visualized in many different ways. Actually, using red, amber, and green is not always the best option because of potential accessibility issues. Deuteranopia, for example (a type of red/green color blindness), would make these colors difficult to use.

The thresholds need clear communication to end users. It can seem a little counterintuitive at first to see one rule showing a less positive color than another rule with a lower score. For example, one rule might have a higher threshold of 99, and a score of 98. This would mean that it has a color code of amber. Another rule might have a score of 90, but because the higher threshold is only 88, it has a color code of green. This is correct, but users will usually need to understand this in training.

When color-coding is used well and is made accessible to those with conditions that affect their color vision, it can really help end users rapidly identify the rules they need to focus on. It can also help ensure that stakeholders remain aligned on what is important.

Further visualizations

The report also provides two further visuals:

- The score over time in comparison to the data quality thresholds
- The number of failed records (current and prior month) by country

The visual showing the score over time is intended to provide a longer-term view of performance on the selected rule. The failed records visual is intended to allow data stewards to focus on the right areas.

For example, the data steward responsible for supplier data in Africa would want to see which of the African countries had the largest number of failed records and consider whether they are appropriately resourced to manage the problem. Here is the report they would use:

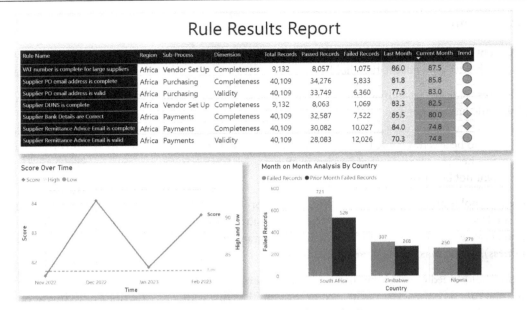

Figure 7.5 – An example of the Rule Results Report

Report interactivity

The Rule Results Report is interactive – when a particular rule is selected in the table, the other visuals are updated:

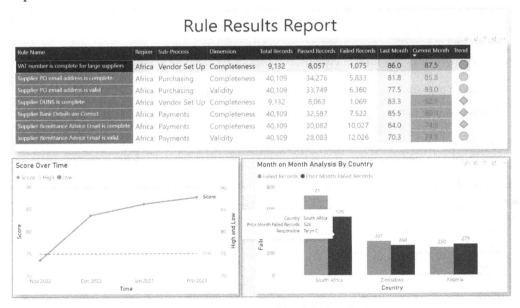

Figure 7.6 – The interactivity of the Rule Results Report

Let us now analyze this report.

In this example, South Africa and Zimbabwe have made some progress in reducing their failed records month to month, but there is actually a slight increase in Nigeria. When looking at the trend over time for the region, you might think that there is no reason to intervene. The score has been steadily improving since November 2022.

In reality, the trend for Nigeria is not positive and may require some intervention. There would be no way of knowing this from the table/trend graph alone, and this gives the Africa data steward useful insight for meetings with the country-level team members. The names of the people responsible for the rules are also visible.

This illustrates how this particular instance of the report can be analyzed. More generally, the users of the report should try to do the following:

- Apply various dimensions and filters to the report to look for outliers. In the previous example, we identified that Nigeria was trending negatively on an individual rule where the overall Africa trend was positive. If we had applied a **Nigeria** country filter to the whole Rule Results Report, we would immediately see the negative trend for the VAT number rule but also for any other rules with a similar trend.

- Find different combinations of dimensions and filters that provide insights and save them so that they can be opened immediately the next time the report is used. In the reports shown in the figures in this chapter, Microsoft Power BI is used. In Power BI, this functionality is called a **bookmark**. Bookmarks allow users to open a uniquely filtered view of a report with a single click. There are many different dimensions and filters, and navigating them all can take time. Using bookmarks for the most important combinations can save time and rapidly provide insights.

- Look for the negative trends on the rules currently above the higher threshold and proactively identify remedial action before the quality deteriorates to a point below the higher threshold. The report uses color to draw attention to the worst items. Items that are currently good but trending toward a less positive position are also worthy of attention.

- Use **Drill through** to the Failed Data Report to see the detailed rule definitions where there is a lack of clarity. The detailed definitions provide all the nuances in the rule design, and this can be necessary to look up and understand less obvious rules.

Just as with the data quality summary, the Rule Results Report allows the user to drillthrough to the next level of detail – the Failed Data Report.

The Rule Results Report is usually the most widely used of all the reports. It is used by senior stakeholders and operational-level people and allows them to speak a common language about the state of the organization's data.

Designing Failed Data Reports

The Failed Data Report is the final level of detail for the data quality reporting. It is intended to be a completely actionable list of records that need correction. This report does not tend to vary much between organizations – it is a simple list of record-level details.

The following sections will provide details of the report, including its features, elements, and the benefits that they provide.

Typical features of the Failed Data Reports

The Failed Data Reports should provide enough detail to do the following:

- Quickly and easily identify the record
- Clearly show the data issue for each record
- Provide as much assistance as possible to the user in correcting the issue

As already mentioned, the report is typically accessed by *drilling through* from the Rule Results Report. The user will select a row of the Rule Results Report and click the number of failed records to see the Failed Data Report. It does not have to be accessed this way, however. Users can open the report directly and open a view that they use regularly – for example, perhaps they save filters on their country, the data object they work on, and a particular rule.

If a user did choose to drillthrough (for example, from the failed data column of the **Supplier DUNS is complete** rule from *Figure 7.5*), they would be presented with a report as shown in *Figure 7.7*:

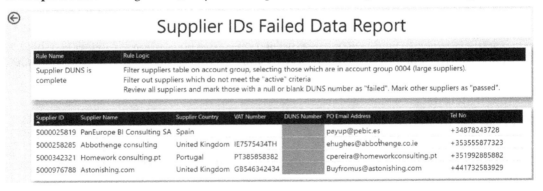

Rule Name	Rule Logic
Supplier DUNS is complete	Filter suppliers table on account group, selecting those which are in account group 0004 (large suppliers). Filter out suppliers which do not meet the "active" criteria Review all suppliers and mark those with a null or blank DUNS number as "failed". Mark other suppliers as "passed".

Supplier ID	Supplier Name	Supplier Country	VAT Number	DUNS Number	PO Email Address	Tel No
5000025819	PanEurope BI Consulting SA	Spain			payup@pebic.es	+34878243728
5000258285	Abbothenge consulting	United Kingdom	IE7575434TH		ehughes@abbothenge.co.ie	+353555877323
5000342321	Homework consulting.pt	Portugal	PT385858382		cpereira@homeworkconsulting.pt	+351992885882
5000976788	Astonishing.com	United Kingdom	GB546342434		Buyfromus@astonishing.com	+441732583929

Figure 7.7 – Failed Data Report for the DUNS number rule

This report includes the following:

Report element	Purpose
Details of the specific rule that the Failed Data Report is for, including detailed Rule Logic, which was not previously seen in the Rule Results Report	Enables the data steward using the report to fully understand why the data has failed. If the rule is flawed, they can see this and alert the team responsible for the data quality reporting.
Supplier ID, **Supplier Name**, and **Supplier Country**	To be able to easily identify the record that has an issue.
The IDs relating to this record (**VAT Number** and **DUNS Number**)	The same Failed Data Report is used for both the VAT rule and the DUNS number rule because all the supplementary details required in this table are the same. In the case of the DUNS number, Dun & Bradstreet can often use a VAT number to obtain the DUNS number. Note that Dun & Bradstreet has a large record of companies all around the world, including their details, addresses, exposure to risk (for example, natural disasters, war, and so forth), and their relationships with other companies. They uniquely identify these companies using the DUNS number and can use other details such as a VAT number to find the matching company in their records.
Contact details (email/phone)	It may be necessary to contact the supplier to get the correct data from them, so these details are included here to avoid the need to go back to the system of record before contacting them.

Table 7.3 – Elements of the Failed Data Report

This set of information should allow an operational-level user to quickly work through each failed record and correct the data as required. There should be minimal need to go from this report to the underlying system of record.

Re-using Failed Data Reports

If the user selects the **VAT number is complete** rule, the Failed Data Report format previously shown in *Figure 7.7* is reused. The report shown in *Figure 7.8* has the same column structure and format as the report in *Figure 7.7*:

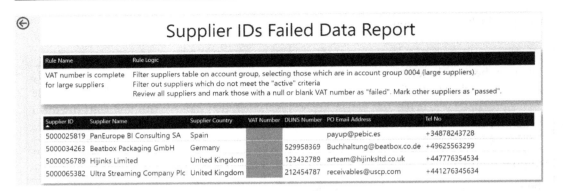

Figure 7.8 – Failed Data Report for the VAT number rule

One important point is to ensure that the conditional formatting that is used to highlight failed data in the report is reactive. In *Figure 7.7* and *Figure 7.8*, the highlight in the cells appears only on the columns that the rule is checking (**DUNS Number** in *Figure 7.7* and **VAT Number** in *Figure 7.8*).

The reuse of these reports is very important to keep the activity to build these reports as lean as possible. If every single rule had its own Failed Data Report, then there would be a large number to build and then maintain. Having said this, the Failed Data Report must be relatively specific to the rules it is attached to. If the Failed Data Report is too generic, it will be hard to use. For this reason, it is important to have multiple Failed Data Reports.

Multiple Failed Data Reports

If a rule that relates to a different part of the supplier record is selected, the Failed Data Report will have different columns. This is essential because if there was only a single Failed Data Report for suppliers, it would have to contain a large number of columns. It would need to include all the supplier attributes for which a rule exists.

This would be confusing and would potentially perform slowly because of the large amount of data included. Where a report unnecessarily includes more columns than needed by the user, there is also a higher chance of running into data security issues.

When different rules trigger different views of failed data, the most relevant information is provided to the data producers, and the reports load rapidly.

If we select the **Supplier Bank Details Are Correct** rule from the Rule Results Report, the Failed Data Report appears as in *Figure 7.9*:

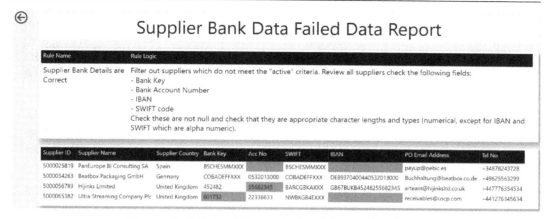

Figure 7.9 – Failed Data Report for band details-related rules

Just as for DUNS and VAT numbers, the report includes a detailed description of the rule logic, sufficient data to identify the record, the columns that include potential failures, and the contact details of the supplier.

Note that, in this case, the report highlights both cells that include data and cells that do not. This is because this rule is checking the validity of the data as well as its completeness. For example, the highlighted account number (**Acc No**) contains an invalid value.

It is crucial to identify the information that an operative would need to correct the data for each rule and ensure there is a Failed Data Report that provides this. Generally, many rules will share a similar set of column requirements for their failed data report and so far fewer failed data reports than rules are required.

The Failed Data Reports are often used in a different way from the Rule Results Report and the Data Quality Dashboard. Each row of failed data may be worked through one by one and progress may need to be tracked outside of the reporting tool. For this reason, the Failed Data Reports may need to be exportable to other tools such as Excel.

Exporting Failed Data Reports

In general, the full suite of data quality reports is designed to be highly interactive, and exporting them is not a best practice. The exception to this is a Failed Data Report. In general, it does make sense to export these, and they are designed to be easily exportable.

The need to export comes from the way these reports are used. They are intended to act as a to-do list for the data producers to collect and correct the data. It is likely that some kind of "status" will need to be documented for each row of data, and clearly, tools such as Microsoft Excel can help with this.

In some organizations, it may make sense to export the data in a format that is designed to be uploaded back into the system of record.

SAP **Enterprise Resource Planning (ERP)** systems, for example, include a tool called **Legacy System Migration Workbench**. This tool allows spreadsheet-based data to be loaded into existing SAP records. If the export is completed using the right column headers and data formats, once the data in the spreadsheet has been corrected, it can be uploaded directly to the SAP ERP system, saving significant effort.

Many stakeholders like to use reports that have been exported into tools that they know well. The most common examples are Microsoft Excel and Adobe Reader formats. It is really important to demonstrate how interactive the data quality reports are designed to be and try to restrict the export of data to just the Failed Data Reports.

Running a Failed Data Report can be quite daunting at times. The report may contain many rows – all of which will need some kind of effort to correct. It is really important to focus only on the failed data that really matters to the organization. Part of doing this is eliminating records that are not needed in the future, such as inactive or duplicate records.

Prior to exporting the Failed Data Report, it is highly recommended that the operative uses the filtering capabilities of the report to reduce the number of rows they will be exporting. For example, the operative can filter based on the region, business unit, and type of data that they are responsible for so that they only export rows that they feel empowered to correct. This will reduce the size of the report file as well as ensure the operative can focus.

Managing inactive and duplicate data

One key aspect of data quality not mentioned in this chapter so far is the management of inactive and duplicate records. The best organizations from a data governance perspective have a clear policy to identify and remove records that are no longer actively being used for transactions in the organization or are potentially duplicated.

However, in reality, these organizations represent just the top few percent. Most organizations are not good at this or are only good at this where they see the greatest risk. For example, a business in a heavily regulated industry might archive production records as soon as they can according to regulations to avoid future inspections identifying flaws originating before the regulatory period.

Managing duplicate and inactive data is a critical part of data quality management. I will explain how managing this properly can reduce the workload of remediation and avoid focusing on old, unused data.

Managing inactive data

When reporting on data quality in an organization with a lot of inactive data, there is a danger that time is wasted on improving the quality of these records.

If a record is inactive (for example, a customer who has switched to a competitor), it usually does not make sense to improve the data. There are exceptions to this – for example, where a former customer is now considered to be a prospect and you want to reacquire their business.

In order to produce a really valuable data quality monitoring solution, it is important to establish a methodology to identify and filter out *inactive* data.

The following section outlines an example of a methodology to help you do the same for your data object and your organization.

Developing a methodology

A methodology for identifying inactive data has to come from the data stewards in the relevant process area. It will vary for each different type of data and different businesses.

Typically, the approach can be quite iterative. For example, a methodology might be developed and, when applied, all but 20% of the data would be identified as *inactive*. This may be considered too extreme and amended.

The following table shows an example of a methodology that might be applied to the supplier data object:

Factor	Typical Parameter	Comment
Recency of last order	Within 13 months = Active	This is often set to 13 months to capture transactions where the order is placed annually, "give or take" 1 month.
Recency of last payment	Within 7 months = Active	7 months captures suppliers where there is no purchase order (for example, utility providers) and payments may be twice per year.
Open transactions	Yes = Active	Open transactions in a system (for example, invoices not yet paid) have to be managed properly. Even if a supplier is otherwise inactive, an open transaction at least requires review and resolution.
Recency of record creation	Within 3 months = Active	If a record has only recently been created, a transaction is likely to be created in the near future, and the record should remain active.

Table 7.4 – Typical active/inactive determination for suppliers

This can equally be applied to product data, as follows:

Factor	Typical Parameter	Comment
Recency of last customer order	Within 25 months = Active	This is usually longer for products than for suppliers because a product might be a component of a critical mainline product.
Recency of shipment	Within 25 months = Active	As above.
Recency of product manufacture	Within 6 months = Active	If a product has been manufactured recently, it is likely that it will be part of a future sales campaign.
Current inventory	Yes = Active	If an inventory exists, it must be managed – either written off or sold – before the product can be treated as inactive.
Recency of record creation	Within 3 months = Active	Similar concept to supplier. Again, the time horizon may need to be longer for a product that takes a long time to produce.

Table 7.5 – Typical active/inactive determination for products

These examples illustrate the type of thinking required to systematically identify inactive data. This thinking can be applied to any type of data.

The impact on the data quality report

When a methodology has been established, then this must be reflected in the data quality reporting.

This will require connecting to the source system and obtaining the relevant data to establish which records are active or inactive in accordance with the methodology established.

For the supplier example shown in *Table 7.4*, the following data would need to be obtained:

- Supplier orders table
- Supplier payments table
- List of open transactions by supplier
- Supplier master data list with "created date"

An extract, transform, and load application would be used to obtain this data and to join it to the supplier records. For each supplier, the transactional data would be checked and an **Active** or **Inactive** flag applied.

This flag is then used in the reports covered in this chapter to ignore inactive data. Usually, users are given the ability to include inactive data if they want to. In some organizations, the parameters like those shown in *Tables 7.4* and *7.5* are placed in a tool where users can edit them and apply the results. For example, a user might reduce the number of months for the last order recency down to 11 from 13.

Adjusting these parameters requires judgment from business users who know the data well and can identify records that the methodology defines as inactive and judge whether this is correct or not.

Once these parameters are well defined, the inactive records can be ignored and this will reduce data that is in the scope of the rest of the data quality reports.

Having dealt with inactive data reporting, we can now move on to consider managing duplicate records.

Managing duplicate data

Just as with inactive data, if there are duplicate records in a system, it is important to avoid spending time correcting two or more versions of what should be a single record.

Duplication occurs very commonly in organizations. It happens when there are no processes to identify duplicates when creating new records, or where these processes are flawed. It also happens when data is migrated from several old systems to a new single system if not enough effort is invested into the migration process.

The following section outlines how duplicates are typically identified and managed.

Detecting duplicates

Just as with inactive data, a methodology is established to detect duplication. This is again very specific to the type of data object involved.

Supplier duplication (for example) is usually detected by looking for commonality in the following fields:

- **DUNS number**
- **VAT or other tax numbers**
- **Postal/ZIP code**
- **Company registration number**
- **Address**
- **Name**

A name and address alone can be very unreliable. For example, a head office might support many different companies within the same group. The address might be the same, but actually, ID fields such as **DUNS number** would reveal that the companies are different.

Typically, a **match confidence level** is determined based on how many of the fields previously listed are a match. The match confidence level indicates whether two or more records almost certainly are the same, or whether there is a higher level of doubt. Almost certain matches will typically result in an automated action being taken to merge records, but lower levels of confidence will go through a manual review process.

Many organizations apply fuzzy matching techniques – meaning that close matches are identified even if not every character is the same.

An example matching strategy would be as follows:

Field	Score
DUNS number	30
VAT or other tax numbers	25
Postal/ZIP code	15
Company registration number	25
Address	10
Name	10

Table 7.6 – Fields to check for supplier duplication with associated scoring

The scoring provides a confidence level for the match. If everything matches, the score would be 100%. If everything except name and address matches, the score would be 83% (95/115). This is calculated from *Table 7.6*, where the total points available are 115, and if everything matches except name and address (10 points are lost for each of these), then the score is 95.

The next activity is to review the matches and determine which records to retain and which to mark as inactive or archived. Sometimes, it is found that all the duplicate records are in use (for example, have open transactions). In these situations, all but one should be blocked for further transactions, and the open transactions related to the unwanted records should be concluded as soon as possible.

It is a good practice to work on duplication first before looking to manage or solve other types of data issues. This will reduce the workload of data remediation activity. If this is not possible and general remediation will take place at the same time as duplication removal, then a filter can be added to all reports to remove all duplicate records from the rule results. This enables remediation to carry on separately.

Eliminating duplicates will provide a significant uplift in the perception of your organization by third parties. Customers will receive better service because all their transactions will be on a single account, for example. The customer account executives in your organization will have a holistic view of customer sales and spending patterns and will be able to use this to provide better service and drive additional revenue. The elimination of duplicates will also make the remediation of other failures against rules faster and more effective.

Now that we have eliminated unwanted records, we can consider how the findings from the reports should be presented to stakeholders in the organization.

Presenting findings to stakeholders

Having worked hard to produce these data quality reports, it is critical to ensure that they are launched successfully and embedded into day-to-day business practices.

Launching data quality reporting successfully

The most important feature of a successful data quality reporting launch is that the rules must be accurate and well tested. If the reporting goes live and immediately is shown to include false data quality failures, it is very difficult to keep people engaged.

Usually through a data quality initiative, you will identify data stewards and data producers who are highly engaged and become almost part of the central team. It is a good practice to release the reporting initially to these users, asking them to monitor the outputs regularly for 1-2 weeks until the confidence level is higher.

These users can often then act as *champions* of the tool when it is released more widely to the business.

It is also highly recommended to make the process to access the tool as frictionless as possible. Talk to your key business contacts and get a list of everyone who would benefit from access. Get all the user accounts created before the go-live and issue them automatically to people. If a license is required, get it assigned to the person before the go-live. With a data quality tool, people can see it as *yet another report* that they have to open regularly and so it needs to be easy for them. Once they open the report and see the results for their area and the failed records, usually, the value starts to become very clear. Data quality reporting is usually very easy to demonstrate and leads to demand for further data quality rules and reports.

Other ways to make reporting easy to access include the following:

- **Automatic report distribution**: Identify the right stakeholders to receive the reports and have them arrive automatically in the inbox of these stakeholders at a regular cadence.

- **Alerts**: Determine a score for a region, a function, a rule, or the whole organization that is the lowest acceptable level. When the score falls below this level, email an alert to the relevant stakeholders. For example, when the procure-to-pay data quality score falls below 85%, send an email alert to the process owner of procure-to-pay and their leadership team.

If the data quality reporting is launched properly and becomes part of the everyday routine of data owners and data stewards, then the chances of effective and long-lasting remediation are much higher.

Presenting to stakeholders on an ad hoc basis in this way is really important. It is also very important to ensure that various governance meetings (for example, management meetings, board meetings, and so on) contain an element of review of these reports.

Embedding reports into governance

For data quality reporting to be a long-term success, it needs to be embedded into business-as-usual activities. There is an entire chapter devoted to this topic later in the book (see *Chapter 9*), but for now, it is important to work with senior stakeholders to get the high-level summary report embedded into leadership meetings as much as possible, such as the following:

- **Executive committee**: A quarterly standing agenda item to review data quality at a high level
- **Regional leadership teams**: A quarterly standing agenda item to review data quality for all processes at a regional level
- **Functional leadership teams**: A quarterly standing agenda item to review data quality for a single process, but for all regions
- **Data governance meetings**: A standing monthly agenda item at a data steering committee

Embedding data quality targets into these meetings, and indeed into the objectives of employees at all levels of the organization, is also very effective.

Summary

This chapter has outlined an example suite of monitoring reports for data quality. This may need to be adapted to your organization but should at least provide an accelerator for the design discussions.

The reports allow anyone in the organization who is given access to them to see an overall picture of data quality and how it is trending over time. They allow people of all different levels to drill right down to record level if they wish. They provide a clear and measurable guide to how data quality really is in the organization.

Of course, they are only as good as the rules that are input into them. Assuming the rules are of appropriate quality, the Failed Data Reports provide an actionable to-do list of data that must be remediated.

The next chapter is all about taking this actionable list and cleaning up the data. This activity will start to reap the benefits that you worked hard to identify when implementing the approach from *Chapter 3*.

Part 3 – Improving Data Quality for the Long Term

As soon as the data quality rules and reports uncover the real data quality position, organizations want to take action to correct it. This part explains how to do that successfully.

However, organizations are often tempted to eliminate bad data through a one-off exercise. This part explains how to ensure that the initial remediation activity is maintained as part of the day to day business activities of the organization.

Once you have completed this final part of the book, you will understand the whole data quality process end to end – from identifying that they have a problem, all the way to correcting the data the long term. You will know which best practices to follow and which common mistakes to avoid.

This part comprises the following chapters:

- *Chapter 8, Data Quality Remediation*
- *Chapter 9, Embedding Data Quality into Organizations*
- *Chapter 10, Best Practices and Common Mistakes*

Data Quality Remediation

In the previous chapter, we described how to set up data quality reporting, which allows you to easily identify bad data. This chapter moves on to correcting the data. As explained back in *Chapter 1*, this does not mean that the organization should aim for perfect data. The aim should be to get the data to the level where it no longer causes significant impediments to the organization achieving its goals.

This is often seen as the most challenging part of the data quality initiative. There is typically a major resource investment and a long lead time to make progress.

In spite of these challenges, this phase is also an exciting one. This is where the organization starts to see the tangible benefits that we attempted to estimate back in *Chapter 3*. As the bad data is replaced with correct data, the issues experienced prior to the initiative finally start to reduce in severity and impact.

Processes become more efficient, resource challenges driven by poor data are relieved, and customers, suppliers, and employees may find that their interactions with the organization become richer. For the first time, it is possible to accurately start to measure the benefits of the work that has been done.

In this chapter, we will outline every aspect of remediation activity, including the following:

- The overall remediation process
- Prioritizing your remediation efforts
- Different approaches to correcting data and the effort and costs associated with each
- Governing the remediation effort
- Tracking the benefits the remediation unlocks

Overall remediation process

The overall process of remediation is typically cyclical in nature. It is usually not possible to work on all the issues uncovered by data quality reporting at the same time. The remediation is usually handled in tranches.

Our process for remediation has the following steps:

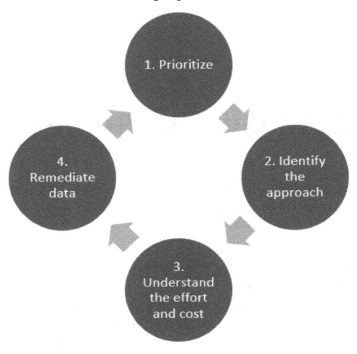

Figure 8.1 – End-to-end process of remediation

The following table provides a more detailed description of each step:

Step Name	Description
Prioritize	Identification of the most important data quality failures so that these can be targeted early.
Identify the approach	There are a number of different ways to remediate data. Here are some examples: • Manual record-by-record corrections • Collection/upload of data from a third party • Automatic rule-based correction The approach identified defines the expected effort level.

Understand the effort and cost	Once the approach has been identified, an approximate level of effort can be defined.
	For example, if 500 suppliers have to be contacted to collect some data, it is possible to estimate the time it will take per supplier on average.
Remediate	Now that both business priority and effort are understood, it is possible to allocate resources appropriately.
	For example, high-priority, low-effort items should be prioritized first.
	Once resources have been allocated, the actual task of correcting the data begins and has to be closely monitored.

Table 8.1 – Details of remediation process steps

Once one cycle of remediation has been completed, the process begins again for the next most important tranche of failures.

Each of the steps outlined in *Table 8.1* will be covered in detail as the chapter goes on.

Prioritizing remediation activities

When you first run your data quality Rule Results Report (or your equivalent), it may be a little overwhelming. There will be failed records for every rule and sometimes the failed records may add up to many thousands. It is not uncommon in larger businesses for 250,000 or more records to fail a rule. For example, if a fast-moving consumer goods organization has a reward card scheme, it can easily have millions of customers. One of the largest of these schemes in the UK has 18 million customers. It would only take a single missing validation on an online enrollment form to generate large quantities of failed data as customers make mistakes when entering data. One organization we worked with required the date of birth of the customer, but did not validate what was entered. Around 1% of customers entered the correct day and month of birth but accidentally entered the current year instead of their birth year. The form was missing a simple validation stating, "customers must be a minimum of 16 years of age to register for this service." Just 1% of customers does not sound much, but when applied to millions of records, it generates a significant amount of work for the issue to be resolved.

Organizations will always only have a limited amount of resources available to remediate data. It will almost certainly not be possible to tackle all the issues at the same time. Therefore, prioritization is key to ensuring that the most value is generated from the available resources.

Having said this, there may be occasions when the focus areas are obvious and formally prioritizing would not be a valuable use of time. For example, one organization referenced in *Chapter 1* was experiencing severe issues with its supply chain because of difficulties with supplier bank details and contact details. These were severe enough to risk the manufacturing processes temporarily being halted at huge cost. An organization like this would have a laser-sharp focus on correcting data quality issues causing these risks. This is typically only a temporary situation and can be tackled through the *early remediation* workstream covered in *Chapter 4*. Once the *burning issue* has been resolved, the organization will usually need to go through prioritization like any other.

It is clear that every organization working on its data quality eventually has to go through prioritization, so the key question we will look to answer in this section is how to choose which failed data to invest resources into correcting.

Revisiting benefits

Chapter 3 outlined techniques to estimate the benefits of resolving data quality issues. Assuming that you did spend some time estimating these benefits, it is very tempting to focus on those areas first. After all, your mandate to deliver the initiative is based on the organization's belief in the importance of these areas and your commitment to making these improvements.

However, it is important to ensure that these are still the top priorities. Many business cases do not include all proposed data quality rules in the benefits calculations. The calculations tend to be based on issues where the following applies:

- The information required to calculate the benefits is readily available
- The benefits calculated are expected to be significant enough to justify the initiative

Often, the benefits calculations can be skewed by political motivations as well – for example, including benefits for business areas with supportive stakeholders over benefits aimed at other less supportive stakeholders.

Additionally, at this point, you actually know how many records failed the rule and this can significantly change the benefit calculation. For example, if you calculated that for every supplier that the organization is missing an email address for there is a cost of $0.50, and you expected 60,000 missing email addresses, then there is a benefit of $30,000. If it turns out that only 10,000 email addresses were actually missing, then clearly the benefit falls to only 15% of what you anticipated in your business case and there could be better areas to apply your focus to.

Usually, as a data quality initiative progresses, new rules are identified as the stakeholders understand the initiative better. These rules can often be the most valuable because they are generated from a more insightful stakeholder group.

Approach to determining priorities

Our favored approach to defining priorities for remediation is to bring together key stakeholders and collaboratively come to an agreement.

Another approach is to quantify business benefits for all the rules and decide on a totally objective *dollars and cents* basis. We do not favor this approach for the following reasons:

- It is very time-consuming – you can typically resolve a significant number of data quality issues in the time it takes to calculate benefits exhaustively.

- It does not take into account subjective or qualitative matters. For example, x value can ignore issues such as reputation or employee retention.

The collaborative approach we favor works as follows:

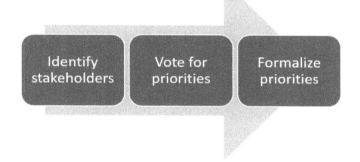

Figure 8.2 – Collaborative approach to agreeing remediation priorities

The following table outlines the steps with more detailed descriptions:

Step name	Description
Identify stakeholders	For each process area (for example, procure to pay) and data type (for example, supplier), one or more stakeholders must be identified who can accurately identify which of the data quality issues will impact their area the most.
Vote for priorities	A presentation of the relevant data quality issues is made to each stakeholder and they are asked to identify their top five (for example) issues in order of priority.
Formalize priorities	Once the individual stakeholder priorities are defined, the whole group meets to review the top-voted rules and to finalize the selection.

Table 8.2 – Details of collaborative approach steps

These steps are outlined in further detail in the sections that follow.

Identifying stakeholders to prioritize remediation

We do mention the identification of stakeholders quite often in this book! Success in the various phases of a data quality initiative is all about having the right people involved at the right times. The remediation phase will include many of the people involved in previous phases, but there may be some others involved as well.

For the approach outlined in *Figure 8.2* and *Table 8.2*, the following is required of stakeholders:

- Knowledge of the business impact of the data quality rule failures
- Being empowered to make priority decisions on behalf of their area

This may be a combination of people – a data steward or the lead of a data producer team may be able to provide the impact to the business, but the data owner may be required to make decisions on priority based on their inputs.

For example, the lead of the procure-to-pay operations team in an organization would understand that missing payment terms in supplier master data means that the team has to go back to the contract to get the payment term before a purchase order can be sent out. They would understand that if 80% of the suppliers are missing the payment terms, this will be a significant drain on productivity. A data owner might not have been able to articulate this themselves because they do not get involved day to day in purchase order release, but they would be able to balance that issue against five other similarly explained issues and make a judgment on what to focus on.

Voting for priorities

The goal of voting for priorities is to identify the issues that are recognized as serious by a range of stakeholders. Issues do not need to be voted for by every stakeholder to be included as priorities, but clearly, the case to include them will be stronger where support is broader. It would be unlikely that an issue flagged as important by a single stakeholder would be compelling enough to be included, but even these should not be ruled out. They might only affect a single team but if a strong case can be made for inclusion, others will take notice.

In order to start the voting process, the central data quality team should bring the appropriate stakeholders together in an initial meeting. This meeting is described in the following section.

Initial meeting

To begin this process, the team responsible for delivering the data rules should run a meeting based on the Rule Results Report (see *Chapter 7*). The aim of the meeting is to do the following:

- Provide a briefing on the data quality initiative to date to give context to the rule results that are presented
- Show the stakeholders the scores and numbers of failed records that the tool has identified

- Train the stakeholders in how to access this information for themselves, so that they can reflect on which issues they consider to be the most important

- Give stakeholders the opportunity to ask questions (and exchange information with one another) on the impact of issues where this is not clear

- Provide context on the steps that will occur after priorities have been established. These include the following:

  - Determining the best approach to remediation.

  - Understanding the effort required to implement that approach

The last point is a little less clear, so here is an example of how this might work. At one organization we worked with, there was a rule called *Correct Delivering Plant for Customer*. Understanding this rule required some knowledge of SAP **Enterprise Resource Planning** (**ERP**) systems. In business terms, the meaning of this is as follows:

- In SAP, every location (for example a warehouse) that can deliver products to customers is called a **delivering plant**

- Each customer can have a particular plant designated as the one that sends them products

The organization had one plant on mainland Spain and another on the Canary Islands. If a customer had the wrong delivery plant, the product might actually be dispatched from the mainland to a Canary Islands location when the same product was located in a warehouse in the Canary Islands already!

During the data quality meetings, it was important to have a member of the logistics team and an SAP expert explain the business impact to ensure that the problem was fully understood and correctly prioritized.

Voting

The next stage of this activity is to ask stakeholders to vote. There are various tools that can be used to gather the votes – ranging from a simple spreadsheet to a survey tool such as **Survey Monkey by Momentive**. The method of gathering the votes is not important. All that matters is the following:

- It is easy to use
- It is easy to aggregate the results

Tools such as Survey Monkey allow anonymous results to be gathered, but in this case, the identity of the person completing the survey is important. The person might need to be asked in the meeting to formalize priorities to explain their vote.

The number of votes allowed depends on the number of data quality rules and the resources available for remediation. If you only have enough resources to focus on data quality improvement for three rules over the next month, then voting from 1-20 (where 1 is the highest priority) would probably be a waste of time. Voting from 1-5 would be sufficient. In this example, voting to 5 might allow a "tie-breaker" for a rule that has received the same number of 1-3 votes. If an additional stakeholder provided the rule with a 4 or 5 vote, then it would mean that rule would be prioritized over the other.

The votes should be collected, ideally, from every stakeholder. Often, one or more stakeholders are late in responding and the temptation might be to exclude them from the meeting to prioritize. We recommend that they are still invited. There is always the possibility that these stakeholders can bring some important information to the final meeting, which might drive a better prioritization that adds more value to the company.

It is important to consolidate the voting results before the final meeting to formalize priorities. It should be possible to determine a rank of rules to be remediated, highlighting rules that are equally weighted to others.

In order to make this as clear as possible, we have created an example. In the example, 15 rules are being prioritized for remediation by 7 stakeholders. Each stakeholder has been asked to rank the rules in terms of priority. 1 is the highest priority, and 5 is the lowest. They will only use each rank once, meaning that they do not prioritize 10 of the rules. This is based on the assumption that there may only be resources initially to work on 5 rules.

Each rank carries a score as follows:

Rank	Score
1	5
2	4
3	3
4	2
5	1
No rank	0

Table 8.3 – Scores associated with rankings

Sometimes, there might be a more complex scoring process. For example, a rank 1 could be given a higher score (for example, 7) because the most important priority for an individual stakeholder may be worthy of additional weight than the next most important priority. Sometimes, a particular stakeholder could be given a higher weighting on their score – for example, if their area is widely understood to be the most badly affected in the company on data quality issues at present.

Once the scores have been provided, they can easily be consolidated. The following figure shows how this might be done:

Score by Rule ID

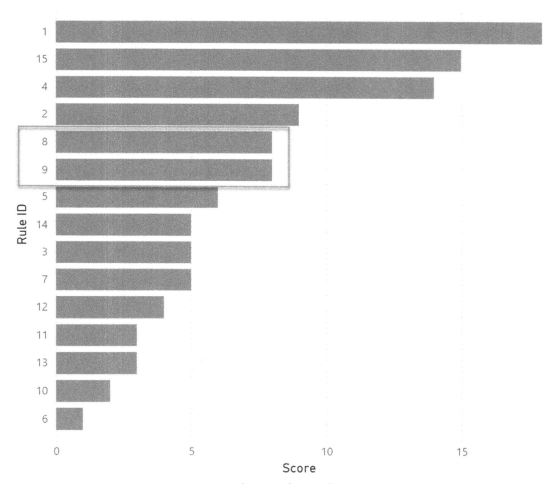

Figure 8.3 – Visualization of scores for each rule ID

In the preceding figure, we see that we have 4 clear priorities – rule IDs 1, 15, 4, and 2. The final rule to be prioritized is unclear because rule IDs 8 and 9 both received the same score. These rules can be discussed in depth in a final prioritization meeting. In order to be best prepared for that, it makes sense to see the breakdown of ranks given for those two scores.

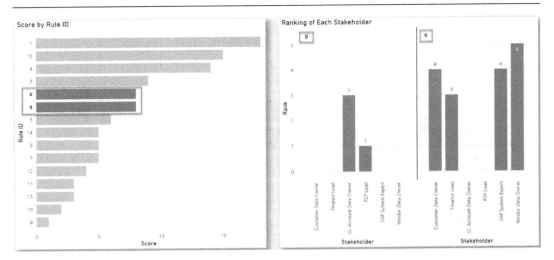

Figure 8.4 – Rankings for tied rules

In *Figure 8.4*, we can see that rule 8 was only prioritized by two stakeholders, but received a relatively high score because it got higher rankings (a top rank and a rank 3). Rule 9 was ranked as important by four stakeholders, but got rankings ranging from 3-5.

This could be useful information for the final meeting. Is having one top ranking more important overall than having many people include the rule in their priorities? In general, it is better to support items where there is consensus, so rule 9 might be a better choice than rule 8.

However, if one of the stakeholders (for example, the **P2P Lead**) has no interest in the rules prioritized already (rules 1, 15, 4, and 2), then it may make sense to include rule 8 to ensure they remain supportive and engaged.

These discussions must take place in a meeting context.

Formalizing priorities

The final stage theoretically should be relatively simple. It is about meeting to discuss the voting results and to formalize the priorities that have already been defined by the voting process. The reality is that this stage is usually the most challenging!

The best-case scenario is that every stakeholder has a "win" from the process – in other words, they have one or more of their priorities included – that is, they do not feel that their area is disadvantaged compared to others.

In reality, it is more common that there will be one or more stakeholders who see none or few of their priorities receiving the highest scores. Where this occurs, it is important to raise awareness of that during the meeting. Most groups of people will understand that compromise may be needed to ensure all stakeholders feel included. Sometimes stakeholders who do not see their issue prioritized will understand that this is best for the business at this time and will support the priorities of others.

The meeting should cover questions such as the following:

- Do participants wish to raise any concerns about the outcomes of the voting? For example, are there business critical issues that did not make the prioritized list?

- Are there functions/data objects that are completely left out of the current priorities? Are the participants comfortable with that?

- Are there any complementary remediation activities that should be prioritized together? For example, if several different issues (some with high priority and some with lower priority) require the organization to contact a supplier, customer, or employee, then all issues requiring this contact should be handled together.

At the end of the meeting (or series of meetings if necessary), there should be a broad consensus on the priorities. For stakeholders that did not see their issues prioritized, there should be a good understanding that there will be later tranches of remediation activity where this might change. If the required consensus cannot be achieved, two strategies can be deployed to move forward:

- **Escalation**: The impasse can be escalated to a senior data governance group if one exists – for example, a data and analytics steering committee.

- **Tactical planning**: If consensus can be reached on a reduced list of priorities (for example, the first two priorities), then a start can be made on these while further discussion is conducted to resolve the impasse.

Once any remaining concerns are resolved and the consensus exists on priorities, the organization moves on to the identification of *how* the issues will be resolved.

Identifying the approach to remediation

Now that the priorities are understood, it is time to work on the approach to remediating the bad data. There are a number of different approaches that can be applied and the effort involved varies hugely.

Typically, each prioritized rule can be categorized into a particular approach. Most often, only one approach will apply to each issue. Sometimes there might be the possibility to apply two or more approaches to a particular issue.

For example, if supplier email addresses are missing in the ERP system to send remittance advice details, three approaches might apply:

1. The data might be in another system (for example, a contract management system) for 40% of the vendors who are missing the data. For these, the data would be migrated across to the ERP system in a batch.

2. The data might be available on previous supplier invoices for a further 40% of the vendors and could be collected and keyed in.

3. The data might have to be collected by contacting the supplier another way (for example, by phone) for the remaining suppliers.

In this example, clearly approach 1 is the least time-consuming, followed by the second, and then approach 3 would be the most resource-intensive.

The following section will identify the typical approaches taken for data remediation and how to decide when each might be applicable in your organization.

Typical remediation approaches

This section will outline the varied approaches that we have seen applied previously. It will cover the level of effort expected for each and examples of where they might apply.

ID	Approach	Explanation	Effort Level	Applicability
1	Applying rules to the data	Sometimes, data can be corrected systematically. In other words, other data can be used to derive the correct or missing value. Going back to our "delivery plant" example in an earlier section, all customers based in the Canary Islands could be given the Canary Islands delivery plant through a batch upload.	Low	This only applies where there is other data that can be relied upon to derive the appropriate value for the field in question and where a very consistent rule can be applied.

| 2 | Collect from internal stakeholders | Often internal stakeholders may have additional information that they can add to a system of record themselves.

For example, a set of cost centers might have out-of- date owners in a system, but the overall head of the division knows which of their leaders own each cost center and can provide the information to then load it in a batch. | Low | Applies where the information is institutional knowledge or where there are regular contacts between internal people and external business partners (for example, where a leader has good knowledge of a supplier, they may be able to provide missing data). |
| 3 | Copying data from one internal system to another | Often, organizations have instances of the same data in different systems. For example, most internal systems have some part of the employee record contained within them (either as the subject of the system or as a user of the system).

Where certain data is missing or incorrect, it is worth asking subject matter experts (SMEs) whether the correct instance of the data already exists in another system of record.

If this is the case, a permanent resolution to the problem would be to create an interface or a master data management system to ensure that a complete record is managed in one place and distributed to other systems as appropriate. | Low | Applicable in organizations where different versions of the same records are held in multiple systems. |

4	Match and merge with a third party	It is possible to export data from your systems (or allow an external connection) and send it to a third party that has a complete and high- quality dataset. The third party uses unique identifiers (for example, company registration numbers, tax IDs, and so on) to match their database and provide complete data in return for a fee.	Medium	The setup effort is high but this can be used to correct any number of records.
5	Obtain from existing internal documentation	Often, missing data may be available already inside the organization, but in an unstructured (non-database) format. For example, employee tax identifiers (for example, social security numbers in the US) might be on a paper form or PDF attachment that the employee has submitted. In some circumstances, documents can be scanned and data can be put into an electronic format using **Optical Character Recognition (OCR)** and then loaded via a batch into a system of record.	Medium	This can be applied any time that the company has paper records. OCR in particular requires that documents have a consistent structure so that the relevant data can be read from approximately the same location each time.
6	Collect missing data manually	This approach involves contacting a supplier, customer, or business partner directly to request from them all the missing/ incorrect information. Once the business partner responds, the data is added to the system of record internally.	High	Applicable when no other options are available. For example, where third parties do not hold this data to be purchased.

| 7 | Online search | Missing data can sometimes be found online. For example, at one organization I worked with, doctors' office address data was incomplete and analysts were able to obtain most addresses through web pages.

Sometimes this data can be obtained in a more automated fashion – for example, by passing an ID to an API and receiving a wider set of information back (usually with a cost involved). | High | Useful where there is a relatively small number of records and where the data collection can be combined with another activity. For example, obtaining an address while preparing goods for dispatch. |

Table 8.4 – Typical approaches to remediation

Table 8.4 is deliberately organized from the lowest level of effort to the highest because that is how you should be thinking when identifying approaches. Clearly, if two approaches could apply, all else being equal, you will select the lowest effort option.

It is not always as simple as this, however, because some of the options involve cost. If cost was not a factor and the number of incorrect records was high, clearly you would select option 4 over option 6 because an automated match and correction of data is far less time-consuming than collecting each individual incorrect record one by one through contact with a business partner. However, if the third party is going to charge a significant amount of money for this service, then this must be factored into the decision.

Matching issues to the correct approach

Every issue identified by the Rule Results Report and prioritized has to be individually assessed at this point. One or several of the approaches above need to be selected to help to resolve each issue.

This section will take some real examples of issues found at organizations we have worked with and outline the possible approaches and those that were actually used in remediation. This should help you understand the thought process required.

Example Issue	Impact	Possible Remediation Approaches	Selected Approach
Two different (inconsistent) payment terms in supplier data	Supplier may be paid earlier than necessary or later than contracted	Contact the suppliers to obtain the correct payment term. Use signed contracts to find the correct term.	The purchasing payment term was sample checked against the signed contracts and found to be consistent. This meant that the financial payment term was deemed to be incorrect and overwritten with the purchasing payment term. Remediation Approach 5.
Supplier bank details incorrect/ missing	Unable to pay supplier	Contact the suppliers to obtain the correct bank details. Use recent invoices received to locate bank details.	Invoices received were used to source this information. In order to reduce the risk of fraud, the bank details were checked across at least two invoices. If two invoices were not available, suppliers were contacted directly – but only when new transactions occurred. Remediation Approaches 5 and 6.
Supplier hierarchy information missing	Unable to leverage potential volume discounts (reductions in price for orders of a specific size) from related companies	Complete a match and merge activity with Dun and Bradstreet. No other options were identified.	D&B were able to match 90% of existing supplier records and provide the ultimate parent company IDs. This transformed spend analytics and led to a reduction in supplier spend of 1.4%. Remediation Approach 4.

Supplier hierarchy information missing	Unable to leverage potential volume discounts (reductions in price for orders of a specific size) from related companies	Complete a match and merge activity with Dun and Bradstreet. No other options were identified.	D&B were able to match 90% of existing supplier records and provide the ultimate parent company IDs. This transformed spend analytics and led to a reduction in supplier spend of 1.4%. Remediation Approach 4.
Employee date of birth incorrect for around 1,000 employees	Issues with taxation, pensions, and identity verification	Contact employees and ask them to update the employee portal. Check background check forms (only available for recent hires).	Affected employees were emailed with a request to update the portal. Line managers were asked to chase where employees were slow to respond. Remediation Approach 6.
Employees incorrectly assigned to a de-activated organizational unit	Issues impacting headcount reporting and HR processes	Check which organizational unit the line manager is associated with and if it is active, move the employee to the same one. Contact line managers and ask them to initiate an organization unit correction for their employees.	The first approach (an example of applying rules to the data) was deemed to be too risky in case the line manager relationship data was also out of date. A proposal of organizational unit changes was prepared and sent to line managers for review/correction with a three-week deadline. After the deadline, data was corrected via a batch upload. Remediation Approach 1.

Missing ship to addresses for several large customers. Note: Customers typically provide the addresses of multiple locations that they would like the organization to ship products to (called ship-to addresses).	Unable to ship product to correct customer locations. (Customer order quotes store numbers rather than addresses because ship to addresses were already provided when the customer first signed a contract.)	Contact customers to obtain the ship to addresses and upload them. Contact account managers to ascertain whether ship to addresses are on file. Contact third-party organizations that can supply address data (for example, Dun and Bradstreet).	Account managers were able to provide documentation from the customers that included the relevant ship to addresses. Remediation Approach 5.
Cost center manager names missing or out of date for 60% of cost centers following a re-organization	Lack of clarity for finance on who to approach to discuss costs and issues with process approvals where the cost center owner is required to provide approval.	Provide the cost center list to senior leaders (that is, heads of functions with multiple cost centers) and ask them to provide appropriate names in consultation with the HR team.	This was the only approach identified and was successfully implemented. Remediation Approach 2.
The organization was awarded a contract to sell to all doctors' offices and pharmacies in the UK and had a very incomplete list of these available in ERP	The organization did not have time for the major data collection exercise as the deadlines to ship products were very tight.	Buy the required data from a third party. Search for doctors' offices online and obtain publicly available details (only really possible one by one).	The majority of data was bought from a third party and loaded into the ERP system as a large batch. The third party did not have a complete and up-to-date record of all customer organizations. Organizations that were flagged as incomplete were manually checked online and calls were made to practices where needed. Remediation Approaches 4 and 7.

A significant number of product weight measurements were missing from the ERP system	Challenges for the logistics team, who were unable to plan appropriate loads for haulage.	Obtain the data from the manufacturing execution system (MES) and copy it to the ERP system.	Data was obtained from the MES and an interface was established to permanently resolve this issue. Remediation Approach 3.

Table 8.5 – Examples of approach application

As *Table 8.5* illustrates, remediation approaches have to be tailored to the individual issue and they are often applied in combination. While 80% of failures of a given rule might be resolved with one approach, the final 20% might require a different way of working.

When identifying possible approaches, it is important to talk with the SMEs in this area. They will usually have the best understanding of the practicalities of resolving the issue. It is critical not to impose an approach on them because then there will be resistance when trying to execute the remediation activity.

However, it must also be recognized that people that deal with this data in operational roles "day to day" may not always be aware of all the possibilities. For example, if they manage the data in an ERP system, they may not realize that the data they are missing is also available in another internal system. People in a customer service role may know that Dun and Bradstreet offer credit checking facilities, but they may not be aware of their match and merge services.

In our experience, if the options suggested are efficient and practical, SMEs will be positive, supportive, and relieved that they do not have to fix the data record by record!

Building a relationship with the SMEs has another important benefit. Often, remediation cannot be fully completed in the data quality initiative itself and the remaining corrections have to be transitioned into the day-to-day activities of operational teams. SME relationships are very important in getting buy-in for this.

Moving remediation to business as usual

In cases where an automated or mass correction approach is applied, often it does not correct all of the data. There may be a difficult 20% of bad data that cannot be automatically matched and where a second approach has to be implemented. Often, difficult decisions need to be made on how far to go in correcting the data. For example, that last 20% might use a manual remediation approach such as 6 or 7. That might be so time-consuming that the cost of implementing it exceeds the benefit. In these situations, it may be most appropriate to apply the approach that gives 80% value and accept (temporarily at least!) the remaining data quality challenge. A "business as usual" remediation method could be applied for the remaining 20%.

To make this a bit clearer, here are further details on the real example in Table 8.5 where supplier bank details were missing:

- An organization's ERP system found 65% of its suppliers were without bank details. This was following a difficult migration from a legacy company system that was then retired.

- Approach 5 was initially applied – using previous supplier invoices to find the bank details, record them in a file, and then upload them to the ERP.

- This resolved the issue for nearly 80% of the suppliers affected.

- The initial plan was to contact the remaining 20% one by one to collect the details. This plan was changed to ensure efficiency.

- The suppliers were blocked in the ERP system for purchasing. This meant that no purchase orders could be raised until the block was lifted. The requester of the purchase order was informed that they needed to request bank details from the supplier prior to the order being placed.

- This meant that the correction of the data occurred organically as the suppliers were transacted with.

There were just a few exceptions (around 100) that needed to be contacted directly because they had a payment due from a purchase order that had already been fulfilled before blocks could be added.

At this point in the remediation process, there should be a clear view of the priority remediation activities and an approach identified to correct each type of data quality issue. It is now possible to accurately estimate the required effort and the time remediation activities will take.

Understanding the effort and cost

Once the approach to each prioritized data quality issue has been identified, an approximate effort and cost estimate should be prepared, along with a timescale and plan for each issue.

- Sometimes it may be necessary to re-visit the prioritization at this point. If any of the issues will be exceptionally difficult to resolve, then it might be better to prioritize a different issue with a simpler resolution. This typically happens in the following situations:

- The approach selected is very manual and will consume more resources than are feasibly available

An approach involving a third party (that is, paying for correct data) is more expensive than initially anticipated

Momentum is important in data quality initiatives. If an issue is problematic, even where the priority is high, it can be better to move on to an issue that can be progressed efficiently.

In order to properly understand the effort and costs involved in remediating a data quality issue, we must first explore the different types of costs involved.

Types of cost in remediation

In *Chapter 3*, we outlined a model to calculate the effort and costs involved in delivering a data quality initiative. Much of what we learned in that chapter also applies when looking at remediation efforts and costs. We must consider people costs and non-people costs, just as we did in *Chapter 3*.

The following table outlines the level of the different types of cost involved in each of the approaches outlined in the previous section:

Approach	People Effort / Costs	Non-People Costs	Likely Cost Level
1. Applying rules to the data	Low: People will be required to determine the appropriate rules and implement a mass update to the data, but there should not be any record-level manipulation.	Low: There may be some support needed from an application development and management (ADM) team (a role that is typically outsourced).	Low
2. Collect data from internal stakeholders	Moderate: Internal people will be required to request the missing data and others will be required to provide it.	None	Moderate
3. Copying data from one internal system to another	Low: Internal people will be required to extract the data from one system and load it into another.	Low: As with approach one, some third-party ADM team support may be required.	Low
4. Match and merge with a third party	Low: Internal people will be needed to check the veracity of the matches made by the third party and to manage records that did not match.	Medium: Third-party suppliers of data typically charge per record.	Moderate
5. Obtain from existing internal documentation	Moderate: It is quite time-consuming to look at the documentation received to find missing data. Each document from each different business partner will have a different format so the process is not always repeatable. If the process can be automated with OCR, this can decrease to "low."	Low: This is usually an internal effort by people within the organization. If OCR is deployed, then the cost of the internal resource will decrease, but technology and consulting costs will increase.	Moderate

6. Collect missing data manually	Highest: Contacting each subject of the data (for example, suppliers) to obtain data is very time- consuming. A level of organization is required because responses must be tracked and chased (if necessary). Organizations may choose to bring in temporary resources to collect data to allow permanent employees to focus on their usual roles. However, this comes with even higher costs.	None	High
7. Online Search	High: Searching for online responses relating to each subject of the data (for example, suppliers) to obtain data is very time- consuming. It may not be as time-consuming as contacting third parties and waiting for responses, however.	None	High

Table 8.6 – Analysis of costs for approaches

Once the approach for an issue has been defined, the techniques established in *Chapter 3* can be applied to calculate approximate effort and costs.

I do not always recommend doing this. At the risk of sounding repetitive, momentum is really important for data remediation activities and if too much analysis is done before deploying resources, that momentum can be lost. For internal people costs, it is usually sufficient to provide simplistic effort estimation – for example, an approximate number of days of effort and a timeline.

External costs (for example, paying a supplier for a match and merge activity) usually require more justification, unless the budget was already set aside. For issues that require this approach, it may be necessary to calculate the effort and cost of an alternative (for example, manual data collection) and prove that the external cost approach is cheaper – or more effective.

Once the stakeholders involved in remediation understand the effort involved, the remediation can begin. In order to monitor progress, appropriate governance then has to be established.

Governing remediation activities

Once the prioritization is complete, the approach has been identified, and the effort involved has been understood, the remediation activities begin. Just as with any other project-style activity, remediation must be governed.

Governance in this instance means the following:

- Tracking the remediation activities against the expected effort/elapsed time

- Reporting to senior leaders on the progress of the activity

- Understanding risks, issues, and "blockers" that need to be managed or mitigated

- Ensuring that when the project activity is done, ongoing work is transitioned into a business-as-usual process

When organizations start to remediate data quality issues for the first time, it has to be managed quite formally. This is simply because the organization has no established processes, best practices, and institutional knowledge in this area. Some organizations that I have worked with have decided to simply assign data quality issues to individuals and not to introduce any further governance. My experiences have shown that in these cases, a few individuals will make diligent progress, but with no oversight in place, most people allow the remediation work to fall down the priority list.

Over time, as the organization becomes more mature in this area, some of the governance may be stripped back – for example, a formal risk and issue log may no longer be needed. As more experience is gained in the remediation of data, the inherent risks associated with some approaches are better understood and can be mitigated before they arise. There is no need to log them and manage them in the same way as before, as the mitigations become part of the institutional knowledge in teams. For example, in one organization that was performing a match and merge operation with a third-party data supplier an issue was formally logged because the match rate was only about 75%. The expectation had been that it would be 95%. This larger-than-expected gap required additional resources to be assigned to improve the match rates and to manage row-by-row correction for the other unmatched records.

When this organization completed similar remediation using match and merge in the future, they had adjusted their expectation of the match rate and planned appropriate resourcing from the start. There was no need to log an issue anymore.

The following section outlines the typical activities required during remediation from a governance perspective.

Key governance activities

The key governance activities for remediation activities are as follows:

Activity	Detail	Examples
Plan	A simple project plan should be developed for remediation. It should cover the following: • Which resources are needed for each activity • Timescales of each task • Dependencies between activities	It may seem trivial to capture the resources responsible for remediation. However, there are usually multiple teams involved. For example, one team may obtain correct data but another team (that owns the system of record) may upload the corrected data. Understanding the workload of the teams at different times of the month can be very important as well. The financial month-end close period often drives a reduction in resources available for remediation and this must be anticipated. The dependencies can be very important as well. For example, there may be five issues on different fields in a single data object. The upload activity of corrected data should only take place once – after all five issues have been resolved.
Governance meetings	At least one regular governance meeting should be established to review progress against the plan and discuss risks or issues that may impact progress or successful outcomes. The meeting should bring together senior leaders responsible for each area involved and also those in their teams leading remediation activities.	The agenda could be as follows: • Review of the latest data quality reporting to see the progress since the last meeting • Update on the plan • Key issues and risks • Changes to approaches (for example, if the first approach does not correct as much data as expected, a new approach may need to be added)

Regular reporting	A regular report should be provided so that anyone with an interest can follow progress – even if they are not invited to the governance meeting(s).	Example content: • Summary • Achievements since the last report • Upcoming milestones • Key risks and issues (as well as a link to a log)
Prevention of re-occurrence	A plan to maintain higher levels of data quality for each issue in the future. This typically includes the following: • Recommendations for permanently resolving an issue • Root cause and potential solutions • Plan to put the solution in place	Prevention of a re-occurrence could include the following: • Adding validation to a data collection form • Re-training staff • Accepting it will re-occur and setting a threshold where a routine remediation process will be implemented periodically

Table 8.7 – Typical governance activities during remediation

Most of *Table 8.7* is commonly found in project management methodology. The main exception is the *Prevention of re-occurrence* activities. These are very specific to the data quality remediation domain and are covered in detail in a dedicated section in *Chapter 9*.

So far in this chapter, we have covered how to approach remediation and how to govern it is ensure that it is a success. Assuming that it is a success, the organization will start to reap the benefits. The next and final section of the chapter is about how to measure those benefits so that you can show those who helped make the initiative a reality that it was worth their time, effort, and funding.

Tracking benefits

Remediation activities are very time-consuming and challenging. It is very common for data quality initiatives to be so focused on this activity that they do not manage stakeholders properly at this stage. The initiative has promised benefits in the business case stage (even if just qualitative benefits). The benefits may have been used to persuade leaders to take resources away from other work to be dedicated to remediation.

It is therefore often very important to start to show that the promised benefits have actually been delivered by the remediation. Where this is done well, you will see the following:

- Leaders encouraging you to continue on to the next process area or data domain

- Previously reluctant stakeholders asking for their area to be added to the roadmap

- Increased investment in related data activities – such as analytics – because the level of confidence in data increases

- Additional areas appointing data stewards/data owners and taking an active part in the whole data management program (if there is one)

The first step when showing progress against benefit targets is to show stakeholders the current data quality position contrasted with the original data quality position. For example, simple metrics such as average data quality score can be very impactful. If the average has improved from 65% to 85% in 6 months, that will usually be recognized as fantastic progress. For this reason, it is very important for data quality reporting to allow historic views and trends. If it doesn't allow this, then at the very least, you should take some exported snapshots of the scores before the remediation activity begins.

It is not always necessary to track benefits. Where an organization has highly visible data quality challenges that are being closely monitored, the benefits should be quickly understood. For example, in one organization I worked with, I already mentioned that supplier data was so poor that payments could not be made to a high percentage. This was leading to supply issues (even for utilities). There was no real need to provide evidence of benefits for this organization. They were already tracking the backlog of supplier payments and this clearly accelerated when the data quality remediation activity made progress. Essentially, the benefits were already being tracked by others.

Where benefits do need to be tracked, the same concepts outlined in *Chapter 3* can be applied. The following example illustrates how this might be achieved.

Quantitative example

In *Chapter 3*, I provided an example quantitative calculation based on missing remittance advice email addresses. *Figure 3.7* showed the detailed calculation of the cost of this to be US$120,000.

This was based on the rate of remittance queries being 5% of all invoices raised. Let's now assume that the query rate is now 1% (because most suppliers now receive an email of their remittance). At this query rate, the cost of managing the queries would be US$25,000, an improvement of US$95,000.

It may be possible to calculate some quantitative benefits that were not previously included in a business case. For example, if the HR operations team lets you know that reduced employee data issues have led to the size of the team being reduced by 2 FTE, and those FTE have been re-deployed to other activities, then these benefits can be highlighted. This approach requires close relationships with the budget holders in the business areas you are collaborating with. They need to understand that you are looking to log benefits attributable to data quality and be willing to share their findings with you.

Benefits that were not specified in the business case can be really valuable where approach 2 (calculating limited benefits and extrapolating) in Chapter 3 was used. This approach relied on calculating a few examples of benefits and then extrapolating across many other known data quality issues. After remediation, it is important to highlight examples of where these benefits did actually get realized. This will give you increased credibility when following this approach in future business case work.

Where approach 3 was used (top-down benefits), it is important to follow actual changes in benchmarks after remediation. For example, how has the "on-time payment rate" or the "cost per invoice" benchmark changed since supplier data was improved?

As always with data quality benefits, quantitative information can be hard to produce accurately. Adding in qualitative benefits to an argument can often make a difference when trying to obtain ongoing stakeholder support.

Qualitative benefit tracking

If the business case promised qualitative benefits, it is important to follow up on these to see what improvements have been made.

This might include the following:

- Re-running the survey for internal employees on how data quality affects them. It can be useful to ask the same questions again but also to ask specific questions about what changes they have seen through the data quality initiative.

- Re-visit the risks that were highlighted in the business case and look for evidence that those risks have been partially or fully mitigated. Here are some examples:

  - How is the organization tracking for net promoter scores from customers following remediation?

  - How many comments from customers referenced data issue issues before and after remediation?

If you manage to link back to the business case and show that the data quality initiative has delivered what was promised, you will give yourself a mandate to continue this work in the organization.

Summary

Remediation has always been one of the most challenging parts of a data quality initiative. It can be incredibly difficult to get sufficient resources to make meaningful changes to data quality scores in a reasonably short period of time. This chapter has outlined how to ensure that the resources allocated are working on what the organization believes are the key priorities and that the approach taken is the most effective possible.

This chapter has outlined how to show stakeholders the progress being made and how to tie progress to the benefits that were agreed upon in the business case chapter.

With successful remediation, you will be asked to continue your data quality initiative into previously unsupportive business areas and deliver even more benefits.

To sustain business benefits, it is critical to make permanent changes to the way the organization manages its data and to embed further data quality improvement into the fabric of its business processes. The next chapter helps to explain best practices when aiming to make this cultural shift.

9

Embedding Data Quality in Organizations

At the end of *Chapter 8*, we established how to go about calculating and publicizing the benefits of the work that's done in the organization to remediate data. This chapter is about how to make those benefits sustainable in the long term. If the organization remediates the data as a "one-off exercise," there will be benefits, but in the medium to long term, the data will return to a low state of quality.

Essentially, sustaining the benefits comes from two areas – firstly, making changes to the way that data is collected in the first place and secondly, continuing the activities outlined in *Chapters 3 to 8*, but on a smaller scale, in a **business-as-usual** context.

I will refer regularly to the term "business as usual" throughout this chapter. The term means the day-to-day operational work to keep an organization running smoothly, excluding all project and one-off activities. For example, one of the activities in business as usual for a sales team is to contact customers and update a CRM system. Implementing a new CRM system would not be considered business as usual because it is a project activity that the sales team needs to dedicate some of their time to.

This chapter is about moving from an intensive "initiative" phase of data quality and moving remaining activities and future maintenance of a high level of data quality into the everyday activities of teams.

In this chapter, we will cover the following topics:

- Preventing issue re-occurrence
- Ongoing data quality rule improvement
- Transitioning to day-to-day remediation
- Continuing the data quality journey

Preventing issue re-occurrence

In *Chapter 8*, we provided a table of the key governance activities that are required during the remediation phase. The last of these was the prevention of re-occurrence. This starts in the remediation phase but becomes a key activity as your initiative transitions from a project-style activity to a business-as-usual activity.

If remediation is completed as a **one-off** activity without understanding why the data quality issue arose in the first place, the issues will simply re-occur in the future. The remediation effort will eventually need to be repeated. It is possible to avoid this with a proper understanding of the cause, a change in systems or processes to resolve that cause, and then ongoing monitoring to ensure the quality remains sufficiently high.

One organization that I worked with used a Big Four consulting firm to complete and correct their supplier data. The work was completed on an entirely manual basis (from detecting the issues to remediation work) and was led remotely by teams in a different country from the subject matter experts. Little or no internal business acumen was applied to the rules or the remediation. There were some successes – notably the addition of missing tax numbers, correction of some address data, and the addition of a supplier hierarchy – but many important issues were missed. The rules did not reflect the individual requirements of the business and nothing was done to ensure the "one-off cleanse" was sustainable. The issues simply re-occurred over time. For example, no process was established to maintain the supplier hierarchy, and it quickly became out of date.

This same organization put in place a data quality initiative similar to the one described in this book. The results were much more specific and permanent. For example, the tax number fields were made mandatory in the supplier creation form and where there was no available tax number, the operative was asked to tick a box and explain why this data was missing. The supplier request was then sent to a data steward to either approve or reject it based on the reason for the missing data. The rule about tax fields was part of the data quality reporting, and trends were continuously reviewed and action was taken if or when they became negative.

If we take the analogy of "closing the stable door after the horse has bolted" and extend it, our data quality initiative essentially helps us do the following:

- Check whether the door is open and whether the horse has bolted (detecting issues and implementing data quality rules)
- Find the horse and bring it back to the stable (remediation)
- Close the door and put in a process to ensure it cannot be left open again (re-occurrence prevention

The next section will explore the different methods that organizations can use to address the risk of issue re-occurrence.

Methods to prevent re-occurrence

Many different types of change might be made to prevent future issues. It is difficult to give an exhaustive list of these because they are very individual to the issue being encountered. However, *Table 9.1* specifies the types of change I have most commonly encountered or recommend:

Type of Change	Details	Applicability
Retraining	This change provides those who create data in a system with better guidance so that they do not make as many mistakes in the future. For example, data producers might receive a training course on how different fields in the system they maintain are used in processes and reporting so that they understand the importance/relevance of the data they are inputting.	This applies when judgment is required in entering data – in other words, it is not possible to put a system validation in place to catch errors. This can happen where such validation checks are too expensive to implement or will take a long time to establish.
Adding/amending system validation	System validation can be added to check the data. For example, a validation can be added to ensure that tax IDs are completed and meet the appropriate formatting rules (length, alpha, and numerical character positions). Sometimes, validations will provide a warning that can be overridden (where judgment may be required) or an error (where no judgment applies). Modern data quality tools can connect to systems of records via APIs and the data can be validated in "real time" against the data quality rules in the tool. This allows the data quality tool to be the "master" system for the data quality rules and can reduce the cost of rule enforcement in systems of record.	This is usually the best solution and applies where there is a "hard and fast" rule for how data should be entered into a field.

Adding an interface between systems	Data can be correct internally in one system but either incorrectly or incompletely replicated in another system. In this case, an interface can be put in place to synchronize the data.	This applies where multiple systems of record need to use a common element of data.
	In other words, the data is created in one system and automatically sent to another by the interface.	
	Note that a **master data management** (**MDM**) solution might be even better in this situation. Where data is shared across multiple systems of record to allow each system to function, it can be good to have a complete "master" record in an MDM tool that is then distributed to all the systems that require it.	
Improving the quality of the data received from a third party	Sometimes, data supplied by a third-party company does not meet requirements.	Where bad data is provided by a third-party company.
	In this situation, the organization can identify a different supplier with better data, or they can engage with the current supplier to discuss the issues.	
	Often, issues occur where the original requirements were not clearly outlined to the supplier.	

| Improving the quality of data input, where it comes directly from business partners (suppliers, customers, and employees) | It is more and more common for suppliers, customers, and employees to be directed to enter data in online forms in "self-service" tools. Where the level of validation is good enough, these can deliver high-quality data. Where the level of validation is not good enough, or where judgment must be applied, problems can occur.

Resolving these issues requires a different approach for the different business partners.

For suppliers, this might be an onboarding pack that explains the data needed and what it does.

For customers, an improved online form with strong validation and high-quality written guidance (for example, tooltips for each field) may be required. For large customers, data entry can be overseen by account managers in the sales teams.

For employees, a data culture needs to be introduced – for example, training on the importance of accurate data as part of the employee onboarding activities. An HR operations team can also be used to check and enhance data from the employee where validations cannot be deployed. | Where data is requested from business partners through self-service tools, such as employee, supplier, or customer online portals. |

Table 9.1 – Typical permanent changes to resolve different types of data quality issues

These changes can create sustainable improvements and help keep the data at the newly improved level after remediation. However, it is not a complete solution to the problem – the following section explains how human error is still a factor.

The ongoing impact of human error

Even if training is completed and validations are tightened up significantly, my experience shows that data quality issues will still occur as data is created and changed. This can be attributed to the **human factor**. The following examples show where training and validation can still fail to prevent issues:

- Different individuals will pay different levels of attention to training and will interpret the messaging in subtly different ways. For example, at one organization I worked with, there was a field for the color of the product. The training stated that this field must be completed and assumed that the end user would input the actual color, such as "black" or "gray." Instead, the end user input "Yes" to indicate that this product had color options available (in other words, that it not only came in a single color, as many similar products did). You may feel that this is quite a remarkable misunderstanding, but I can tell you first-hand that it occurs more than might be expected. (Note that this particular example can be resolved by improving the training or by adding a drop-down list of color values to the forms.)

- System validations cannot be completely exhaustive. Having a set of validations that cover every conceivable circumstance would be extremely expensive, and some data just cannot be validated. For example, if a customer is inputting their email address, a complex validation might check that the email includes the @ sign in the appropriate position and that the domain after the @ sign is a real domain (by using a domain lookup service). It cannot check that the email account at that domain exists. For example, `invalidemail@packt.com` is a valid email address from a validation perspective. We still rely on end users to carefully and responsibly input some data elements.

As a result of this human factor, it is still important to continuously monitor data.

What is important here is to ensure that the time between the issue occurring and the detection of the issue is minimized. The next section outlines a simple strategy to accomplish this.

Short-horizon reporting

Typically, our data quality reporting shows a full population of the data in the scope of a particular rule. For example, all suppliers that are currently active are checked to ensure that they have correct address data and tax details. Failures that are observed from this reporting will show errors in suppliers created even 5 years before. What this does not tell you is how the operatives currently creating and changing the data in your systems of record are performing. To achieve this, I recommend the use of **short-horizon reporting**.

This is where your data quality reporting (see *Chapter 7* for examples) includes a date filter so that the horizon you report over can be limited. For example, you might look at data quality scores for data created/changed in only the last 2 business days.

If the scores on some rules are worse than the long-term average, then you will see that a problem is going to worsen over time. The user ID of the person who created or changed the data can be included in the reporting. If you can see that a particular operative or team is currently making errors that worsen data quality scores, then you can target training very specifically for that team.

In this section, we learned how to deploy strategies to avoid errors re-occurring. We learned that even after deploying these strategies, further errors will still occur. We also learned about short-horizon reporting, which can help identify these errors without delay. Now, we will turn our attention to the fact that the data quality rules we are monitoring cannot stand still. As the business evolves, its priorities and objectives evolve with it. Source systems will change to respond to the shifting landscape, and the data quality rules must change with them. The next section explains how to ensure your team is aware of these changes and can ensure data quality is at the heart of them.

Ongoing data quality rule improvement

Once a data quality initiative is completed and a set of valuable rules are in place, it is critical to maintain these. It would be wonderful if the rules could remain consistent for a few years at least, but in my experience, this is never the case. Some rules may stay consistent for 10 years, while others will change within months (or even weeks!) of being initially established. The rules that stay consistent for longer are generally those that address long-standing legislative requirements such as taxation. Those that change more regularly are those most closely tied to how the business operates.

For example, product data tends to evolve quite quickly. If you consider an organization that makes technology products such as mobile phones, the level of change will be high. For example, in 2010, the network capabilities of a phone were limited to 2G and 3G and a rule might have checked that every handset had one of these values. In 2023, 4G and 5G are also relevant and the rule will have needed to change. Later in this decade, I do not doubt that this rule will have to change once again as new technology is introduced.

The logical conclusion to this is that the data quality team responsible for the rules must find a way to learn early on of changes to ways of working, processes, and systems. These changes must be assessed to see which of them will result in new rules or changes to existing rules. The following section outlines some strategies to do this.

Strategies to identify rule changes

To ensure that you have advance notice of data quality rule changes, data quality has to be a discussion topic at the forums where these changes are debated and approved. It has to be "on the radar" of the stakeholders who approve these changes. In an ideal world, these stakeholders should ask the project managers and solution architects who are changing systems and processes to engage with the data quality team and budget for data quality rule changes as part of the project. If this happens, this is a real sign of the senior stakeholder support that will drive success in data quality work.

Here are some strategies that I have successfully used when looking to identify rule changes:

Strategy	Details
Presence in architecture review boards	Many organizations have an **architectural review board** (**ARB**) or similar. These boards review every new project that will change the system landscape of an organization. They ensure that different groups in the organization engage with one another for the greater good. For example, if a project proposes to introduce a new application, it must engage with the IT security team for an assessment to ensure that the application is safe to use from a cybersecurity perspective. This strategy is about establishing a similar link in your organization's ARB equivalent for data quality. The ideal outcome is for the ARB to have a standard question about the impact that a project may have on data quality rules. The ARB can mandate that the project considers this impact before approval is given. If possible, a data quality representative should join this board or at least be given access to the presentations and minutes.
Presence in system governance committees	For each major system in an organization, there is usually a governance forum that discusses the future of the system, including upcoming projects. If possible, a representative should join these meetings periodically and be given access to presentations and minutes. The representative can present the changing scope of the data quality tool regularly so that the committee is aware of where their system impacts data quality rules (or where new data quality rules might help them).
IT security teams	Typically, the IT security teams will approve every project with a system implication – even those that might be too small to be on the radar of a major board such as an ARB. Where you cannot get a presence in the ARB, the IT security team may be a good proxy because they will have oversight of all project work.

IT ticketing systems	Every organization has an IT ticketing process of some kind. These tools allow people to raise requests or incidents about processes and systems that they use to get support.
	These tools have a catalog of services that run in an organization. The team that owns this catalog will have visibility of projects that are going to need new services in the ticketing system in the coming weeks and months.
	Therefore, they can help give a view of the portfolio of change that might affect data quality. However, this is a sub-optimal option compared to ARB or system governance committee attendance. IT ticketing systems tend to be updated only in the go-live phase of a project, so the advance notice of the change might be only a few weeks.
Use a network of data stewards	In previous chapters, we established that, ideally, data stewards will regularly meet to discuss data quality. These data stewards will also have roles in other forums. Many of them will be part of system governance committees, for example.
	Therefore, the data quality forums can be used to send a message to the data stewards so that they can closely observe their other meetings and look for upcoming changes that will affect data quality. If the data stewards feel truly accountable for their data quality rules, they will do this naturally and without prompting.
Utilize town halls and other large public meeting spaces	Organizations will usually run town hall-style meetings. These are sessions where a large group will meet to hear updates from leaders. The groups may be for a single community (for example, research and development) or they may be for a whole company.
	One strategy is to ensure that data quality is an occasional topic at these meetings and to include a few minutes on the importance of the data quality team keeping up with change. This may only provoke a few stakeholders to get in touch and provide details of the changes, so it needs to be used in combination with other strategies.

Insert data quality into organizational templates	As introduced in *Chapter 3*, many organizations have a standard set of templates that must be completed when making changes to processes or systems. These might include the following: • Project initiation documents • Architectural assessments • IT security assessments • Change requests • Project plans • Test plans • Communication plans In some organizations, I was able to successfully introduce a data assessment or add a data assessment to either the project initiation document or the architectural assessment. This requires that the reviewers of these documents are aware of what should be entered concerning data quality and that they enforce that this is done well.
Insert data quality into the business case template for all new projects	This strategy ensures that data quality is considered from an early stage. It ensures that the budget is set aside for any required data quality changes. The challenge with this approach is that if data quality is one of the many entries that needs to be considered in the business case, the business case template becomes hard to use. End users of the template start to ignore the extraneous elements or provide (ironically) poor-quality data.

Table 9.2 – Strategies to ensure data quality is considered in process and system change

As with many other tables in this book, each strategy can be implemented independently or in combination.

The strategies in *Table 9.2* should help the data quality team identify a roadmap of changes and their approximate timeline. This enables them to conduct an impact assessment. Once the impact of the changes is known, the emphasis shifts to how the changes will be delivered. Typically, in my experience, organizations do either of the following:

• Ask each change owner to fund the effort required for data quality for their project

• Retain a small amount of data quality development capacity internally or through a partner so that a certain level of change can be delivered

It is much easier for the data quality team if some permanent capacity can be retained. Without this capacity, the data quality lead has to influence every change owner to find a budget for data quality, and as soon as budgets are stretched, this becomes a challenge. Any activity that doesn't directly contribute to the change owner's immediate objective (to get their change completed) is dropped. This leads to a mismatch between the reality of systems and the data quality rules. In the medium term, this will lead to new data quality problems and greater required investment in the future. The best model is to provide permanent capacity that covers around 80% of the typical demand level and ask the largest projects to provide additional budget or resources to cover their requirements. Usually, the permanent capacity can be discussed as part of the annual budgeting cycle in the organization. Alternatively, it can be added to the business case as one of the impacts of the initiative. It does not help the business case get approved (because it points out an increase in the permanent cost base of the organization), but organizations that see the importance of data quality will recognize the need to support it more permanently.

Once there is consensus on how the changes will be delivered, the process of updating data quality rules can begin.

Updating data quality rules

In a business-as-usual context, creating and changing data quality rules must be managed slightly differently. We now have a set of live data quality rules that must not be disturbed by project-related changes until the project goes live.

As with any IT system, it is important to manage these changes through a proper change management process that ensures this is the case.

The new or changed rules must be developed in a development environment and tested in a test environment before they're released to the live system.

Assuming that data stewards are accountable for the rules, they should review the changes to the rules in a design document and they should see evidence of testing completed to ensure the rules work as expected.

The data stewards need this level of involvement because if changes reach the live system and they no longer fully recognize the rules they are accountable for, then that accountability will be less meaningful for them.

The data quality rules must be communicated appropriately to end users so that they understand changes in scores caused by rule changes. If a new rule is introduced, it will stand out on the Rule Results Report (see *Chapter 7*) because it will not have a "last month" figure. Some changes to existing rules can cause a "jump" (positive or negative) in results and this may need some commentary.

The following is an example of a rule change that could cause a "jump" in rule results:

- Consider a rule that checks that all products have a weight in kilograms.

- The business decides to no longer maintain weights for raw materials, and these are filtered out of this rule.

- Previously, there were 50 raw material codes in the system, with 25 of them failing because of a missing weight.

- There were 100 finished goods material codes, with 10 of them missing the weight.

- The total number of records checked was 150, with a failure rate of 35, leading to a data quality score of 77%

- After the rule change, only 100 materials would be considered because the 50 raw materials would be filtered out. Therefore, the new data quality score would be 90%.

- The score would go from 77% to 90% overnight when the rule change was made live.

This level of change would need to be explained to ensure that end users did not wonder if it was a mistake in the data quality tool. In my experience, if they are not well informed, users will raise tickets to request that a jump like this is investigated.

In this section, we learned how to ensure that the data quality team is well informed about changes that affect data quality rules. We also learned how to make sure that these changes are made with due consideration to the existing live rules since end users depend on them.

In the next section, we will discuss how to ensure that data quality failures are routinely corrected as part of the day-to-day work of internal teams.

Transitioning to day-to-day remediation

Sometimes, organizations that have just completed their first data quality initiative lack the building blocks required to make remediation part of their employees' day-to-day responsibilities. When the intensive project-based remediation ends, there is no mechanism to "pick up the baton" and continue. As described in *Chapter 8*, often, it is not practical to complete all the data correction required against a particular rule, so some proportion of the work remains. The hope is that the amount of work remaining is small enough (or of a reduced urgency) so that a business-as-usual team could manage it.

This section is about how the work should be transitioned from a project phase into business as usual and what mechanisms and building blocks must be set up to accommodate this. The starting point is to outline what is required for success and how this might be put in place.

Requirements for success

For a team to be successful in incorporating data quality remediation into their day-to-day activities, they need the following:

- Sufficient time

- Sufficient knowledge of what is good and what is bad data

- Cooperation from business partners (other employees, suppliers, and customers)

- Sufficient access to systems to make corrections

- The right culture in the team

In the following section, we will explain the importance of each of these, as well as ideas that might help ensure that they are put in place.

Sufficient time

Teams that will need to take on an element of data remediation have typically not been sized correctly for this task. They are sized only for the original day-to-day tasks allocated to them. This means that data quality work will be an unanticipated workload in many cases.

Sometimes, this issue will resolve itself automatically. The workload of the team will have been artificially increased by the data quality issues present before project-stage remediation took place. For example, consider an accounts payable team that has an issue with remittance advice email addresses. Their suppliers won't receive remittance advice documents and won't know when they are going to be paid. Therefore, they would send unnecessary queries to the team. If the remittance advice documents are now being received, the number of queries will reduce, and this should create some capacity.

If this is not the case, and there is no available capacity, the data quality team may need to approach the leaders of the relevant team to discuss priorities. They can make a case that data quality remediation will reduce their long-term burden and it is worth prioritizing as a result.

It may also be possible to identify that the data quality issues that need to be corrected by one team are impacting another team so heavily that a temporary arrangement involving the affected team may make sense.

Consider a team that creates customer master data but has a large number of customers where no delivery time window (in other words, a period where their premises are open for deliveries) has been captured in their customer record. The logistics team spends 2 days per week on average managing re-delivery scheduling for these customers. There may be a case for the logistics team to support the customer master data team by allowing logistics staff (if the security team agrees) to add the delivery windows when they find them upon contacting the customer after a failed delivery.

In some situations, there may be a case for the team needing to take on remediation activities to increase in size – either temporarily through contract or consulting staff or permanently through employees. If this is the case, some of what we outlined in *Chapter 3* would be relevant here. The team can outline the benefits of the data quality improvement that they would be able to make to get their additional resource requirement approved.

If no resource is available to resolve the issues, and no solution can be found to this, the data governance forums described in *Chapter 2* can be used for escalation. At the highest level, the data owners would come together and hopefully identify a solution with the influence and resources at their disposal.

The next requirement for success relates to the knowledge level of the team working on business-as-usual remediation.

Sufficient knowledge of good and bad data

For a business-as-usual team to be successful with remediation work, they must understand what they need to do very clearly.

They must have a very clear understanding of the data quality rules and what specifically causes failed records to appear. They must be able to translate that to the screens that they see when entering or changing data.

For example, if three different tax numbers are captured in the system of record for a supplier in a certain country, there must be clear guidance and then training on which number goes where and the appropriate formats.

This is the basic requirement in terms of knowledge, but I also recommend that a greater level of depth is imparted to these teams. This greater level of depth includes the following:

- Understanding how fields are used in processes
- Understanding how fields are used in analytics
- Understanding how fields are important for compliance and the impact on the organization if the required standard is not met

Most employees want to feel connected to the organization they work for. This connection can be particularly strong in organizations that have a strong sense of purpose – for example, medical research that might one day cure a terrible disease. If employees clearly understand how their actions can impact the organization, it is often possible to leverage their connection to motivate them to work harder on data quality.

For example, consider a scarce medicine that must remain in cold storage to remain viable. This cold storage limit can be exceeded if the product is not delivered on time. Suddenly, the customer premises opening times become critical. The employee understands that the scarce medication could be wasted if they get the opening times wrong and they feel a greater sense of connection and responsibility.

This connection can also be achieved through the bonds between teams. If an employee is well connected to their colleagues right across the organization, helping them understand how the data quality issues in their area can affect their colleagues' success can be a powerful motivator.

Sometimes, the best way to connect an employee to a particular target (such as a data quality target) is to build it into their objectives and financial reward. In my opinion, this is usually a short-term incentive, but a useful one nonetheless.

Data quality remediation is never an individual activity. It requires cooperation between teams – including fellow employees and sometimes also third parties such as suppliers and customers.

Cooperation from business partners

Often, the teams who add data directly to systems need to gather information from others. For example, a new supplier will need to provide their address and bank details. The procurement team will need to agree terms (timing) of payment and other contractual details. These details may be passed to a master data team for input into a system, or data might be entered directly into a portal. In either case, the quality of the data is impacted by the contribution of the business partner.

As a result, the training and education process will often extend to a large group. Sometimes, the members of this group only go through the process once every few years and therefore have no chance to retain any information they are given. For this reason, this is one area where centralized master data management may play a role.

An MDM tool (such as Informatica Master Data Management or SAP Master Data Governance) can provide a guided experience through carefully designed forms with validation and an automated process that moves each step of data collection between the different groups involved.

For example, a supplier master data process may look like this:

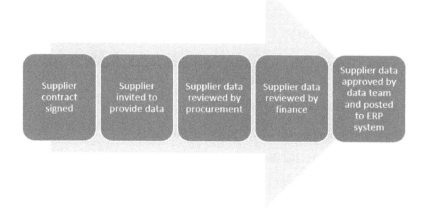

Figure 9.1 – Typical master data management process for a supplier (simplified)

This process validates data throughout and informs each person entering data when they have made a mistake. The next person in the process can send the data back to the previous person (or persons) if they see an issue with the data that was not managed by the validations.

This is similar for HR master data teams who rely on employees to provide appropriate quality data, and for commercial master data teams who rely on their customers to register accurately.

For organizations that are not ready to invest in MDM tools, the same principles apply. Any form used (even if just in Microsoft Excel) should contain as much validation as possible and guide the user on what to input. This process should be explained to all parties and there should be the opportunity to return the form to the previous contributor if the data is not correct.

Sufficient access to systems to make corrections

Sometimes, the existing access level of the teams who are picking up responsibility for business-as-usual remediation will not be sufficient. For example, they may have access to create or change a single record at a time when it would be much more efficient to make governed and tested mass changes – that is, changes to many records at once.

When additional remediation responsibilities are being assigned to an already busy team, it is critical to make the work as accessible as possible for them. By this, I mean that they should not have to raise individual requests to system owners for access. This should be organized at the team level and agreed upon before the start of the additional work. In some cases, it may be necessary to change controls related to creating and changing data to accommodate the required pace.

For example, mass changes may have been reserved for an IT support team and not made accessible to master data teams. This might have been a control to ensure that mistakes did not affect a large range of records. If this mass change capability is now made more accessible to a larger number of people, the risk can still be mitigated, but the controls might look a little different. A log of the changes made might be reviewed by a team leader, or the changes themselves might be routed to a supervisor for approval before they are made.

The right culture in the team

This is a much less tangible success factor, and perhaps a little out of place in a book called *Practical Data Quality*, but nonetheless, it is important to consider.

The right culture in this context means the following:

- The team is passionate and proud of the quality of their data
- The team feels that they own the data
- Mistakes that are made in the team are treated as learning opportunities
- The team makes compromises where required for the good of the organization

This is not easy to achieve and takes exceptional leadership. Here are my recommendations to achieve this:

- Celebrate the progress that the team makes and link it to the benefits that it brings. For example, if an improvement in product master data leads to a customer getting great service, have the commercial team speak about the benefit achieved at a team meeting.

- Assign specific elements of the data to specific people or sub-teams. For example, if your team owns asset master data, break it down into different types such as computers, furniture, and more, and assign one type to each team member. Allow them to present their progress and challenges.

- When mistakes are made when attempting to correct data, ensure that employees feel supported in public and in private discussions. For example, praise them for having the courage to mention the mistake and for the steps they have taken to correct it or prevent it from happening in the future. It is important to ensure mistakes are discussed openly because it is highly likely that others in the team are making similar mistakes.

- Sometimes, individuals will have ways of working that they are reluctant to give up. For example, one master data team member might prefer to create a new product by copying from an existing record that has similarities, whereas others may create the new data "from scratch." If the organization has noted that a higher percentage of errors are made on records created using the copy functionality, then it might be better to stop this practice. In a team with the right culture, the employees will make this change because they care about the overall performance of the team.

Culture may be the most intangible of these points, but it is possibly the one that can make the most difference.

In this section, we discussed the different factors that need to be in place for remediation to be successfully taken on by a business as usual team. The next section will explain how to plan for a successful transition.

Planning for a successful transition

As outlined in *Chapter 8*, during a well-managed data remediation phase, several supporting mechanisms will be in place. These include governance bodies, managed reporting processes (where senior leaders are kept abreast of status and progress), management of risks and issues, and a formal plan (often led by a project manager). At the end of the data quality remediation phase, all of all of this support may end – or at least be dramatically reduced.

As explained previously, it is unlikely that every issue will have been completely solved. Often, there will be a residual number of records that will need to be corrected one by one by contacting a customer, supplier, or another third party. These issues are transitioned into business as usual teams but without the previous intensive level of support. So, how do organizations manage this?

The first part of answering this question is planning. A plan must be created that documents the activities required to accomplish the following objectives:

- All remaining data quality issues are documented
- Owning business as usual teams are identified
- Knowledge transfer sessions are carried out
- Business-as-usual status reporting is established

This section will explain each of these objectives in turn and what is required to accomplish them.

Documenting remaining issues

During the remediation phase, a lot of thought will have gone into the best way to remediate each data quality issue. As the remediation work has now been carried out, there has likely been further learning and experience to add to this body of thought. Documenting this ensures that the organization will continue to benefit from this.

If a particular data quality issue starts to worsen again, this thinking can be leveraged to quickly move into action. The following key information should be captured:

- The status of the issue – how many records were incorrect to begin with, how many have been corrected, and how many remain? Of the remaining issues, are there any that have a higher priority (for example, active records) than others?
- The remediation approach selected (see *Chapter 8*) and whether this approach worked as expected.
- The proposed next steps to continue the remediation activity. If the selected approach did not work as expected, has an alternative recommendation been agreed upon? Has the original approach succeeded as far as possible, and now a different approach is needed for the remaining records? This element must include an agreed pace of remediation for the issue. There should be some anticipation of the progress expected so that it can be measured as time passes.

Here is a real example of this from an organization I worked with in the past (note that the number of failed records and scores are not accurate as I only had access to this information when I worked for this organization):

Information	Example
Data quality issue	Customers were part of a hierarchy where hospitals might have been part of a hospital group. To understand which hospital group they were in, an external identifier was required, but it was missing or incorrect for the majority of customers.

| Status of the issue | A starting point was provided – a score of 45%, with 5,000 failed records without a valid ID.

At the end of the remediation phase, 400 records remained with incorrect or missing IDs. |
| --- | --- |
| Approach selected | The customer data (which consisted of the 5,000 failed records) was sent to a third party to be matched to their database. The third party then returned the IDs for a fee.

The approach worked well, but 450 records could not be matched to the third-party database. A further 50 records were corrected through direct contact with the customer. These 50 further corrections were prioritized because the customers ordered in the last 6 weeks. |
| Proposed next steps | The existing customer data for the 450 unmatched records was not good enough. For example, the name and address data needed to be improved before it could be matched to the third-party database.

The additional 50 prioritized customers were contacted directly for all missing/incorrect data, including the required ID.

Of the 400 failed records, only 200 of these ordered products in the last 3 months. These 200 should be contacted one by one proactively.

The remaining 200 should be flagged in the CRM system and contacted for the missing data when they next place an order.

The remaining 200 are expected to be improved at a rate of 25 every 4 weeks, with a residual of 75 customers who may not place a future order. This is based on the typical rate at which customers place orders. |

Table 9.3 – Example of the documentation for data quality issues during a transition

The preceding example is interesting because it shows that a proportion of customer records had other data issues than just missing or incorrect IDs. The name and address data must have been sufficiently inaccurate that it did not match a record from the third party. This is a typical complication when working with a third-party database and can uncover wider data issues.

Once this level of documentation has been completed, the next step is to identify who will take responsibility for the issue in the business as usual team.

Identifying owning business as usual teams

During the remediation phase, it is likely that one or two members of a business as usual team will have been involved in the remediation effort. For example, from a team of 10 procure-to-pay analysts, two might have been temporarily assigned to remediate data quality issues.

This does not necessarily mean that this team will want to (or be able to) permanently own this issue in the future. Some organizations will decide that a central team will own data quality issues in the future – for example, an operational excellence team. In other cases, it might be agreed that a particular team *should* own an issue, but they may have reasons to decline this work – insufficient resource levels or insufficient expertise, for example.

It is hard for me to advise how to resolve this in this book. The issues will vary across each organization and need to be addressed on a case-by-case basis. In general, if a team agrees that it *should* own an issue, but has a reason that it cannot, then data governance forums should be able to help. The issue can be escalated to those who can help remove any impediments that prevent ownership of the issue.

During this phase, the best course of action is to identify all data quality issues that an owner cannot be found for and to raise those in one meeting of the appropriate data quality forum. It might be agreed that some data quality issues remain unresolved for now (in other words, the business accepts the risk) while others are seen as a priority and the impediments must be removed. At the very least, you must have a documentation trail that you can explain which issues should be moving forward and which are agreed as accepted risks.

Once the teams who will take on the responsibility have been identified, the next step is to ensure they have all the knowledge they need to be successful.

Knowledge transfer sessions

As mentioned in the previous section, the business as usual teams have likely played some part in the remediation effort so far.

This practice offers a valuable advantage as it ensures the presence of experts within the teams who are familiar with the activities and approaches used thus far. However, it is still very important to have a full knowledge transfer to every other member of the team.

Usually, the kind of activities that are not completed in a full remediation phase are those that require record-by-record correction. This means that every member of a transactional team must take part in business as usual remediation. They need to use every opportunity they have within the routine of their job to correct a data issue on a record. For example, every time a procure-to-pay analyst opens a supplier record (for example, to look up the commitment level on a purchase order), they should check whether it is on the list of failed records and can be corrected synergistically alongside their core work.

Where the team has not been involved in the remediation work at all so far, the knowledge transfer will need to be more extensive – including a full explanation of the data quality tools and reports, as well as the background of the data quality initiative and its scope.

A technical element may need to be included in the knowledge transfer in terms of access to tools and training. These access requirements may include the following:

- Elevated access to systems of record to be able to correct data in tables that were previously not used by the business as usual team

- Access to the data quality tool so that the data quality position of the data which the team manages can be reviewed and failed data can be downloaded into a "to-do" list

Once the knowledge transfer is complete, it is important to keep track of whether teams are taking on the work that has been explained to them.

Establishing business as usual status reporting

During the remediation phase of an initiative, formal status reporting will be put in place. In business as usual, this may no longer be in place and therefore there may be less visibility of data quality status. Visibility is a large part of success in data quality management. If senior leaders are no longer exposed to the information on status (or a lack of it!), then progress may stall.

It is important to revisit where data quality status and issues will be communicated to senior leaders after the initiative is complete. As discussed in previous chapters, this will typically be in established data governance forums with data owners and stewards, but also at departmental leadership meetings. If data quality is a very high priority, summary-level reporting may even be included in board information packs, or reviewed quarterly in board meetings.

Having worked through all these elements of the plan, the transition can be conducted and teams will hopefully be able to make progress with residual data quality issues – albeit at a slower pace than during the initiative phase because of their other responsibilities. Once the transition is complete, it is important to look at key aspects of the work that's been completed to identify if the transition has been a success.

Indications that the transition has been successful

When around 4 weeks have passed since the transition, it is important to check certain indicators to see whether the transition has been successful.

These indicators include the following:

- **The pace of remediation**: Ideally, all issues that were transitioned to a business as usual team should show improvement in line with the expectation set in the "proposed next steps" element in the *Documenting remaining issues* section. The pace should be examined at an overall level. If most issues are progressing at the pace expected, but a few issues have stalled, this is less worrying than if only a few issues are on track.

- **The rate that new issues are arising**: If new data quality issues are arising (for example, rules with previously good scores have a worsening trend), this may indicate that the team is struggling with their new workload now that data quality remediation has been included. This should be explored with team leaders and remedial actions should be proposed.

- **Progress on business KPIs that relate to data quality issues**: If a data quality rule that has been handed over to the business as usual team relates to a business KPI, assuming that the data quality issue resolution is on track, then there will hopefully also be a positive trend on the business KPI. For example, the *processing time per invoice* KPI might reduce as the *supplier payment terms completeness* data quality issue is resolved. This is because when the team that inputs the invoice cannot see the correct payment term on the supplier master data, they will need to consult a contract in a separate system. This takes longer than trusting and using the payment term in the supplier master data and drives up invoice processing time.

If any or all of these indicators do not show the trend that you expect, then the transition may have failed to a certain extent. The typical reasons for this are as follows:

- **Resource issues**: Teams found the new workload overwhelming and were not able to make it a priority or a new project took the capacity that was intended for data quality remediation.

- **Access issues**: The transition does not provide the necessary access to systems that the business as usual teams need and they are unable to complete their remediation work.

- **Political challenges**: A lack of leadership support means that teams do not feel fully accountable for the data quality issues and decide not to prioritize them. There is little or no consequence associated with this decision when leaders are not truly engaged in data quality.

- **Engagement challenges**: With extra activities such as data quality remediation, work must be done to ensure that teams are engaged. As discussed previously, this may include connecting the work with the success of the organization. It may also include recognition rewards or similar benefits for analysts who make the best progress with data quality issues.

Once these indicators show positive trends, then the transition is complete, and so long as the data quality team continues to publicize the status and progress made, and recognize the teams who do a fantastic job, then a major milestone on the data quality journey of the organization will have been achieved. Even after achieving this milestone and moving on to other priority business areas, it's very important that the business as usual team closely monitors the data of the improved area. Unfortunately, over time, all data deteriorates if it is not closely monitored.

If you can achieve this "steady state" data quality improvement for the scope of your first data quality initiative, then it is time you consider broadening your work to another part of the organization that needs your support.

The following section will outline how to identify the next initiative and get support for it.

Continuing the data quality journey

Chapter 2 showed that data quality work usually takes place through multiple iterations of a cyclical process. We have just described the final step in that process – the transition to business as usual.

The next step is to return to the beginning again (apologies to anyone who thought that they were finished!) and start to scope further data quality work in a new initiative.

This section describes how this can be approached.

Roadmap of data quality initiatives

A single data quality initiative (as described in *Chapters 3* to *8*) will include a range of different people – from project managers to data quality rule developers. These initiative-based resources will typically leave the organization or return to their original roles when the initiative ends. If there is only ever a need for one initiative, then this is fine, but if it is expected that many initiatives will be needed, then this adds additional cost to the next initiative and can hamper progress. For this reason, it is critical to start scoping the second initiative before the first is complete.

If this is done successfully, then resources can move from one initiative to another seamlessly. The benefits of this are as follows:

- The knowledge and experience that the initiative team members have gained will be rolled onto the next initiative.

- The onboarding and knowledge-building time will be reduced to almost nothing.

- Any underutilization of resources at the end of the first initiative can be used to start the second initiative. For example, if you retain data quality rule developers to handle corrections to rules for a month after going live, they may have idle time if no corrections are required. This time can be filled with work for the next initiative.

To obtain these benefits, the data quality lead must start working on the next initiative around the stage where rules have been developed and can be demonstrated in meetings, but where they are not yet live. This gives the whole go-live and remediation phase for a new initiative to be scoped and get started.

Ideally, a full roadmap of data quality initiatives should be identified – with initiatives scoped for 18 months or even longer. This can allow organizations to include these initiatives in their budget cycle so that when the business case is created, it is to obtain allocated funds rather than to request net new expenditures. This is typically very hard to obtain outside of an organization's budget cycle.

Identifying the next initiative

In *Chapter 5*, we explained how to start with business objectives and make the link to data quality issues. When completing this activity, usually there are several areas where data quality challenges are identified, and one or a few of these are prioritized for an initiative.

This means that there should have been a bank of other areas that were a high priority but did not get included in the initiative for one of several reasons (for example, a lack of stakeholder support in that area).

This work can be revisited to consider whether one of those business areas is now ready for an initiative. In reality, the conversations with stakeholders from these business areas should have continued on a regular cadence (for example, monthly) to ensure that data quality remains on their agenda. This is part of the role of a data quality lead – *keeping the next business area warm*.

For example, at one previous organization, I was part of a team that completed an initiative for customer, supplier, and finance data. In the discovery phase, we found that HR and product data needed attention, but neither of these business areas was ready for an initiative at this point. We met with leaders from both areas regularly and agreed on actions to prepare for an initiative. This included discussing the source of the budget, who might be involved, and what prerequisites might need to be in place before starting an initiative. When our first initiative ended, it was relatively straightforward to engage with both of these teams for the next initiative. The HR team came first because their data quality problems were more pronounced at the time.

Complementary initiatives

There can sometimes be enhanced benefits if the next data quality initiative has some overlap with the first one. For example, if the first initiative included supplier data, and the contract data and purchase order data have known issues that could be part of another initiative, there may be many synergies. Here are some examples:

- Knowledge of the stakeholders in that business area already.
- Data that was integrated into the first project may be valuable for the second initiative. For example, purchase order data was already required in the first project for the Inactive Report (see *Chapter 7*) for suppliers. This existing integration can be reused and the data can be run through rules that you develop in the new initiative.
- Existing rules may be enhanced because of the complementary data. For example, if a rule existed to check the supplier payment term was not "pay immediately" or missing, this rule could be enhanced to check that the payment term was identical to the one in the contract. This is a much better rule.
- The data for the next business area may come from some of the same systems as for the first initiative. In these circumstances, access and integration patterns will already be in place and significant time will be saved.

These benefits should be taken into account when you're selecting the next business area.

When you do suggest to the next business area that they join an initiative, they may be supportive because of previous conversations, or you may still encounter resistance. The next section is about how the work in the first initiative can help you gain stakeholder support for the second and subsequent initiatives.

Obtaining support

Where a business area with data quality challenges still needs some convincing before a commitment is made to an initiative, the data quality lead must work to obtain the required support.

This is usually much easier in the second initiative for several reasons:

- Having at least partially completed a first initiative, a set of data quality rules in a suite of reporting can be demonstrated to the stakeholders in the new business area. These reports usually look very impressive during a demonstration. At one organization, I came across a very senior leader when traveling from one meeting to another. I was able to show him the data quality dashboard for the first initiative on a stairwell over 2 minutes. Even this very short demonstration caught his attention and he supported our work to start an initiative on the data in his area (although he did say he would avoid me on future stairwells!).

- If the initiative has progressed well, it should be possible to get business stakeholders to co-present with you. This is often very powerful because they can articulate the benefits of the work as they see them, and are seen as offering a more independent opinion.

- Significant work will have been done on identifying the business benefits of the work at this stage. These prospective benefits will have been given authenticity by the data quality reporting.

Hopefully, with this information to help with these conversations, it should be far easier to get support for a second initiative than it was for the first.

What if no further initiative is sanctioned?

Sometimes, when organizations go through unexpected change, initiatives that were previously well supported may end prematurely. Here are some examples of this:

- Significant changes at the board level (change of CEO, for example)

- Significant trading headwinds (increased costs or reduced revenues or margins, for example)

- Regulatory or political change (Brexit in the UK, for example)

Data quality initiatives are often quite high on the list of initiatives targeted to finish early in these circumstances. This is because the benefits are usually less tangible and harder to prove (as already explained at length in *Chapter 3*).

If the data quality initiative ends after the first iteration, the responsibility of the data quality lead is to ensure that the legacy of the first initiative is protected. Protecting this legacy involves doing the following:

- Working with business-as-usual teams to ensure they continue to monitor the quality of the data

- Ensuring that the application management and support teams understand the tool and what must be changed when source systems change

- Working with data owners and stewards in the area involved in the first initiative to ensure that they monitor the state of data and work with the business-as-usual teams and application management and support teams to "keep the lights on

Now, let's summarize this chapter.

Summary

In this chapter, we learned about what needs to happen with data quality after the intense effort of a budgeted data quality initiative. We learned what causes data quality issues to re-occur and how we can minimize that recurrence. We also learned about the need to keep up with business change and manage the baseline of rules effectively as time passes. Then, we learned about how to transition data quality remediation from a fully managed initiative-based process to an embedded activity in a business as usual team. Finally, we learned how to transition from a single initiative into a longer-term roadmap of activity that fully transforms the data quality of your organization.

We've now been through the entire data quality improvement cycle that we outlined in *Chapter 2*. In the final chapter, we will highlight the key best practices and the most commonly made mistakes in data quality work before finishing this book by looking at how innovation might change the field of data quality in the coming years.

10

Best Practices and Common Mistakes

The opportunity to write a book about data quality has allowed me to reflect on my work across several different organizations and industries. It has driven me to identify the commonalities between the different initiatives and focus hard on what went well and why. Conversely, I have also had to reflect on what didn't go well and why, which was a less enjoyable experience!

In doing this, I have identified several best practices that I would like to highlight. I have also organized the examples where initiatives didn't go to plan into common themes.

The entire book is about identifying best practices and common mistakes. Where they already exist elsewhere in the book, they will be referenced rather than repeated, but I felt it was useful to have everything in one place here in this chapter. Some completely new items did not fit with the context of the other chapters.

In each case, the best practice or mistake has been selected because it can transform the success of your initiative – either positively or negatively.

Finally, I have reflected on how emerging technologies will disrupt the data quality field in the near future.

Therefore, this chapter will cover the following topics:

- Best practices
- Common mistakes
- The future of data quality work

Best practices

The difficulty of this section is in selecting the most useful best practices to highlight. To select the best practices for this chapter, criteria were created, and each best practice was scored against these criteria.

Selecting the best practices

The criteria were as follows:

- **Level of impact**: How significantly the best practice could influence the success or failure of the initiative. Best practices scoring highly were essential, with the initiative risking failure if they were not implemented.

- **Tangibility**: How easily the best practice can be translated immediately into action. Best practices scoring highly could be introduced without delay or preparation.

- **Duplication**: This factor was about assessing which best practices had already been covered in previous chapters. Best practices scoring highly would have only been mentioned in passing in previous chapters, or not yet mentioned at all.

- **Quality of available examples**: This is linked to how tangible the best practice is. The highest-scoring best practices were the ones where I knew I had multiple good examples to explain them.

- **Fit with other best practices**: Some of the best practices are linked. Some best practices scored more highly because they were important to include to strengthen the overall picture.

Each best practice was scored between 1 and 10 against these criteria, where 10 was the highest score. The outcome of this exercise was the following list of best practices, which will be outlined in detail:

- Manage data quality primarily at the source

- Implement supporting governance meetings

- Include data quality in an organization-wide education program

- Leverage the data stewards and producer relationship

These best practices are new and have not been a key focus in this book so far. At the end of this section on best practices, *Table 10.4* highlights key best practices covered elsewhere in this book.

Manage data quality primarily at the source

Throughout this book, the assumption has been that data quality is being assessed in the ultimate source system. The ultimate source system is the system in which the data was created. For example, invoices from suppliers are posted first in an ERP system, and the ERP system is the ultimate source of this data.

However, in many organizations, data quality is assessed against a secondary source. A secondary source is a system that receives the data from the ultimate source but is not where the data originates from.

Secondary sources can include systems that use the data for another process or analysis. For example, a data warehouse takes data from multiple ultimate source systems and combines it for analysis. Often, the secondary source transforms the data in some way before it is used. This can hide data quality issues, or in some cases cause or worsen them.

For example, at one organization, I was required to build a report that showed the analyzed sales pipeline. One of the key dimensions that needed to be analyzed was done by the salesperson. The organization wanted to understand how successful different salespeople were when they had different levels of experience and different backgrounds. Unfortunately, I found that a high percentage of sales in the source data were missing the salesperson's name or any other identifying attribute. To meet the requirement, I used the location of the customer and mapped this to the geographic regions that each salesperson covered. I was open with the end users that this would lead to a 95% accurate result – because I knew that sometimes sales that were made in the geographical area of one salesperson would have been made by another salesperson due to pre-existing relationships or staff absence. This was good enough for the requirement.

This is a very common practice in the world of analytics. Data engineers, data scientists, and data visualization specialists face data quality issues every day. In my experience, it is very rare for these data quality issues to be reported. People in these roles are creative and have a lot of clever tools at their disposal that can transform data. It is far quicker to create a workaround (which is essentially what I did in this example) than to wait for the data quality issue in the source to be resolved. My example was problematic (you might argue that I should know better!) because my workaround was used by others for their own data visualizations. While I knew the small inaccuracies that would occur and briefed my audience on these, others did not.

In my example, I closed the data quality gap only in the secondary source of the data (the data warehouse). The risks associated with this are as follows:

- The data is still used from the primary source for other secondary sources (other data warehouses or other systems that need the data).

- The "fix" to the data in the secondary source is incomplete or misleading. Corrections can be made in a secondary source that would not be possible in the ultimate source of the data.

The fixes that are applied to the secondary sources are very often inappropriate or temporary. Here are some types of fixes that can cause problems:

- Fixes that only correct the data quality issue at a certain point. For example, when the issue was detected, one population of data was incorrect, and only that set of data was corrected. The time between the creation of the failed data list and the end of the remediation process can be several months. During this time, a significant additional set of failed records can be created by business-as-usual processes, and this can lead to the fix breaking down.

- Fixes that only work at an aggregate level – for example, the category of spend is not captured for a certain percentage of transactions with suppliers. To resolve this, each supplier is given an overall categorization (for example, consulting, capital purchases, travel, and so on), and all transactions are allocated to this category. This enables reporting at the aggregate level, which involves looking broadly at how much the organization spends on the different categories. It does not enable reporting at a supplier or category level though. This reporting requires a finer degree of accuracy. In reality, many suppliers will provide products or services from different categories.

Correction of data in the secondary source is not recommended. However, it is important to recognize that sometimes, secondary source fixes are required. In the preceding example, where I did this, there was a pressing deadline for the reporting, the level I was able to provide was sufficient for the requirement, I explained the inaccuracies clearly to the audience, and finally and most importantly, I reported the data quality issue in the primary source. I followed the issue throughout its life cycle until I eventually saw it resolved. I then re-engineered the report so that it used the primary source salesperson rather than the location mapping. Under these conditions, it can be acceptable to correct the secondary source as a temporary workaround.

In some organizations, there was internal pressure to monitor data quality in the secondary source, rather than the ultimate source. This was because the secondary source (as a data warehouse) contained a lot of data from various sources. This would have reduced the amount of integration required between the varied ultimate sources and the data quality tool.

The best practice outlined in this section is intended to help you explain why connecting to the ultimate source is important. The data should be monitored in the source, it should be corrected in the source, and it should then feed the secondary source(s) with high-quality data that can be used without workarounds. The reduction in workarounds will make the data engineers, scientists, and data visualization specialists much more productive.

There is still a case for monitoring the data in the secondary source as well. Monitoring is very different from that which is described in this book though. The monitoring required includes the following:

- Checking that data is complete – all jobs that load feeds of data have been completed successfully. For example, if there are different feeds of data for the sales in every country that run every 24 hours, then a failure of any feed will leave a gap in the data used in reports.

- Checking that data has arrived in the correct formats – for example, fields that should contain a date and time are formatted as datetime.

- Checking transformation jobs have run correctly – these jobs are used to take raw data from sources and prepare them for reporting.

This last point leads to a direct touchpoint with data quality as outlined in this book. In *Chapter 2*, in the *Data quality dimensions* section, we covered the *consistency* dimension. Data transformation jobs in data warehouses carry the risk of accidentally introducing data quality issues, such as duplication or missing data. Therefore, it can be valuable to assess data in the data warehouse and apply a set of consistency rules.

However, the primary assessment and correction of data should always be in the ultimate source.

Implementing supporting governance meetings

A key part of *Chapter 2* was to outline all of the roles that you might need to interact with in a data quality initiative. It is a best practice to find people to fulfill these roles, even if unofficially.

What *Chapter 2* did not cover was the various governance meetings that need to be in place to ensure that there is an effective way of bringing people in these roles together to drive the data quality agenda forward in the organization. This best practice will cover that in depth.

Role of governance meetings

You might be wondering why data quality governance meetings are even needed. The data quality tool provides effective reporting of the state of the data and produces a list of failed records for each actionable issue. Each person running the data quality reports can conclude and take action.

This is true, but the governance meetings are still critical. They ensure the following:

- Data quality risks and issues are properly assessed, and appropriate actions are put in place

- Critical risks and issues are appropriately escalated to the most senior leaders in the organization

- There is consistency in how the organization responds to data quality problems – for example, all parts of the organization bring data quality issues to the same groups, where they are subject to the same processes and actions

- Where the approach or action that must be taken is not clear, appropriate people engage in working groups to find the path forward and share best practices

Without the data quality governance meetings, data quality risks and issues won't be addressed properly– at least in the parts of the organization that are not as engaged in the data quality effort.

Even where engagement is high, if efforts are not coordinated, they run the risk of being inefficient. For example, if a data quality remediation activity includes contacting suppliers to obtain missing or incorrect data, it is really important to only contact them once. If they are contacted by different teams looking for different information, it makes the organization look chaotic and inefficient. Alternatively, when approaching a third party to collect data for a large batch of records, the request must be as complete as possible.

For example, consider a situation where the finance and procurement teams are both collecting missing information about suppliers. Finance needs maximum recommended supplier credit limits, and procurement needs contact details and supplier hierarchy details. If procurement decides to pay a third party for the missing data, then it would be easy to add the additional finance requirement to the request and it would probably cost only fractionally more. If the two functions approach two different third parties, then the result might be a total spend of double what would have been required for a coordinated approach. It is also possible that one function would approach a third party while the other contacted suppliers directly. Both of these possibilities are bad for the organization.

Having outlined the potential benefits and risks related to data quality governance groups, it is time to outline the details of the groups themselves.

Recommended data quality governance groups

To finalize this best practice, the following table lists the recommended data quality governance groups, outlining their membership and their role. For brevity, the term **data quality** will be shown as **DQ** in the following table:

Group	Role	Membership	Inputs	Outputs
DQ Steering Group (quarterly)	To oversee all DQ activities and make key decisions. Operates at a portfolio level –overseeing every active DQ initiative, no matter which stage they are at. To discuss DQ issues and risks escalated by other bodies or data owners. A broader group (such as a Data Governance Steering Group) might include the agenda of this group rather than a separate group being established.	**Chief Data Officer (CDO)** (Chair) Data Governance Lead DQ Lead Data Owners Data Stewards (by invitation, depending on the scope of issues under discussion)	Escalated DQ issues or risks. Status reports for any active initiatives. Commentary on the latest Data Quality Dashboard (as described in *Chapter 7*). Changes in organizational priorities that might impact the direction and scope of DQ activities.	Decisions on the DQ initiative's scope. Final ratification of implementation and support supplier and tool selections. Agreed actions to manage active DQ issues and risks. Financial support where members of the group have budget available.
DQ Working Group (every 2 weeks)	To review the portfolio of data quality initiatives and identify opportunities for improved coordination. To determine the appropriate reaction to data quality issues and risks and to escalate those that require executive attention. To discuss remediation priorities and identify the appropriate approach to improve data.	Data Governance Lead (Chair) DQ Lead Data Stewards (Data Owners may attend upon invitation if an issue critical to their area is being discussed).	Status reports for any active initiatives. Commentary on the latest Data Quality Dashboard (as described in *Chapter 7*). DQ issue and risk log.	A shortlist of critical DQ issues and risks to escalate. Recommendations for initiative scope decisions. Recommendations of implementation and support supplier and tool selections. Agreed approaches for remediating poor-quality data with defined timelines.

DQ Initiative Steering Group (monthly)	To manage a single active DQ initiative. The group aims to ensure that the initiative delivers its stated objectives on time and budget.	DQ Lead (Chair) Project Manager Data Owners and Stewards involved in the initiative DQ Architect	Initiative status report Initiative-specific issues and risks Initiative actual spend versus budget.	List of issues and risks that require further escalation to the DQ Working Group or the DQ Steering Group. List of actions agreed to mitigate initiative issues and risks. List of agreed actions to respond to schedule, budget, or quality issues in the status reporting. Approval or rejection of initiative change requests.
DQ Initiative Project Meeting (weekly)	To manage the day-to-day activities of a single active DQ initiative. The group aims to support all members of the initiative to deliver their activities from the project plan on time and with the right level of quality.	Project Manager (Chair) DQ Architect DQ Developers DQ Testers Data Stewards (during business-facing phases such as design and testing)	Initiative status report. Initiative issues and risks. Any relevant initiative documentation, such as a report summarizing the testing that's been completed.	Preparing change requests where the initiative needs to change the scope or increase the budget. Agreed actions to address issues that are preventing the progress of any member of the initiative team. List of issues and risks to escalate to the DQ Initiative Steering Group.

Table 10.1 – Typical data quality governance groups

The proposed meeting cadence is included in parenthesis after the meeting title. These will vary from organization to organization, but these suggestions are quite typical in my experience.

Every organization will be different and the recommended list can be adapted as appropriate. What is important is that the activities outlined in the **Role** column are all covered by the various groups that are put in place. The split of these activities between different groups (or other groups not listed here) is irrelevant, but coverage is important.

The Data Quality Steering Group in particular carries a critical role. It contains several senior stakeholders, with the CDO and Data Owners being present. These individuals have a good understanding of what is happening in the organization and where changes to the direction and strategy might affect data quality. As such, they have a responsibility to ensure that data quality work changes direction where appropriate when the focus changes.

For example, when a political change occurs (such as Brexit in the United Kingdom), it is important to react. At one organization I worked with, Brexit resulted in a need to create facilities in the Netherlands to continue frictionless access to the European Union market. This required significant changes in the ERP data and a host of new data quality rules to ensure that the data remained correct. Any data quality issues in this area could lead to regulatory issues and delays in getting the products to the marketplace. In this scenario, the steering group is responsible for making it clear that this requirement is a top priority, and giving authorization for team members to de-prioritize other work to support this new priority.

Without this group, and all the others listed in *Table 10.1*, data quality work is likely to fail, or at least be far less effective than it could otherwise be.

This best practice has outlined the case for having these groups and the activities that they should take responsibility for. The next best practice is about how to ensure that awareness and interest in data quality is high right across your organization.

Including data quality in an organization-wide education program

The vast majority of people in a modern organization interact with data in some way. Some will be producing data, and some will simply be using it. Either way, a data quality team needs to get a simple and clear message to everyone about their conduct concerning data.

Every organization has an education program of some kind. I am sure everyone reading this will have completed training on topics such as the following:

- Anti-bribery
- Anti-money laundering
- Conflicts of interest
- Health and safety

These are typically completed by everyone on at least an annual basis and for all new starters. On top of this, organizations often assign role-specific training to people. For example, a finance professional who has information about financial results and position before it is publicly available will receive in-depth training on avoiding insider trading. An employee who works in a laboratory will have training on how to complete mandatory documentation of the test that they are completing.

This best practice is about adding training on data quality to this portfolio of training. There should be two types of training:

- Generic training assigned to everyone
- Role-specific training assigned to employees in specific roles (data owners, data stewards, data producers, and so on)

In the rest of this section, I will outline the purpose of the training and the key messages that it should deliver.

Generic training

Provisioning generic training across the whole organization can be a contentious topic. Some people will argue the following:

- Adding training to everyone is expensive for the organization because it takes up time from a **lot** of people
- Evidence shows that many people often *click through* generic training rapidly to remove an obligation rather than take important knowledge away
- Generic training like this is usually reserved for compliance with laws and regulations – and a topic such as data quality does not belong
- Data is only important for people in data roles

There is merit to some of these arguments. I particularly agree with the second point – that people do not give generic training the attention that the organization might want. People are often "ticking a box" when completing this training. For this reason, my recommendation is to keep the data quality generic training very simple, as I will outline ahead.

However, I fundamentally disagree with the final argument – which is the one heard most often. Data is not just for people in roles that are data-focused. Those people need to be trained in more depth, but I would argue that everyone needs to take an interest in data for an organization to be successful in improving it.

You can take any role in an organization and find a link to data. Here are some illustrations of this:

- Every employee is responsible for the accuracy of their data – their bank details, their address, their emergency contacts, and so on. If employees do not take good care when entering this data, it will make them less productive and waste the time of their colleagues in HR.

- Almost every role engages with data in some way:

  - Here are some obvious examples:

    - Product testers in a pharmaceutical company must check the product to ensure it is within tolerances to be used on humans. They have to carefully document what they tested (which batch) and precisely what the test result was. The rules around this kind of data capture are very strict.

    - Finance clerks who are asked to post journals to allocate transactions to the correct part of the general ledger play a critical role in data accuracy. A very simple and easy-to-make mistake (such as the transposition of two numbers) can create a significant negative impact.

    - An HR professional who enters out-of-cycle amendments to salaries has to be extremely accurate with their data entry to avoid an impact on the employee or the organization.

  - Here are some less obvious examples:

    - A building receptionist who captures a list of guests entering and leaving a building. Their records are very important in the event of an emergency. Additionally, they may supply entrance badges that enable people to access the areas that they need to. If these badges are not activated correctly, then significant employee or visitor time can be wasted.

    - Marketing managers who organize marketing campaigns through various types of media. Marketing managers will often be responsible for requesting the addition of new suppliers to the organization's systems. They will also need to be able to assess the effectiveness of their marketing campaign by looking at the engagement from the target audience.

The generic training is part of a wider set of activities that help build a positive culture in the organization to support high-quality data. The training may not change every employee's behavior. There will be some who simply "click through" the training. However, even if only 25% take away the key points, that should cause a noticeable increase in awareness of the importance of data quality.

The generic training has the following characteristics:

Purpose	Key Messages
To raise awareness of the impacts of poor data quality on the organization	Ideally an introduction from the CDO or Chief Executive Officer. The definition of data quality. Examples of how it impacts the organization and how data quality rules and reports can help. Examples of how every role has a responsibility for high-quality data. Examples of how poor data quality can negatively impact the experience of the employee and their colleagues. *Here are some basic rules around data:* • Raise issues that you see with data • Ask for help when you do not know what to enter into a system
To provide every employee with information on raising data quality concerns to the appropriate person	Explain what the organization is doing about data quality. Explain the role of the data steward. Provide links to the list of data stewards for each area, and what information they need to be provided with before they can work on a data quality issue.

Table 10.2 – The purpose and key messages for generic training

This training should be no more than 15 minutes in length. For some organizations, there might be longer data management training, which encompasses the data quality element outlined earlier.

The next section will explain what should be contained within the role-specific training.

Role-specific training

The role-specific training should be much more detailed and targeted. It will be targeted at the spoke roles (as outlined in *Chapter 2*, in the *Different stakeholder types and their roles* section). The central hub (for example, the Chief Data Officer and so on) will not typically have data quality training created for them. There are usually only a handful of roles and they will have been filled with people who have extensive data quality experience and have been responsible for creating the data quality initiatives and their related messaging.

The role-specific training is intended to make sure that people in the spoke roles are given a consistent message from the hub about data quality.

The role-specific training has the following characteristics:

Purpose	Key Messages
To explain the hub and spoke data governance organizational model, and how each role fits within it. This element of the training would be the same for data owners, data stewards, and so on.	An outline of the difference between the hub and the spoke. The overall expectation on each spoke team. The support that they can expect from the hub team. The governance meetings outlined in the previous best practice. An outline of the responsibilities of each role in the model.
To explain the specific role in depth. This would be tailored to the specific role it was assigned to – for example, the data owner.	A detailed outline of the specific role that the training is aimed at. (This outline can be found in *Chapter 2* in the *Different stakeholder types and their roles* section). Each person coming out of the training should have a clear idea of how they need to help move the data quality agenda forward in the organization.

Table 10.3 – thinner borders etc

It is very hard to measure the success of a data quality training program, but I observed plenty of anecdotal evidence of the success of the training at organizations I saw deploying it.

This was most evident when reaching the testing phase of a data quality initiative. This stage usually requires significant input from the data stewards and other business-focused people from the spoke team. In an organization where training was in place, the level of input was much lower. They already understood what the initiative was trying to achieve and what a data quality rule was. They were much more engaged in the work needed of them because they knew that correcting data would eventually make their day-to-day work easier.

This brings us to the final best practice, which relates to two of the roles in the spoke (the data steward and the data producer), and making sure that their interactions are handled correctly.

Leveraging the data steward and producer relationship

The two most critical roles in the spoke part of the organization are the data steward and the data producer. If you can get these two roles working effectively together, then there is a much higher likelihood that your data quality work succeeds.

The data steward role is the "make-or-break" role of the spoke. If the person appointed as a data steward is ineffective for any reason (often, this can be because their existing day job is too demanding), this will severely hamper any contribution from that spoke.

The data producer role is generally the one that can have a hands-on impact on the data, both day to day when creating or changing records, and also during remediation. The data producers are usually the people tasked with correcting the data quality issues after they have been identified.

Therefore, the relationship between these two roles is key. They are usually people who are well known to one another because they are in a similar part of the business. Sometimes, it means they are already allies and used to supporting one another. Sometimes, they might be in different teams in the same area, but they do not support one another very well. If it is the latter, then the hub roles may need to spend some time working with the two groups to improve their interactions.

Their interactions will be critical in the following ways:

- Data producers can often be the ones causing some of the data quality issues. When they are entering data, they may not have the knowledge, training, or support that they need, or they may have insufficient time to enter the data carefully. Data stewards need to get an understanding of this and advocate for the data producer teams to get them the help that they need.

- Data producer teams are often asked to drive the remediation of data on top of their existing responsibilities. They do not necessarily have the skills to correctly estimate the time that the additional remediation work will take, and therefore cannot communicate that either their existing work or the remediation will not progress at the desired rate. The data steward, on the other hand, typically does have these skills and can get the required information from the data producer teams to explain this to the data owner.

- Data producer teams are often broken down by function when the data that they support is cross-functional. For example, supplier data has procurement elements and finance elements, and data producers are usually based within a single function. This means that two different groups of data producers need to cooperate to deliver high data quality for supplier data. Often, this cooperation is problematic. Individual teams may not agree on the ownership of data quality issues and some may fall between the two teams. The role of the data steward in these circumstances is to bring the teams together and encourage cooperation.

The data producers will also likely be involved in the design and testing activities in a data quality initiative and the data steward will be asked to broker their engagement. Therefore, it is key for the data quality lead to work well with the data steward and to support them to work well with the data producers.

So far in this section, I have outlined four new best practices that have not been covered in previous chapters. To conclude the best practices section, I will now point out the most important best practices that are covered elsewhere in this book as a quick reference guide.

Best practices throughout this book

This whole book is intended to provide you with best practices. In the following table, I will highlight those that I see as most important and provide the parts of this book that outline these in detail:

Best Practice	Why It Is Important	Chapter and Section Reference
Track the benefits achieved	While it is difficult to estimate the benefits that a data quality initiative will deliver beforehand, tracking the benefits once the rules have been delivered is easier. It is important to do this to show that the first initiative did deliver value and to encourage investment in further activity.	*Chapter 8*, the *Tracking benefits* section.
Start with a business strategy	Too many organizations start their data quality initiative by looking at the details of the data and trying to see "what is wrong with it." The right approach is to understand what the business is trying to achieve and to work out where data issues might impede this. It ensures that data quality work will be truly impactful.	*Chapter 5*, the *Understanding strategy, objectives, and challenges* section.
Define the rule scope carefully	Data quality rules are only effective if they are tightly scoped. Generic rules tend to produce a lot of unwanted failed records, and business users start to ignore the results. Once business users lose faith in what they see from a data quality tool, it is hard to restore engagement.	*Chapter 6*, the *Introduction to data Quality rules* section (the *Rule scope* subsection).
Test rules thoroughly	Linked to the preceding best practice, data quality rules must produce completely accurate results. All records that should fail should appear as failed data, for example. Just as for the previous best practice, this is about ensuring that the business users feel that they can rely on the rules and reports.	*Chapter 6*, the *Testing data quality rules* subsection.

Build a range of reports for different stakeholders	Each stakeholder needs to see different information in the reports that they use to monitor data quality. For example, if the information was the same for each, data owners would struggle to quickly understand the current data quality position for their area.	*Chapter 7*, the *Introduction to data quality reporting* section (the *Different levels of reporting* subsection).
Re-prioritize before remediation	The original scope will be based on an assessment of the expected benefits. In other words, the data quality rules with the highest expected benefits will be in scope, and rules with the lower expected benefits will have been de-scoped. This often means that remediation activities start based on the order of priorities originally assigned to rules. This can be a mistake because the actual rule results can be a surprise (for example, far fewer failed records than anticipated), or the business can have changed in a way that makes another issue more important. Re-prioritization before starting remediation can avoid focusing on the wrong issues.	*Chapter 8*, the *Prioritizing remediation activities* section.
Preventing re-occurrence	Most data quality issues will re-occur if the root cause is not fully understood and changes are made.	*Chapter 9*, the *Preventing re-occurrence* section.

Table 10.4 – Best practices found throughout this book

You may notice that no best practices have been selected from some chapters. This does not mean that they do not contain best practices. It is just that those best practices do not necessarily stand out as much as these seven.

This section has outlined the key best practices for any organization looking to move the data quality agenda forward successfully.

I explored some new best practices not found elsewhere in this book, and then put the spotlight on seven key best practices from various chapters in this book.

The next section will examine the most commonly observed mistakes from data quality initiatives and how to avoid making them.

Common mistakes

Data quality initiatives are not easy and unfortunately many fail to deliver real value. I have had many difficult moments over the last 16 years where mistakes have been made. I have seen initiatives that have done the following:

- Overspent or been delayed

- Never been completed

- Delivered as planned but failed to capitalize on greater opportunities that presented themselves during implementation work due to a lack of flexibility

This section reflects what was learned from each of these experiences.

Failure to implement best practices

This section is noticeably briefer than the best practices section. This is partly because many of the common mistakes in data quality initiatives involve a failure to identify and implement the best practices. In other words, the mistake is the inverse of the best practice.

This section will highlight just two of the best practices from the previous section and outline the potential cost of missing these. These two have been highlighted in particular because failing to implement them can bring your data quality work to an early end.

Failure to track benefits as they are realized

The first of these is the failure to track the benefits achieved early enough. This is a very common mistake because the work required to start to track the benefits comes at a very inconvenient time. Remediation activity (as outlined in *Chapter 8*) is usually at its busiest point, and people in the organization are still getting used to using the data quality rules and reports – and therefore have many questions. It is difficult to spare people to work on calculating benefits, and it does not feel productive at the time. Instead of delivering further future benefits, you are working on calculating the benefits of work you have already done.

However, it is essential to work on benefits tracking contemporaneously. To illustrate this, I will revisit the example used in both *Chapter 3* and *Chapter 8* (in the *Tracking benefits* section). To calculate the accurate benefits, we needed the following:

- The rate of remittance queries (the percentage of queries against all invoices raised – both before and after the improvement to the remittance advice email address data)

- The total number of queries raised for a period before the data was corrected

- The total number of invoices raised for a period since the data was corrected

It may be possible to obtain this information months later, but in many cases, it may not. For example, the organization might not actively track the number of queries being raised by suppliers about remittance advice. The team tracking the benefits would need to ask the procurement to pay the team to track that for a certain period before and after the data fix so that accurate benefits could be calculated.

The benefits calculations are fundamental to the continuing data quality journey. In many cases, you have asked the organization to take a leap of faith in giving you the budget that you need (because it is so hard to accurately calculate quantitative benefits before the extent of data quality issues is known). To get further support to continue the work you are doing, it is critical to be able to show that the first initiative was valuable.

Failure to test rules thoroughly enough

This is the single most common mistake in data quality initiatives. The level of testing required for rules in data quality tools is higher than the level of testing for most other software implementation activities.

The rules are intended to show where the data is wrong. Those who have been responsible for the maintenance of that data sometimes find this difficult to accept. They see it as criticism (when the root cause is usually a lack of time or training) and react negatively. Psychologically, they are looking for any reason to reject the findings of the tool. If the rules themselves are wrong, and a proportion of the records that failed the rule are correct, you are giving the detractors "ammunition." In the worst cases, utilization of the tool can drop to a level where the investment no longer makes sense.

The *Implementation of data quality rules* section of *Chapter 6* gives all the details you need to ensure that testing is of a high standard. From the many recommendations made in this book, ensuring rigorous testing is probably the most important of all.

A lack of practicality

This book aims to provide a step-by-step approach to data quality based on the data quality improvement cycle outlined in *Chapter 2*. Most chapters represent one key phase of that improvement cycle.

Chapter 4 is a departure from that structure. That departure was intended to recognize that data quality initiatives do not run in a step-by-step sequence as we would like them to.

Before starting any initiative, a lot of time will have been spent on the planning, and your business case may depend on delivering by a certain date. This can lead to a rigid approach, where the initiative does not react to what is going on around it. This is a common mistake in data quality initiatives and must be avoided.

Examples of where an initiative must react

An initiative must be willing to be flexible both in terms of schedule and scope. The triggers that might require flexibility include the following:

- Discovery of a pressing data quality issue that needs remediation before a full set of data quality rules has been designed, built, and tested. A way of responding to this is covered in detail in the *Early workstreams* section in *Chapter 4*.

- A major change that affects the whole organization – such as political change, a change in leadership, a change in ownership, an acquisition, or a major shift in the marketplace.

- A major change in business or IT strategy.

Where early remediation is required, this can affect the ability of the initiative to deliver its full scope because resources are re-deployed from the originally planned work. It does not affect the overall aims of the initiative.

Major organizational, strategic, or political change must be treated differently. They may completely change the scope of the initiative. For example, if a company is acquired and a decision is taken to integrate its data into the existing systems of the organization, this can change scope overnight. Consider the impact on an initiative that was aiming to improve employee data- if the number of employees is about to double, a re-plan is needed. You might choose to continue with your work but extend it to the new company as well. To keep the same scope, you will either need to increase the budget or time scales. It might be better to reduce the number of rules but to apply those that are developed to both the existing and the acquired company. If you ignore this major change in circumstances, you might do a fantastic job in cleaning up the data of the existing employees, but still be left with a major data quality gap when data from the newly acquired company is migrated into your systems.

A major change in business or IT strategy can have a similar effect. For example, if you have invested in a data quality tool that fits well with the rest of the IT architectural estate, but that estate undergoes major change, you might need to re-think. Organizations sometimes choose to move from one provider of software to another on a wholesale basis (often when IT leadership changes), and this can affect all in-flight initiatives. If all the development and testing is complete and you are about to launch your data quality tool, it will not make sense to change direction. However, if you are not yet into the development phase, then it might make sense to check that your choice of tool still makes sense. It should be possible to proactively avoid uncertainty like this by staying well engaged with business and IT leaders, but what is important is that you react properly when change does take you by surprise.

A common theme in this book is that data quality work has to be tightly integrated into what the business needs. This applies both to this common mistake and also to the following one – which is about implementing rules that truly impact business stakeholders.

Technically driven data quality rules

The selection of data quality rules for an initiative needs to be driven by business strategy, and rules need to come from important business requirements.

A common mistake in data quality work is for data quality or IT professionals to identify and develop rules in isolation from business subject matter experts. This is what happens when organizations treat data quality work as an IT activity.

This typically leads to the following:

- Superficial rules that do not reflect the reality of business requirements. This, in turn, leads to a lack of ownership and buy-in from business stakeholders.

- Technically focused rules.

- An incomplete set of rules.

- Incorrect prioritization of rules.

The following table provides some real examples of IT-driven rules seen in various organizations:

Type	Example	Comment
Data needs to be sent from one system to another via an interface. Data quality rules are set up to identify data that has a longer field length in the source than is possible in the target.	Supplier names in the Supplier Relationship Management system have to be 35 characters or less to successfully integrate into the SAP ERP system.	This is not a real data quality rule. This kind of rule can be built into the integration tool that is sending the data from the source to the target. It does not have a real business meaning.
The "mandatory" fields for a given record are identified and checked in a data warehouse and any missing data is considered to be a failure. This is to identify where an ETL process may have removed data that the business needs for reporting.	Supplier data has to contain the following: • Name • All address fields (including zip/postal code) • Tax numbers • Email address	This is a very superficial rule. It does not consider the appropriate rule scope (as outlined in the *Rule scope* section of *Chapter 6*). For example, some small suppliers will not have a tax number. Zip or postal codes do not exist in every country.

| Rules are prioritized that make IT business-as-usual activities easier. These are prioritized ahead of important business-facing rules. | Rules that support interfaces or support jobs to transform data in a data warehouse are implemented.

Rules that would improve customer experience or the ability to ship products on time are not prioritized. | While it is important to run IT effectively and efficiently, the rules that make a "game-changing" difference to an organization are those that have a clear business impact. |

Table 10.5 – The result of technically driven data quality rules

To have the greatest opportunity to change your organization for the better with improved data quality, there must be a very close relationship between the data quality team and the business subject matter experts.

The next common mistake continues this theme. An IT-driven approach without full business integration can often lead to activities being completed as a "one-off" rather than a repeatable, embedded business activity.

One-off remediation activity

In *Chapter 9*, the *Prevention of re-occurrence* section clearly outlines that a one-off approach to remediation activity will only lead to a temporary improvement. That chapter provides the relevant detail and an example, but this is such a common mistake that it needs to be mentioned here for completeness.

Many organizations have a culture of intensively working on an activity to solve a problem, and then moving on to another pressing topic. This does not work for data quality. An initial high level of effort has to be followed up with a long-term and consistent approach that makes the data quality improvement sustained.

Restricting access to data quality results

Exposure to poor data quality can be a sensitive topic in organizations. Some leaders will campaign for data quality results to be restricted just to themselves or a handful of trusted leaders in their teams. In my experience, this leads to a lack of rapid remediation activity in this area.

Part of the motivation to resolve data quality issues comes from competition with other functions and competition in geographical regions. It also comes from appropriate pressure from peers and the most senior leaders. If you allow challenging stakeholders to restrict the results for data quality in their area to just a few people, the competition and pressure do not drive prioritization and progress may be limited.

Avoid silos in data quality work

Data in organizations does not work in isolation. There are complex relationships between different types of data. For example, customer data is linked to order data. Order data is linked to product data. Product data is linked to suppliers (who may provide raw materials). Supplier and product data are both linked to purchase orders.

It is critical to recognize this in data quality work and to look for opportunities to break down silos. Many organizations run a data quality initiative on customer data to try to improve the customer experience. At one organization that did this, I observed that the biggest drain on customer experience was a lack of rapid availability of the product. The root cause of this issue was related to issues with both the product and purchase order data. This was seen as the responsibility of the supply chain team, but the supply chain team did not have any budget to run a data quality initiative of their own. It would have been better for the customer experience if the commercial team used their budget to help their supply chain colleagues improve the product and purchase order data.

So far, this chapter has outlined the key best practices and common mistakes made in data quality initiatives. I hope that providing these gives you the opportunity for first-time success in your initiatives. To complete this chapter and this book, the following section will outline how I anticipate data quality work changing over the years.

The future of data quality work

Up until this point, this book has been based entirely on my experience across the various organizations I have worked with. This final section is different. It is my conjecture and theory about how working in data quality will change over the next 10 years.

Over the last year, we have seen much wider public recognition of the potential of **artificial intelligence (AI)**-driven **large language models (LLMs)**, such as OpenAI's Chat-GPT. When combined with major ongoing growth in the perceived importance of data in organizations, there will be a significant shift in how we do data quality work in the future.

This section outlines the key trends I expect to see, and what we as data quality professionals need to do to be prepared.

LLMs

LLMs are a capability driven by AI. They have been trained by being exposed to large quantities of publicly available information via the internet. This training and access to information allows them to respond meaningfully to inputs from a human being. Essentially, it means that a human can input a request or question and get a valuable and insightful answer in response.

For example, when I ask Chat-GPT (OpenAI's highly successful LLM) to define data quality within the field of data governance, it provides this response:

"Data quality is a critical aspect of data governance, which refers to the overall management and control of an organization's data assets. Data quality specifically focuses on ensuring that data is accurate, consistent, complete, reliable, and relevant for its intended purpose. In the context of data governance, the field of data quality encompasses various processes, practices, and strategies aimed at maintaining and improving the overall quality of data within an organization."

It goes on to document all the different components of data quality – including data profiling, data cleansing, and so on, with a definition of each.

Models like this have been around for many years, but the work of OpenAI on Chat-GPT and then GPT-4 has been so successful that it has focused the media and the public on this field and how it might be applied to our lives. Large organizations have been rushing to add LLM capabilities to their existing products.

Microsoft, for example, is adding capabilities called **Copilots** to many of its products. These are embedded LLMs that will allow users to leverage the capabilities of these models in their day-to-day work. For example, in Microsoft Excel, shortly, instead of typing a formula, I may be able to write a request in natural language that the Copilot interprets and creates the formula for me, as shown in the following figure:

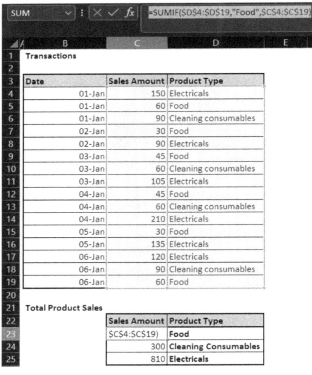

Figure 10.1 – Simple example of the application of LLMs

In *Figure 10.1*, we have a simple list of sales transactions by date and product type. There is a table below this that aims to aggregate the data so that we can see the total sales by different product types.

In Excel, the formula for each of the totals is calculated by a SUMIF function, meaning that the row is only included in the total if a certain condition is met. In the future, it will be possible to use the co-pilot to write "sum all the sales amounts for food products only," and Excel will produce the formula automatically.

This is a very simple example with a simple formula, but consider formulae that are multiple lines in length, with many different levels of nested functions. This can become a major time-saver.

I see multiple potential applications of LLM technology for data quality work, and these are outlined next.

LLM use cases in the world of data quality

Like other software vendors, I believe that data quality tool suppliers will be rapidly introducing LLM capabilities into their tools.

The capabilities I expect to see are as follows.

Automatic generation of code for rules

Many data quality tools were introduced with the idea that business users could create data quality rules themselves, rather than defining what they want the rule to be and asking a developer to build the rule. For example, in SAP Information Steward, it is possible to "right-click" on a pattern in a profile that looks correct and select **Create rule**. The tool then provides simple code automatically.

Unfortunately, in my experience, this approach only works for a small proportion of the rules. Most rules have a level of complexity that requires code to be written rather than generated, and this has historically required skilled developer resources.

With LLMs, I expect to see the dependency on developers decrease, and business users learn how to create "LLM-friendly" rule descriptions that can successfully generate the code.

By *LLM-friendly*, I mean that the rule description will need to be more carefully curated so that the model can understand it.

For example, in *Table 6.3* in *Chapter 6*, there is the following rule description: *Employees of type "contractor" must have an end date within 18 months of today's date.*

For an LLM to properly produce rule code for this rule, I would expect that the rule description would need to be written as follows:

"Check the employee table <Table Name> and filter out all employees except those with the type "C". Check their end date from the field <field name>. Mark records where the end date is less than 18 months from today's date as "passed" and records where the end date is greater than 18 months from today's date as "failed.""

I appreciate that this looks much more complicated than the previous simple business rule. I believe that if there is a strong business glossary in place, with a mapping of business terms to underlying metadata, that simplicity could be maintained. For example, the term "contractor" could be mapped from the glossary to the relevant employee type in the data source ("C" in this example), and the LLM could read the mapping and understand the term "contractor." The same would be true of the other table, field, and value names.

This emphasizes the points in *Chapter 2* – while a strong wider data governance program is not a mandatory prerequisite for success in data quality work, it must develop over time. If work on metadata management progresses at the same rate as data quality work, then LLMs will be an invaluable part of creating data quality rules.

If these rules can be derived from simple business descriptions, then the role of the developer (and the expense of the developer) will be significantly reduced. You would still need a developer, but their role would be to review the LLM code and make improvements for supportability and consistency purposes where necessary.

Rule generation goes from being the remit of the developer to being the remit of the business user. The business user would need to learn how to feed information to the LLM correctly. There are training courses already appearing on how to write high-quality prompts for LLMs.

It is possible to use an LLM today for this purpose. If you can ascertain the type of code that your data quality rule uses (for example, C#), then you can ask the model for the code. For example, I typed the following statement into Chat-GPT:

Write the following statement in C# code:

- Employees from the EMPLOYEES table should be filtered so that only the CONTRACTOR employee type remains.

- Then, the remaining rows of data from the EMPLOYEES table should have their end date from the END_DATE field checked against today's date.

- If the row of data has an END_DATE field within 18 months from today, then the row should be marked with a status of PASSED. Otherwise, the row should be marked as FAILED.

Chat-GPT returned a block of code that can be found in the GitHub repository for this book at https://github.com/PacktPublishing/Data-Quality-in-Practice/blob/main/ChatGPT%20code%20example.txt.

If you review the code from GitHub, you will see that Chat-GPT is intelligent enough to make assumptions. For example, it assumes that there is a column in the database called STATUS and can write the PASSED or FAILED value to that column. It also assumes it is connecting to a SQL database, and leaves a comment showing where to insert the actual connection details for that database into the code.

This is something that you could attempt in Chat-GPT today. The results must be carefully tested to ensure they give the right result. For example, you may notice that Chat-GPT assumed that the number of days in each month is 30. This will create a slightly inaccurate result and may need to be improved upon.

Automatic generation of rule descriptions

The next possible use of an LLM in data quality is the inverse of the first to some extent. Producing good quality data quality rule descriptions is sometimes neglected in initiatives. The rules are written in computerized code from workshops with the business. The rules are good quality because they come from real business requirements, but they are not properly understandable and documented for business users.

LLMs will be able to read the code and produce a simple business description to match it. These descriptions would need to be reviewed by a subject matter expert but would at least provide a strong starting point.

Additional coding opportunities

There are other opportunities in a data quality initiative for LLMs to help with coding. Data quality tools need to import data from data sources so that it can be tested according to the rules. These **extract, transform, and load** (ETL) jobs contain code, and wherever there is code, LLMs can accelerate activities. I believe that developers will still be required to create ETL jobs, but they can be encouraged to use LLMs to accelerate their workflow.

In addition to this, there is quite complex logic involved in assessing which records might be duplicated in a dataset and which records are inactive. The rules around duplication and inactivity are usually documented in data governance policies (see the *Data quality in the wider context of data governance* section in *Chapter 2*) and these can be read by LLMs and logic in the appropriate language could be created as a "starting point."

Recommending rules from data definitions and a data profile

Data quality tools usually contain both a profiling and data quality rule creation capability. Some tools already provide rule recommendations from data profiles today. I expect that when tools have greater AI capabilities built into them, these rule recommendations will become more sophisticated.

The risk here is that the rules become divorced from the priorities and strategy of the business. In the fullness of time, I expect that LLMs can be used to read and understand the business strategy. We should then consider that the following information can also be available for an LLM:

- A full set of data definitions (which provide what information *should* be in the field)

- A mapping of the definitions to the underlying data source fields

With all this information, there should be a great opportunity for LLMs to suggest rules that add real business value. They must be in line with the priorities associated with the strategy, based on a business-led data definition, and take into account a real snapshot of the data from the profile.

These suggestions will become a crucial input (and accelerator) for business conversations and make the design phase less resource-intensive.

Remediation of data

One of the most resource-intensive parts of a data quality initiative is the remediation of bad data. LLMs and other forms of AI and automation technology should be able to help accelerate some remediation activities. The following list provides some ideas:

- AI could be used to look for internal inconsistencies in the data and propose corrections. For example, if products had a missing or inaccurate product category value, but had a valid product sub-category value, then the appropriate product category could easily be proposed.

- Optical character recognition could be used to scan supplier documents to find missing details such as tax numbers, email addresses, and similar and automatically recognize when the data held in internal systems is out of date and propose corrections.

- LLMs with access to existing internet resources could be fed a file of data and asked to check it against authoritative free external resources. For example, a list of customer address data could be checked against company websites to identify errors and organizations that are now out of business. Most websites contain a list of offices or stores for an organization and these are freely accessible by LLMs.

- LLMs could interact with suppliers, customers, and employees to obtain missing details. For example, new employees with missing or incorrect details could be contacted via an internal chat tool (for example, Microsoft Teams) and asked to provide the appropriate details. The model could then post the correct details to the system of record automatically.

I am sure that you have additional ideas to add to this list!

I am very excited about how LLMs will change data quality work over the coming years, and I feel it is very important for data quality professionals to do the following:

- Stay in touch with what data quality tool suppliers are doing to integrate this technology into their tools

- Start to work with LLMs daily so that when these innovations become part of their day-to-day work, they are well prepared

The phases of a data quality initiative will remain the same, but most phases have the opportunity to be significantly accelerated. This will reduce the cost of data quality initiatives and make it easier to get them off the ground. People in key data roles (such as data quality leads) will need to adjust. They will need to gain experience in how to get the best results from LLMs and how to partner with people who use LLMs effectively. For example, a new breed of developer will be required – someone who can understand and debug code effectively, but can use an LLM to draft it rapidly. There will be a need to educate business stakeholders on LLMs and where they are being applied. This will be required because business users will need to see the outputs from LLMs (for example, rule descriptions) and be able to critically appraise them.

I hope that this section has encouraged you to research LLMs and start thinking about how they could be applied in your data quality work – even from today. The next section is about how organizations will continue to demand more from us as data quality professionals.

Greater emphasis on high-quality data in organizations

Data quality has grown significantly as a discipline in the 16 years that I have worked in the field. I expect to see this growth continuing and accelerating even further. The previous section was all about how LLMs can accelerate data quality processes.

This is a conversation that's going on for many different processes in organizations. There are groups of people in most organizations looking into how LLMs can accelerate their strategy and reduce their cost base.

The impact of poor-quality data on the benefits of LLMs cannot be overstated. If data quality is not high, then LLMs will not generate useful results. For example, the previous section covered an LLM generating data quality rules based on strategy documentation and data definitions. If the data definitions are missing or incorrect, then the rules that are generated will be useless.

Another example is customer master data. LLMs should be able to provide good customer service 24 hours a day, 7 days per week. However, they are dependent on good quality customer master data, good quality order history data, good quality product and inventory data, and an understanding of customer service and returns policies. If any of these aspects of data are of poor quality, then the LLM will not deliver the expected outcome. If a customer would like to return a product, but the LLM is unable to access the order history (showing that they bought that product), then the conversation with the customer will be difficult and a poor customer experience will occur. A human being would also struggle if this data were missing, but at this point, humans are still better at finding *workarounds* and using judgment.

An AI-based solution would also provide instant analytics – for example, showing where processes could not be completed as expected because of missing or incorrect data. This will expose the issue of poor data quality more quickly than before and increase demand from executives to resolve this.

I am expecting demand to grow even more quickly for data quality work as generative AI makes its mark.

To summarize, the impact of LLMs will be profound on data quality work. We, as data quality professionals, will see significant opportunities arise from this. Opportunities to deliver our initiatives at lower cost or with a broader scope, opportunities to take some of the mundane and repetitive work involved in data quality and automate it, and finally, opportunities to grow our skills – learning from the LLMs that support us. I recommend we all try to take those opportunities.

Summary

In this final chapter, we have highlighted the best practices that, if followed, will lead to the best possible outcome for your data quality initiatives. We also identified the most common mistakes made in data quality initiatives. If these mistakes are not avoided, initiatives may not achieve their objectives as fully as they might have done.

We also considered the impact of LLMs on data quality work – which I expect to be transformative in the next few years.

Data quality has been a passion for me over the last 16 years, and I have seen concerted and well-supported initiatives truly transform the ability of organizations to achieve their strategic goals. I've put everything I have learned into this book in the hope that it helps others get their initiative right the first time. I wish anyone starting an initiative after reading this book every success!

Index

Packtpub.com

Subscribe to our online digital library for full access to over 7,000 books and videos, as well as industry leading tools to help you plan your personal development and advance your career. For more information, please visit our website.

Why subscribe?

- Spend less time learning and more time coding with practical eBooks and Videos from over 4,000 industry professionals
- Improve your learning with Skill Plans built especially for you
- Get a free eBook or video every month
- Fully searchable for easy access to vital information
- Copy and paste, print, and bookmark content

Did you know that Packt offers eBook versions of every book published, with PDF and ePub files available? You can upgrade to the eBook version at packt.com and as a print book customer, you are entitled to a discount on the eBook copy. Get in touch with us at customercare@packtpub.com for more details.

At www.packtpub.com, you can also read a collection of free technical articles, sign up for a range of free newsletters, and receive exclusive discounts and offers on Packt books and eBooks.

Other Books You May Enjoy

If you enjoyed this book, you may be interested in these other books by Packt:

Principles of Data Fabric

Sonia Mezzetta

ISBN: 9781804615225

- Understand the core components of Data Fabric solutions
- Combine Data Fabric with Data Mesh and DataOps frameworks
- Implement distributed data management and regulatory compliance using Data Fabric
- Manage and enforce Data Governance with active metadata using Data Fabric
- Explore industry best practices for effectively implementing a Data Fabric solution

Data Literacy in Practice

Angelika Klidas, Kevin Hanegan

ISBN: 9781803246758

- Start your data literacy journey with simple and actionable steps
- Apply the four-pillar model for organizations to transform data into insights
- Discover which skills you need to work confidently with data
- Visualize data and create compelling visual data stories
- Measure, improve, and leverage your data to meet organizational goals
- Master the process of drawing insights, ask critical questions and action your insights
- Discover the right steps to take when you analyze insights

Packt is searching for authors like you

If you're interested in becoming an author for Packt, please visit `authors.packtpub.com` and apply today. We have worked with thousands of developers and tech professionals, just like you, to help them share their insight with the global tech community. You can make a general application, apply for a specific hot topic that we are recruiting an author for, or submit your own idea.

Share Your Thoughts

Now you've finished *Data Quality in Practice*, we'd love to hear your thoughts! Scan the QR code below to go straight to the Amazon review page for this book and share your feedback or leave a review on the site that you purchased it from.

https://packt.link/r/180461078X

Your review is important to us and the tech community and will help us make sure we're delivering excellent quality content.

Download a free PDF copy of this book

Thanks for purchasing this book!

Do you like to read on the go but are unable to carry your print books everywhere?

Is your eBook purchase not compatible with the device of your choice?

Don't worry, now with every Packt book you get a DRM-free PDF version of that book at no cost.

Read anywhere, any place, on any device. Search, copy, and paste code from your favorite technical books directly into your application.

The perks don't stop there, you can get exclusive access to discounts, newsletters, and great free content in your inbox daily

Follow these simple steps to get the benefits:

1. Scan the QR code or visit the link below

https://packt.link/free-ebook/9781804610787

2. Submit your proof of purchase

3. That's it! We'll send your free PDF and other benefits to your email directly

www.ingramcontent.com/pod-product-compliance
Lightning Source LLC
Chambersburg PA
CBHW080625060326
40690CB00021B/4817